NEW WORLD

NEW WORLD

*The Heart of the New Testament
in Plain English*

by

ALAN T. DALE

MOREHOUSE-BARLOW CO., INC.
WILTON, CONNECTICUT 06897

© Oxford University Press 1967

First published in the United States of America 1973
by
Morehouse-Barlow Co., Inc.
78 Danbury Rd, Wilton, Connecticut 06897
ISBN:0-8192-1149-4

Printed in the United States of America

Foreword

by the Rev. Canon C. F. D. Moule,
Lady Margaret's Professor of Divinity in the University of Cambridge

I REGARD Mr. Dale as a wizard, and I wish I knew the secrets of his art. He takes phrases from the New Testament, which, to me, are extremely familiar, because I happen to have studied them all my life, and he holds them up at a particular angle or gives them just a little tilt, and suddenly they shine with a new lustre and freshness. I say to myself, 'But is that really what it means?'; and when I ponder over it, I generally have to admit, 'Yes, of course, it is; but I had never looked at it like that before'. Mr. Dale has something of a poet's imagination, combined with an extremely practical and realistic way of asking 'What were things really like?' and a genius for the apt modern analogy. He has evidently thought so deeply about the meaning of New Testament words and ideas that he is able to paraphrase freely without losing the essentials.

A poet's vision; a realist's grasp of facts; and, we must add, a parent's understanding of the family. For this, too, makes him an effective interpreter. He knows his boys and girls so well that he can not only give them the story in lively, contemporary shape, but also suggest things for them to do, which will help them to think out the meaning of the Christian story for themselves and begin to make it their own.

It is remarkable how large a proportion of the New Testament is retained in these racy paraphrases and modernized presentations. From unexpected angles and in clever disguises, it comes back at the reader and startles him with its freshness and relevance.

I count it a privilege to be allowed to write this little foreword to volumes which, I am sure, are going to help to kindle genuine reverence for Jesus Christ and to show readers how real and contemporary the Gospel is.

Clare College,
Cambridge.

Preface

THE New Testament is comparatively short. Unlike the Old Testament which spans a thousand years and more, it is the creation of only three generations of a small and scattered community. Short though it is, it can be intimidating for the ordinary reader. He turns the pages over: twenty-seven books—'gospels', letters, 'revelation'; some passages crystal-clear, some strange and remote and obscure even when he has read them two or three times. One incident is unforgettable—the plain and moving report of the death of a young man one Friday afternoon outside the walls of the capital city of an occupied country on the eastern borders of the Roman Empire. Four times that story is told, the climax of each of the first four books. That death in the afternoon is the obvious clue to the whole collection of writings.

I was once that ordinary reader, and *New World* has grown out of the plain guide I made for myself. I wish someone had made it for me and put it into my hands when I first picked up the New Testament to read it for myself. It was that death in the afternoon that started me reading. I wanted to know why, for these last two thousand years, it was a death men could not forget.

New World, therefore, is a translation of the essence of the New Testament as I now see it, made with a controlled vocabulary. The first three parts tell the story; the last two parts show how Christians tried to make sense of it and so came to their characteristic convictions. This, for me, is what the New Testament is about.

By 'essence of the New Testament' I mean this: first, an account of the ministry of Jesus; secondly, what Jesus himself had to say about it all; thirdly, a shortened version of the first great history of the origins and spread of the Christian community; fourthly, an account of what Christianity meant to one man—Paul; and finally, a survey of Christian convictions as seen in the letters of Paul and the gospel of John.

Here, in more detail, is the pattern of the five parts of *New World*.

The Beginning gives the account of the ministry of Jesus as it is found in the earliest gospel, *The Gospel according to Mark*. *The Gospel according to Matthew* is an enlarged edition of *Mark*; on a first reading of the New Testament it need not detain us, for Matthew's important additions are chiefly concerned with sayings of Jesus apparently unknown to Mark, and we shall be dealing with these in part two. The substance of what Luke had to say will be dealt with in part three, for Luke set his hand to something not attempted before.

The Message sets out what Jesus himself had to say. Modern scholarship enables us to go behind the collections of the sayings of Jesus which we find scattered throughout the first three gospels. It has given much attention to the *form* in which Jesus spoke, and I have therefore arranged his sayings according to their *form*. I have tried to let Jesus speak for himself—to let his words make something of the living impact he first gave them.

I give first what Dr Vincent Taylor has called 'Pronouncement Stories'— stories about Jesus which were remembered because of something he said. Note his informality. Then I give the parables and the poems. That Jesus was a poet, in the proper sense of the word, is one of the great insights of our times, the significance of which we have not yet adequately realised. To me, it makes all the difference to the way we approach him and listen to him.[1] Finally, I give individual sayings, each of which must be considered separately in the light of his total vision (the original occasions on which he said these has been forgotten) and the two poems in which he summed up what he lived and died for.

From Galilee to Rome gives a shortened version of Luke's two-volume work, written some fifty years after the death of Jesus, which might carry a title such as *The Origins and Convictions of the Christian Community*. Its two parts, *The Gospel according to Luke* and *The Acts of the Apostles*, were separated in the second-century arrangement of the New Testament. Luke sets the story of the first forty years against its world-wide background and shows how the friends of Jesus came step by step to grasp his fundamental conviction—that the Good News was for everybody everywhere. Nothing less than the reading of Luke's whole work will bring home the richness and range of his argument and the many issues with which he was concerned. I have tried, in this shortened version, to let his main argument speak for itself.[2]

The story of the ministry of Jesus and the spread of Christianity has now been told. What did this story mean to those involved in it?

In *Paul the Explorer* I have tried to set out what Christianity meant to one man, Paul of Tarsus: first, in his own words; and then in the words of his friend, Luke—'My doctor', he called him—in his account of Paul's

---

[1] This insight has been accepted by scholars ever since Dr C. F. Burney published his book, *The Poetry of our Lord*, in 1925. Those who wish to look more deeply into the matter will find a straight-forward account of Hebrew poetry in Dr T. H. Robinson's *The Poetry of the Old Testament*; should consult Dr T. W. Manson's *The Teaching of Jesus*, pp. 50–56, especially the last paragraph; and can read a fascinating account of the nature of Hebrew poetry and the effect of its discovery in the eighteenth century (by Dr Louth, Professor of Poetry at Oxford) on the development of English poetry in Murray Roston's *Prophet and Poet*.

[2] In my selection from Luke's two-volume work, I have omitted many of the sayings of Jesus which he quoted (these will be found in *The Message*) and the passages from *Mark* with which he later expanded his own account (these have already been used in *The Beginning*); and I have kept some of his stories about Paul for part four, *Paul the Explorer*.

ten years in the cities of the Aegean and of his defence before the courts in Palestine.

In *Jesus, Leader and Lord* I give the interpretation of Christianity offered by the two outstanding thinkers of its first century of expansion— Paul and the author of the Fourth Gospel.

In making this selection and arrangement, one central conviction has sustained me. It could not be better put than in the words of Dr Manson: 'Christianity had at its heart a person and a life before it had a creed and a code; and the thing that is characteristic of the great documents of the New Testament is their passionate devotion to the Person and their spontaneous reproduction of the life. 'For me to live is Christ and to die is gain' . . . The New Testament has not attained to the dignity of a creed and a code; it has what is much better—a passionate love of Christ and a living fellowship of the brethren.'[3]

I have tried to avoid in any way distorting or misrepresenting what the New Testament has to say; I have made the selection and arrangement in the light of modern New Testament scholarship. I have long been troubled by the way in which, as ordinary readers, we keep apart our reading of the New Testament itself and the insights and discoveries of New Testament scholars. I think this is due to the fact that unless we can actually see what the text, in the light of such insights and discoveries, reads like, we find it difficult to relate what we read *about the New Testament* to what we read *in the New Testament itself* in the full editions of the Bible we normally use. I have, therefore, embodied, as far as I could, the work of scholars to whom I myself stand in great debt for what understanding of the New Testament I may have; this will be seen both in the translation itself and in the arrangement of the text. The reader who wishes to examine the reasons on which my decisions rest will find them in the books I have used.[4]

I have also tried to help the reader to approach the records of the most important story in the world with critical awareness as well as with imagination. The clear intention of Jesus was to call everybody to fearless thought as well as to splendid living. He would have agreed with Socrates that 'the unexamined life is unlivable' ('If you can't ask questions, you

[3] *On Paul and John*, p. 117.

[4] These are the chief books: *The Beginning*, T. W. Manson, *The Servant-Messiah*; *The Message*, C. H. Dodd, *The Parables of the Kingdom*, J. Jeremias, *The Parables of Jesus*, and T. W. Manson, *The Sayings of Jesus*; *From Galilee to Rome*, V. Taylor, *The First Draft of St. Luke's Gospel*; *Paul the Explorer*, J. Knox, *Chapters in a Life of Paul*; *Jesus, Leader and Lord*, C. H. Dodd, *The Epistle to the Romans* (Moffatt Commentary), *The Interpretation of the Fourth Gospel* and *Historical Tradition in the Fourth Gospel*; as background for the whole volume, C. F. D. Moule, *The Birth of the New Testament*. I have, of course, used these books quite simply; but I am sure that to look at the New Testament through the eyes of such scholars is as important for the ordinary reader as for a teacher like myself.

might as well be dead'). He was not concerned with proselytizing or indoctrination but with human maturity. He gave himself to help ordinary people to live as sons and daughters of God their Father. He didn't want 'Yes-men'; he wanted people to 'judge of themselves', 'to know what they believe and to love what they know'. Only so can he become for us either Leader or Lord.

A few notes about the controlled vocabulary I have used will make clear what I have tried to do.

In the later years of the nineteenth century scholars became aware that the language of the New Testament was largely the spoken language of the Mediterranean world. Whatever the faults of our twentieth-century translations, made in the language we ourselves speak, they have recaptured for us something of the directness and freshness of the colloquial idiom of gospel and letter.

I can remember a railway journey across England, lost in the pages of a Moffatt *New Testament* I had bought at a railway bookstall; and the Saturday morning when I went out and bought a copy of E. V. Rieu's *The Four Gospels* and felt as if I were reading *Mark* for the first time. Paul must have first come alive for many of us in the pages of J. B. Phillips' *Letters to Young Churches*—the very title was an inspiration.

As a teacher, I have always coveted for my students such an experience. What I said to them mattered only in so far as it sent them to read the New Testament for themselves and catch something of the same excitement.

So here I set myself a limited linguistic aim. The full edition of *New World* is intended for young people in Secondary Schools; if all of them were to read it without hindrance, I had to use a controlled vocabulary. I have tried to see how much of the heart of the New Testament can be put into very simple speech. I have not watered anything down (so I believe) though I have had to simplify wherever I could. I wanted them to be able to read it as I read Moffatt in the train. I have tried to face the issues straightforwardly, using, as far as I could, the work of New Testament scholars. I have had to come down on one side of the fence, of course, where there is still debate among competent men; but I have done so openly.

Paraphrase, especially in Paul's letters, has been unavoidable. I have done what I could to keep it within bounds. The problems which a translation with a controlled vocabulary raises troubled me most in *Jesus, Leader and Lord* with its richness of language and soaring argument. I hope that I have not entirely lost, in the search for simple language, the thrill I myself felt, and that the reader will be inspired to go on to read the full New Testament. For *New World* is not intended to take the place of the full text; it offers the reader a simplified version—first steps to the full translations.

PREFACE

I have found the making of this translation an exhilarating experience. Putting the New Testament into simple language has forced me to reconsider my own Christian convictions and to see the plain story of what happened in a fresh light. I hope that the reader will catch something of the excitement and enlargement I felt.

I have been helped in my work by many people. My colleague, the Rev. D. R. Jones, has kept me to my task whenever my spirit seemed to flag. I must acknowledge how much I owe to my students for whom the first tentative translations were made; to many teachers in different parts of the country who have tried the translation out in their schools, tested it, and made many suggestions about vocabulary and arrangement; and to the young people themselves who were not slow with comment and criticism— they will recognize their own contributions. I am grateful to Dr. K. Lovell, Lecturer in the Psychology of Education in the University of Leeds Institute of Education, who tested the language used in *The Beginning*.

To four people I am particularly grateful for detailed help: to the Rev. Rupert E. Davies who read through the text of the translation and saved me from many pitfalls; to the Rev. Canon C. F. D. Moule who encouraged me when I sent him an early draft of *The Beginning* and has kindly written the foreword to the first four volumes; to Dr. C. H. Dodd, who read through the final volume and gave me invaluable criticism and suggestions; and to Mr. Peter Spicer, of the Clarendon Press, who has been a steady and candid guide and whose thorough and persistent criticism has meant more to me than he will admit. Mr. F. D. A. Burns, of our Department of English Literature, has read the translation through and helped me with many questions of vocabulary and idiom; I am very grateful to him. My debts to those I have named will be obvious, but I alone am responsible for the errors and misjudgments the volumes still contain. I fear to think how many more there would have been but for their help.

I must add a word about the illustrations. I would like to thank Mr. Bernard Brett, not only for the excitement of his paintings, but also for the stimulation of many conversations; and Miss Susan Cooper, of the Clarendon Press, for her help in choosing the photographs.

ALAN T. DALE,
Dudley College of Education

May, 1965.

Acknowledgments

IN making this translation, I have been helped by many people. My colleague, the Rev. D. R. Jones, has kept me to my task whenever my spirit seemed to flag. I must acknowledge how much I owe to my students for whom the first tentative translations were made; to many teachers in different parts of the country who have tried the translation out in their schools, tested it, and made many suggestions about vocabulary and arrangement; and to the young people themselves who were not slow with comment and criticism—they will recognize their own contributions. I am grateful to Dr. K. Lovell, Lecturer in the Psychology of Education in the University of Leeds Institute of Education, who tested the language used in *The Beginning*.

To four people I am particularly grateful for detailed help: to the Rev. Rupert E. Davies who read through the text of the translation and saved me from many pitfalls; to the Rev. Canon C. F. D. Moule who encouraged me when I sent him an early draft of *The Beginning* and has kindly written the foreword to the first four volumes; to Dr. C. H. Dodd, who read through the final volume and gave me invaluable criticism and suggestions; and to Mr. Peter Spicer, of the Clarendon Press, who has been a steady and candid guide and whose thorough and persistent criticism has meant more to me than he will admit. Mr. F. D. A. Burns, of our Department of English Literature, has read the translation through and helped me with many questions of vocabulary and idiom; I am very grateful to him. My debts to those I have named will be obvious, but I alone am responsible for the errors and misjudgments the volumes still contain. I fear to think how many more there would have been but for their help.

I must add a word about the illustrations. I would like to thank Mr. Bernard Brett, not only for the excitement of his paintings, but also for the stimulation of many conversations; and Miss Susan Cooper, of the Clarendon Press, for her help in choosing the photographs.

ALAN T. DALE,
Dudley College of Education

May, 1965.

Contents

CONTENTS

List of Illustrations

Most of the photographs in Book V have been taken from *The Family of Man,* an exhibition organized by Edward Steichen for The Museum of Modern Art, New York, in 1955, and show the people of our twentieth century world. As we look at them, let us look at them through the eyes of Jesus. Can the family of man become a real family—the family of God? Jesus believed that—with God's help—it could. He lived and died and rose again to make it such.

BOOK ONE

THE BEGINNING

PALESTINE
Centre of the Known World

BRITAIN

GAUL

SPAIN

ITALY

Rome

GREECE

Carthage

Amber route

Boundary of the Roman Empire

ASIA

PALESTINE

Babylon

Alexandria

EGYPT

ARABIA

AFRICA

Ivory Route

PARTHIA

Silk Route

CHINA

INDIA

Pepper and Spices Route

N

Mercator's Projection

On the Banks of the River

THE story of Jesus began in the hot Jordan Valley, on the banks of the river. Not very far to the south was the Salt Sea. It was a long way from Nazareth, the village in the north where he had grown up and lived as a builder.

Jesus was probably about thirty years of age. He had come south to join the hermit John and his friends.

John the Hermit had been living in the wild hills that rise to the east of Jordan River. He believed that God had called him to tell the Jewish people to change their ways and live in his Way.

People all over the country were talking about John and what he was saying and doing. Great crowds went out to listen to him. The news reached Nazareth. When Jesus heard it, he left his village and his family and friends, and went to meet John on the banks of Jordan River.

THE HERMIT JOHN

There is an old poem in the Bible, written in far-away Babylon a long time before our story begins. The Jewish people were prisoners there, but they were soon to be set free to go back across the desert to their homeland. The poem is about the journey home, and it begins like this:

> The voice of a man
> shouting in the lonely desert—
> 'Get God's road ready,
> make his paths straight'.

John appeared, like the man in the poem, on the lonely moorland, calling people to change their ways so that God might forgive them. He told them to wash themselves in the water of Jordan River as a sign that they had really changed their ways.

All sorts of people went out to hear him—country people from Judea and town people from Jerusalem; they were washed by him in the water of Jordan River, saying that they were sorry for the wrong things they had done.

John lived as his desert ancestors had lived: he had a cloak of camel's hair and a leather belt round his waist, and he used to eat locusts and wild honey.

JORDAN RIVER—near the place where Jesus was baptized. Near the river, trees and bushes grow luxuriantly, as you can see; it was called 'the jungle of Jordan'. But beyond the river, the land is dry and barren.

'A Stronger One than I am comes after me,' John told the people. 'I am not good enough to bend down and untie his shoe-laces. I have used water as a sign that your hearts shall be made clean; he will really give you God's own power.'

JESUS HEARS GOD'S CALL

When the crowds were going out to hear John, Jesus left his home in Nazareth and was washed by John in the water of Jordan River.

As Jesus was coming up out of the river, he saw, as it were, a flash of lightning across the skies; and, with the gentleness of a dove, God filled his heart with peace. Into his mind came God's words:

'You are my only Son; with you I am very pleased.'

Then God's Spirit sent him out on to the lonely moorland, and he stayed there many a long day. His only company was wild animals, but God looked after him.

In Galilee

WE do not know how long Jesus stayed in the south after he heard God's call. But when King Herod had arrested John and put him in prison in his lonely castle of Machaerus, high on the mountains on the eastern side of the Salt Sea, Jesus went back to his homeland of Galilee. The stories here are all about what happened in Galilee.

The work of Jesus in Galilee was brought to an end when the soldiers of the 'Resistance Movement' tried to make Jesus their leader. Jesus knew that this was not God's Way. He had been telling the people what God's Way really was, but they had not listened. Even his own friends did not understand. When the 5,000 men met Jesus at a lonely spot on the shores of Galilee Lake, Jesus knew he would have to leave Galilee. The Desert Meal was the end of his work there.

THE GOOD NEWS

Jesus came into Galilee telling everybody the Good News about God. This is what he said:

> The Great Day is here.
> God's Kingdom has come;
> change your ways
> and trust in the Good News.

THE JUDEAN DESERT—the lonely moorland where Jesus went after his baptism. It was wild country. Robbers could lie in wait for travellers. It was here that soldiers of the Resistance Movement could meet out of sight of Roman soldiers.

A DAY IN THE LIFE OF JESUS

Jesus and his friends were in Capernaum, a fishing town on the shores of Galilee Lake. It was Saturday, the Holy Day of the Jews, and Jesus and his friends went along to the Meeting House and took part in the Service of Worship. There was a madman among the people who had gathered there.

'What are you bothering us for, Jesus, coming here from Nazareth?' he shouted out. 'Have you come to get rid of us? I know you—you're God's Holy One!'

'Be quiet,' said Jesus severely, 'and come out of him.'

The mad spirit in the man threw him on the ground, and, shouting out loudly, came out of him. Everybody was taken by surprise, and started talking about Jesus and what he had said and done:

'What's this?'

'It's not like anything we've heard before!'

'He talks to mad spirits as though he was their master!'

'And they do what he tells them!'

THE MEETING HOUSE IN CAPERNAUM. The one Jesus knew was destroyed in an earthquake; these are the ruins of the one built in its place, probably with some of the old stones.

THE HILL COUNTRY OF GALILEE. These are rolling hills, like the hills in the south of England. In the time of Jesus, the hillsides would be covered with trees. These have since been destroyed.

Jesus and his friends left the building and went along with James and John to the home of Peter and Andrew. Peter's mother-in-law was in bed with fever. They told Jesus about her, and he went to her and took hold of her hand and lifted her up. The fever left her and she looked after the visitors.

At sunset, when the Holy Day was over, people brought all who were ill in body or mind to Jesus. The whole town crowded round the door of the house. Jesus made them all better, whatever their illness was.

Early next morning, while it was still dark, Jesus got up and went out of the house to a lonely place. Peter and his friends hunted him out and found him—praying.

'Everybody's looking for you,' they told him.

'Let's get away,' said Jesus, 'and give them the Good News in the near-by market-towns. That's why I came out here.'

JESUS AND HIS HOME FOLK

In Nazareth

One day Jesus went back to his own village with his friends. On Saturday, he spoke to the people in their Meeting House. Everybody listened to him with amazement.

'Where does he get it all from?' they said.

'What's this learning he's been given?'

'He does such wonderful things!'

'Isn't he the builder, Mary's son? Aren't James, Joses, Judas and Simon his brothers?'

'And aren't his sisters here with us?'

Because they knew him so well, they couldn't believe he was anybody special. They didn't want to have anything to do with him.

'You know what people say,' said Jesus. 'A man of God is always well thought of—except in his own country and among his own relatives and in his own home.'

He could do no wonderful things there. He could only put his hands on a few sick people and make them better. What surprised him was that the people of his own village didn't trust him.

In Capernaum

Jesus was at home in Capernaum, and people came crowding to him; he and his friends had no time even to eat their meals.

News of all this came to his family. They came over to look after him; they thought he was out of his mind.

His mother and brothers came and stood outside the house, and sent somebody in to ask him to come outside. The crowd was sitting round him.

'Look!' they said to him. 'Your mother and brothers are outside asking for you.'

'Who are my real mother and brothers?' asked Jesus.

He looked at those who were sitting in a circle round him.

'Here are my real mother and brothers,' he said. 'He who does what God wants him to do is my real brother and sister and mother.'

JESUS AND HIS FRIENDS

Five Friends

One day Jesus was walking along the seashore; he saw Peter and his brother Andrew casting their nets into the sea—they were fishermen.

'Come with me,' said Jesus. 'I'll show you better fishing than this—for men, not fish.'

And they left their nets and went with him.

A little farther on James and his brother John were getting their nets ready in the boat. Jesus called them, and they left their father with his men in the boat and went away with him.

Some time later Jesus was again out walking and he saw Levi at work in the tax office.

'Come with me,' said Jesus.

Levi got up and went with him.

A Would-be Friend

When Jesus was out on the road again, a man ran up and kneeled down in front of him.

'Good Sir,' he said, 'what must I do to take my place in God's New Kingdom?'

'You use the word "good",' said Jesus. 'Why do you use it about me? You can only use that word about God himself, for only God is really good . . . You know the Ten Commandments, don't you?'

'Sir,' he said, 'I've kept the Ten Commandments ever since I was a boy.'

Jesus looked at him and liked him very much indeed.

'There's only one thing you must do,' he said. 'You want to be really rich. Well then, sell what you've got and give it to people who haven't got anything, and come and join my company of friends.'

The man's face fell when he heard this, and he went away very sad; he was a very rich man.

'How hard it is,' Jesus said, 'for a rich man to live in God's way.'

ANOTHER VIEW OF THE HILL COUNTRY. The little villages nestled in the valleys between the hills, and round them were the fields and the orchards. But there were no stone walls or hedges to separate the fields from one another.

His friends were amazed to hear him talk like this.

'You know,' Jesus went on, 'you haven't grown up yet. You think it's easy to live in God's way. But it's hard for anybody to live like that. It's easier for a camel to get through the eye of a needle than for a rich man to live in God's way.'

His friends were really amazed.

'Who then can live in God's way, if a rich man can't?' they said to one another.

Jesus looked at them.

'You forget,' he said. 'What men by themselves can't do, God can. Don't you remember what the Bible says about God—"I know that You can do everything"?'

Peter started talking.

'Look!' he said. 'We've given up everything to come with you!'

'And I give you a solemn promise,' said Jesus. 'Nobody has left his home, or brothers or sisters, or mother or father, or children or fields, for me and the Good News—for nothing. He won't have an easy time; he'll have to be ready to face prison and death. But here and now he will get a grand reward: more homes, more brothers and sisters, more mothers, more children and more fields. And in the New World that's coming, he'll have a place in God's Kingdom.'

The 'Twelve'

Jesus went into the hills and called the men he wanted and they went out to him. He chose a small company of very close friends, and he called them the 'Twelve'.

He wanted them to be with him, and to go out telling the Good News about God and making sick people better.

These are the 'Twelve' and some of the nicknames Jesus gave them:

Simon	'Rock' (we say 'Peter')
James and John, the sons of Zebedee	'Thunder and Lightning'
Andrew	
Philip	
Bartholomew	
Matthew	
James, the son of Alphaeus	
Thomas	
Thaddeus	

Simon   'Rebel'
Judas

(Judas was called 'Iscariot' like his father; this is the friend who handed Jesus over to the Jewish Government.)

Jesus sent the 'Twelve' out, two together, into the villages; and he gave them power to make sick people better.

His orders were: 'Travel light with staff and sandals, no food, no bag, no money in your belt, and only one shirt.'

The 'Twelve' went off and told people the Good News about God and called them to change their ways. They made mad people better; they put ointment on other sick people and made them better too.

Then they came back and met Jesus again, and told him everything they had done and what they had said to the people in the villages.

A Stormy Night

Jesus had been talking to a crowd of people from a boat, and it was getting dark.

'Let's go across the Lake,' he said to his friends.

They left the crowd and took him along with them in the boat just as he was. Other boats, too, put out to sea with them. Suddenly there was a wind storm, and the waves were breaking into the boat and filling it with water. Jesus was sleeping on a cushion in the stern.

They woke him up.

'Sir,' they shouted, 'doesn't it matter to you that we're sinking?'

Jesus woke up.

'Silence!' he said to the wind and the sea. 'Be quiet!'

The wind dropped and there was a dead calm.

'Why are you cowards like this?' he said to his friends. 'Don't you trust God yet?'

They had been very frightened indeed.

'What sort of man is this?' they asked one another. 'He's master even of wind and sea!'

PEOPLE JESUS HELPED

A Leper

One day a leper came to Jesus and knelt down in front of him.

'If you want to,' he kept saying, 'you can get rid of my leprosy.'

Jesus was angry and stretched out his hand and touched him.

'Of course I want to,' said Jesus, 'be clean.'

The man's leprosy left him and he was better. But Jesus sent him off.

'See you don't tell anybody,' he warned him sternly. 'Off you go to the Temple and take what the Bible orders you to take, so that everybody can see you're really better.'

But the man went off to spread the news far and wide.

A Cripple

One day some men brought a cripple to Jesus, and four of them were carrying him. The crowd was so great that they could not get anywhere near him. So they stripped the flat roof off the house where Jesus was, dug a hole and lowered the mat with the cripple on it.

Jesus saw how these men trusted him.

'I'm speaking to you,' he said to the cripple. 'Get up, pick up your mat and go home.'

The cripple got up, picked up his mat and walked out.

Everyone kept looking at him in amazement and thanked God for his goodness.

'We've never seen anything like this!' they said.

A Madman

One day Jesus and his friends sailed to the far shore of Galilee Lake.

A madman lived among the graves there. Nobody had been able to tie him up even with chains. He had often been tied up with handcuffs and chains, but he had torn the handcuffs apart and smashed the chains. Night and day he lived among the graves and on the hills, shouting out and striking himself with stones. Nobody could tame him.

Jesus got out of the boat. The madman saw him from a long way off, ran to him and knelt down at his feet.

'What are you bothering me for, Jesus, Son of the Most High God?' he screamed at the top of his voice. 'I beg you, in God's name, don't torment me!' For Jesus was already saying to him—'Come out of the man, you foul spirit.'

'What's your name?' asked Jesus.

'I'm the Roman Army,' he said. 'There are thousands of us.'

He begged Jesus over and over again not to send the foul spirits

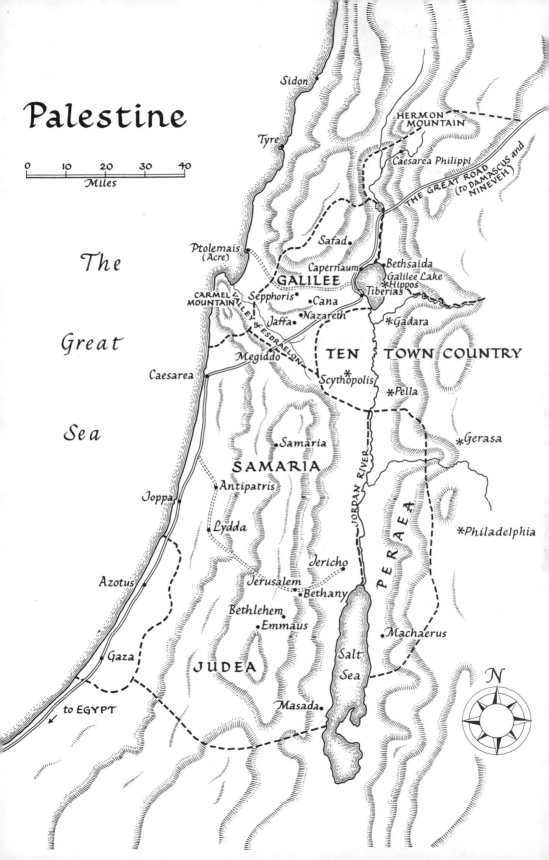

Palestine

0   10   20   30   40
Miles

The

Great

Sea

Sidon

Tyre

HERMON
MOUNTAIN

Caesarea Philippi

THE GREAT ROAD
(to DAMASCUS and
NINEVEH)

Safad

Ptolemais
(Acre)

Capernaum
Bethsaida
Galilee Lake
*Hippos
Tiberias

GALILEE

CARMEL
MOUNTAIN

Sepphoris
Cana
Jaffa
Nazareth

*Gadara

Megiddo

TEN   TOWN COUNTRY

Caesarea

Scythopolis

*Pella

Samaria

*Gerasa

SAMARIA

JORDAN RIVER

Antipatris

Joppa

PERAEA

Lydda

*Philadelphia

Jericho

Azotus

Jerusalem
Bethany

Bethlehem
Emmaus

Machaerus

Gaza

JUDEA

Salt
Sea

to EGYPT

Masada

N

away from the graves and the hills. A great herd of pigs was feeding on the hillside.

'Send us into the pigs,' said the spirits. 'Let us get inside them.'

Jesus let them go, and the foul spirits went off into the pigs. The herd rushed down the steep bank into the sea—all 2,000 of them—and were drowned.

The herdsmen ran off and told the news in town and country; everybody came out to see what had happened. They came to Jesus and looked at the madman now sitting down, wearing his clothes and quite sane, the very man who had called himself 'The Roman Army'. They were very frightened. Those who had seen what had happened told the others about the madman and about the pigs; and they all begged Jesus to go away. They didn't want him there.

As Jesus was getting into the boat, the man himself begged to join his company of friends; but Jesus wouldn't let him join them.

'Go home to your own people,' he said, 'and tell them what God has done for you and how he has had pity on you.'

Off he went, and everywhere in 'Ten Town Country' he told people what Jesus had done to him. It amazed everybody.

A Little Girl

One day a great crowd gathered round Jesus on the seashore. An officer of the Meeting House called Jairus, who had a little girl twelve years old, came along. When he saw Jesus, he fell down at his feet.

'My little girl's dying. Come and touch her with your hands,' he begged over and over again. 'Then she'll get better and live.'

Jesus went along with him and was talking to him when people came from his house.

'Your daughter has died,' they said. 'Why go on bothering the Master?'

Jesus took no notice of what was being said.

'Don't worry,' he said to Jairus. 'All you must do is to trust me.'

He let nobody go with him except his three friends, Peter, James, and John. When he got to the house, he saw the uproar that was going on there and the paid mourners weeping and wailing loudly.

He went in.

'What's all this uproar and weeping for?' he asked. 'This little girl isn't dead; she's asleep.'

Everybody made fun of him, but Jesus turned them all out. He took the father and mother and his friends, and went into where the little girl was lying and took hold of her hand.

'Little girl,' he said, 'get up.'

She got up and walked about. Her father and mother were too amazed to know what to do. Jesus gave them strict orders that nobody must know about it and told them to give her something to eat.

A Sick Woman

One day a great crowd was following Jesus and pressing round him. A woman who had suffered from bleeding for twelve years was among them. The doctors hadn't helped her very much. All her money was gone on doctor's bills, and she was no better; indeed she was much worse. She had heard people talking of Jesus and she had joined in the crowd behind him.

'If I touch just his clothes,' she kept saying to herself, 'I shall be better.'

She touched his clothes. Her bleeding stopped, and she felt better in herself at once. Her trouble was over.

Jesus noticed that power had gone out of him; he turned round in the crowd.

'Who touched my clothes?' he asked.

'You see all this crowd pressing round you,' said his friends, 'and you ask who touched you!'

Jesus looked all round him to see who had done it.

The woman, frightened and trembling all over, knew what had happened to her; and she came and fell down in front of him and told him everything.

'Daughter,' said Jesus, 'your trust in me has made you better. Go home and don't worry; your trouble won't bother you any more.'

A Deaf and Dumb Man

One day some people brought a deaf and dumb man to Jesus and begged him to touch him with his hand.

Jesus took him away from the crowd by himself. He put his finger in his ears, and spat and touched his tongue. Then he looked up and sighed.

'Be opened,' he said.

The man began to hear and use his tongue, and he talked quite clearly. Jesus told the man's friends not to tell people about it. But

JAFFA today, a village two miles west of Nazareth. In the time of Jesus, this was the head village of the area, and a headquarters of the Resistance Movement.

the more he told them not to talk about it, the more they spread the news. They were too amazed to obey him.

'How well he does everything!' they said. 'He even makes deaf people hear and dumb people talk!'

A Blind Man

One day Jesus was passing through the village where Peter had grown up as a boy. People brought a blind man to him, and asked him to touch him and make him better.

Jesus led the blind man by the hand outside the village. He wet his eyes (as doctors often did in those days) and touched them with his hands.

'Can you see anything?' he asked.

The blind man looked up.

'Yes,' he said. 'I can see people—but they are like walking trees!'

Jesus put his hands on the blind man's eyes again. Now he could see quite clearly. He was blind no longer, and he could see the hills on the other side of Galilee Lake as plainly as anybody else.

Jesus sent him off home.

'Don't tell anybody else in the village,' he said. 'Don't go back there.'

Boys and Girls

One day parents were bringing boys and girls to Jesus for him to touch them; his friends told them to go away. When Jesus saw them doing this he was angry.

'Let the boys and girls come to me,' he said. 'You mustn't stop them. God's Kingdom is made up of the young like these. I am sure of this: anyone who does not welcome God's Kingdom like a little boy or girl won't get inside.'

JESUS AND THE CROWDS

People everywhere were amazed at what Jesus said; when he spoke, you had to listen. Everybody was talking about him in all the country towns and villages. He used to speak to them in their Meeting Houses and make sick people better. He couldn't go into any town without people crowding round him; he had to stay out in the countryside and people used to come to him from the villages round about.

They came to him from all over Galilee, from far in the south, from the other side of Jordan River, and even from the foreign cities of Tyre and Sidon.

When Jesus was at home in Capernaum, people crowded together so that the space about the doorway could no longer hold them.

He used to go out by Galilee Lake. Crowds came there too, and he used to talk to them.

One day, on the seashore, the crowds nearly crushed him; he had to tell his friends to keep a boat ready for him to get into. Once he had to get into a boat and the great crowd stood on the land at the water's edge.

Jesus made many sick people better. They pressed on him to touch him, and wherever he went—into villages, towns, and farms—people put the sick in the market-places and begged him to let them touch the hem of his clothes. Those who touched him got better.

OUR WAYS AND GOD'S WAYS

Jesus at Home

One day Jesus was having a meal at home with his friends. Quite a number of tax-collectors and ordinary people had been invited. Some Jewish Leaders, who had been 'shadowing' Jesus, noticed who was there.

'Why is he eating with such people?' they asked his friends.
Jesus heard them.
'Healthy people don't need a doctor,' he said, 'but sick people do.'

Religion isn't Dull!

One day, during the Fast Days, the friends of John the Hermit
were fasting. Some people came to Jesus.
'Why do John's friends fast,' they asked, 'but your friends don't?'
'Can guests at a wedding leave the wedding breakfast uneaten?'
asked Jesus. 'What would the bridegroom think?'

In the Fields

One Saturday, the Holy Day of the Jews, Jesus was walking
through the cornfields, and his friends were picking the ears of
corn as they walked along.
'Look!' said the Jewish Leaders. 'Why are you doing what's not
allowed on our Holy Day?'
'You don't know your Bibles very well,' said Jesus. 'Don't you
remember what King David and his soldiers once did when they
were hungry and starving? He went into God's House and ate the
special bread that was kept there. That wasn't "allowed" either,
you know; only the priests are "allowed" to eat that bread. He
gave it to his soldiers too!'
'Our Holy Day,' Jesus went on, 'was made to be a help to men
and women; men and women weren't made just to keep the Holy
Day. What is more, they themselves can say what can and what
can't be done on our Holy Day.'

In a Village

One Saturday, Jesus went to a Meeting House. A man with a
crippled hand was there. The Jewish Leaders watched Jesus closely
to see if he would heal him, though it was a Holy Day, so that they
could report him.
'Stand up for everybody to see,' said Jesus to the man.
He turned to the Jewish Leaders.
'What's the right thing to do on the Holy Day? A good thing or a
bad thing?' he asked. 'Make someone better or let him die?'
They said nothing, and Jesus looked round at them in anger;
he was very sad because they were so hard-hearted.
'Stretch out your hand,' he said to the man.

GALILEE LAKE and the Plain of Gennesareth, looking south. The Roman Road from the coast of the Great Sea came down to the lake through the valley in the distance; and on the plain to the right was the village of Magdala from which Mary of Magdala came. 'The Hill' where Jesus met his friends alone was probably one of those in the distance.

The man stretched out his hand and it was strong again.

The Jewish Leaders went out and met with other Leaders in the south, to see what they could do to get rid of Jesus.

Old Customs

The Jewish people still kept some old customs.

They never ate anything without 'washing' their hands up to the wrist. If they bought anything to eat from the market, they sprinkled themselves with water. In the same way, they 'washed' cups, pots, and copper pans. This was not a proper wash, but just sprinkling; they thought that this was the sort of thing God wanted them to do. If anything had been sprinkled, they called it 'clean'; if it had not been sprinkled, they called it 'dirty'.

The Jewish Leaders noticed that the friends of Jesus ate their food with 'dirty' hands, and they came to talk to him about it.

'Why don't these friends of yours keep the old customs?' they asked. 'Why do they eat food with "dirty" hands?'

'You're just playing at being good,' said Jesus. 'The old words of the Bible might have been written about you—

> These people talk, talk, talk!
> They don't really love Me.
> What they do to 'please' Me
> doesn't mean anything;
> what they say 'God wants'
> they have made up for themselves.

'You make people do what you want them to do,' said Jesus, 'not what God wants them to do. Here's an example. God said: "Respect your father and mother"; you say: "If a man says to his parents, 'I know I ought to give this to you, but I'm going to give it to the Temple', he needn't do anything for his father or mother." So your "old custom" takes the place of God's command. I could give you many other examples.'

What matters

One day Jesus called the crowd to him.

'I want you to listen to me,' he said. 'I want you to be quite clear about what's "clean" and what's "dirty", what God wants and what God doesn't want. It's not "outside things" that matter, but "inside things".'

When Jesus got home, away from the crowd, his friends asked him about this strange saying.

'Can't you see it, either?' asked Jesus. 'Isn't it clear that what's "outside" a man can't make him "dirty"? It doesn't go into his mind, only into his body. These things make a man "dirty": real badness, stealing, murder, greediness, wickedness, lying, indecency, selfishness, saying untrue things about people, having high and mighty ideas about yourself, not knowing what God wants you to do because you never tried to find out. All these wrong thoughts come out of a man's mind; they come from "inside" him and make him "dirty".'

LAST DAYS IN GALILEE

The Desert Meal

Everybody seemed to be coming and going; there was not time even to eat.

'Come,' said Jesus to his friends, 'it's you who need a holiday, away from the people, by yourselves.'

So off they went in a boat right away from everybody. But a lot of people saw them going away and recognized them; the crowds who had come from near-by villages hurried along the shore and got ahead of them.

Jesus put the boat back to land and got out.

He looked at the great crowd of people—5,000 men—and he was very sorry for them. He remembered the words from the Bible: 'Like sheep without a shepherd to look after them'. That's what this crowd was like; they had no leader. Jesus talked to them for quite a long time.

By now the afternoon was passing.

'This is a very lonely place,' said his friends to Jesus, 'and it's getting very late. Send the crowd off; they can find their way to the farms and villages over there and get some food.'

'You feed them,' said Jesus.

'What!' they said. 'Do you want us to go and buy £50 worth of bread to feed them?'

'How many loaves have you got?' asked Jesus. 'Go and see.'

They found out.

'Five,' they said, 'and two fish!'

Jesus told the men to sit down in groups on the green grass, and they sat down in companies, some one hundred and some fifty strong.

Jesus took the five loaves and the two fish, and looked up and said Grace over them. He broke the loaves and gave the pieces to his friends to give to the people; and he shared the fish with them all, too. Everybody had enough to eat, and they gathered what was left of the crumbs and the fish into twelve baskets.

Then Jesus straight away made his friends get into the boat and go ahead of him over to the far shore of the lake, near Bethsaida. He stayed behind to get the crowd to go home. When he had said good-bye to them he went away up into the hills to pray.

The Night at Sea

It was now dark. The boat was out at sea and Jesus was alone on the land.

Hours passed and it was just before dawn. The men in the boat were in a bad way. A sudden storm had come down on the sea and they were struggling against the wind. Jesus saw them and came to them, walking on the sea. He was level with the boat, when they saw him. They thought he was a ghost. They yelled out in terror; all of them were staring at him.

'Cheer up!' said Jesus. 'It's me. Don't be frightened.'

He got into the boat with them and the wind dropped. They were utterly amazed; they didn't know what to make of it.

When they got across to the land, they were back again on the west shore where they started. They brought the boat into the harbour. They had just got out of the boat when the people recognized Jesus. They ran round the countryside and carried on mats those who were ill to wherever they heard he was.

In the Northern Highlands

JESUS now left Galilee and crossed the border into the countryside which was governed by the foreign cities of Tyre and Sidon. The countryside they governed stretched right across the mountains from the sea to the Jordan Valley. When he left this foreign countryside, Jesus still stayed outside Galilee. He went into 'Ten Town Country', the country governed by the great Greek cities; and then into the countryside of the new city which the Governor Philip had built in the highlands. Here he climbed snow-capped Hermon Mountain with Peter and James and John.

Jesus spent most of the time alone with his friends. He was trying to help them to understand what God's Way was really like.

JESUS IN HIDING

After the Desert Meal, Jesus left his own country, Galilee, and went over the border into the countryside which belongs to the foreign city of Tyre. He stayed in a house, because he did not want people to know where he was, but he couldn't hide away so easily.

He left the countryside of Tyre and went through the country-side of Sidon, through 'Ten Town Country', across the mountains to Galilee Lake.

JESUS AND A FOREIGNER

While Jesus was in the countryside of Tyre, a foreign woman, whose little girl was sick in mind, heard about him. She came and fell down at his feet, and asked him to make her daughter better.

'Children get their food first,' said Jesus to her. 'You don't give the children's food to your little dogs.'

'Of course, Sir,' she said, 'but the little dogs under the table get the crumbs the children drop!'

'You're right,' said Jesus. 'You can go home, your daughter's better.'

The woman went home and found her daughter lying in bed, quite better.

The ruins of one of the foreign cities in Palestine. This is the square of the city of Jerash. These foreign cities were built just like the cities in Greece and Asia, with the same sort of buildings and streets.

ON A COUNTRY ROAD

Jesus and his friends went out into the countryside near the new city which the Governor Philip had built in the highlands.

'People are talking about me,' said Jesus to his friends, as they were walking along the road. 'Who do they say I am?'

'Some say John,' they told him. 'Others say Elijah, and others say one of the great men of God.'

'But you,' said Jesus, 'who do you say I am?'

'You're God's chosen Leader!' said Peter.

Jesus warned them not to say this to anybody.

He went on to tell them that he himself—and his friends as well—would have to go through hard times. He would be treated as an enemy of the Jewish Leaders and would have to face death; but his death would not be the end. He was quite open about it.

Peter took Jesus on one side and talked seriously to him. Jesus turned round and saw his other friends. He spoke seriously to Peter.

'Out of my sight, Tempter!' he said. 'You're not thinking of what God wants. You're talking like everybody else.'

A MOUNTAIN WALK

A week later Jesus took his three friends, Peter, James, and John, and led them up into a high mountain. They were all alone together.

High up the mountain, Jesus was changed.

His friends were still with him. His clothes were gleaming white; no bleacher on earth could make them whiter. His friends saw two other men talking with Jesus: Moses, who had led the people out of slavery in Egypt, and Elijah, who had stood up to a king in God's name.

Peter didn't know what to say, so he started talking like this.

'Sir,' he said. 'It's grand for us to be up here. Do you want us to make three shelters, one for you, one for Moses and one for Elijah?'

Peter and James and John were terrified.

A cloud rolled round them. God's words came into their minds. 'This is my only son. You must do what he says.'

The three men looked round. There was nobody there but Jesus.

As they went down the mountainside, Jesus told them not to talk

THE PORT OF SIDON—the foreign countryside Jesus visited when he crossed the border of Galilee.

about what they had seen to anybody, 'until I have risen from the dead.'

It was this saying they could not forget. They talked again and again among themselves about what 'rising from the dead' could mean.

At the Foot of the Mountain

Jesus, Peter, James, and John had left their friends behind at the foot of the mountain. When they got back, they saw a great crowd round them and the Jewish Leaders arguing with them.

'What's the argument about?' asked Jesus.

'Sir,' said one of the crowd, 'I brought my boy here. It's you I wanted to see. He has fits and loses his speech. Every time he has a fit, it throws him on the ground. He foams at the mouth and grinds his teeth and becomes stiff. I asked your friends here to make him better, but they couldn't do anything.'

'What little trust you've got!' said Jesus. 'How long have I got to be with you? How long have I got to put up with you? Bring him to me.'

They brought him to Jesus, and the lad fell on the ground in a fit and rolled about foaming at the mouth.

'How long has he been like this?' Jesus asked his father.

'Ever since he was a child,' he said. 'It's thrown him many times into the fire and into water. He might have lost his life. If you can do anything, have pity on us and help us!'

' "If you can"!' said Jesus. 'Everything is possible to a man who trusts.'

'I trust!' cried the boy's father. 'Help me if I don't trust enough.'

Jesus noticed that the crowd was running towards him. He spoke severely.

'You deaf and dumb spirit! Come out of him, I tell you, and never go into him again.'

With a scream, the lad had a terrible fit and the spirit left him. He lay as if dead.

'He's dead!' everybody was saying.

Jesus took hold of his hand and lifted him up; and the lad stood on his feet.

The countryside near the new city the Governor Philip had built in the highlands. This is the source of Jordan River, near Hermon Mountain.

The Journey South

JESUS now left the north country and went south. But he did not want people to recognize him and come crowding round him to listen to him or be healed by him. His work in the north was finished. So he passed quickly through Galilee and Samaria. He had to tell the people in the south the Good News about God, as he had told it to the people in the north.

What God wanted him to do was clear. But he knew it would be dangerous. Jerusalem, the capital city, was in the south. Here was the headquarters of the Jewish government; and here, during the Great Feast, Pilate, the Roman Governor, and his soldiers came to keep order.

SETTING OFF

Jesus left the northern highlands and crossed Galilee. He did not want either the Jewish Leaders or the people in the villages to know about it. He was still trying to get his friends to see the danger he was in.

Three things were clear to him. First, he would be caught by the Jewish Leaders; secondly, if he was caught, they would kill him; thirdly, if they killed him his death would not be the end—he would soon 'rise'.

His friends did not know what he was talking about and they were afraid to ask him any questions.

A QUARREL

Jesus and his friends had been out on the road.

'What were you arguing about as you came along the road?' he asked them when they were back in the house.

They said nothing; they had been arguing with one another about which one of them was the most important.

Jesus sat down, and called the 'Twelve'.

' "Number One" among my friends,' he said, 'doesn't mind being of no importance at all and spending his time looking after other peoples' needs.'

He took a boy and stood him among the grown men and then picked him up.

'Whoever welcomes one of these young ones, because that's the sort of thing I would do,' he said, 'welcomes me; and whoever welcomes me, welcomes not me—but God who sent me.'

OUTSIDERS

'We saw a man making sick people better and using your name,' said John to Jesus one day. 'He doesn't belong to us, so we stopped him.'

'Don't stop him,' said Jesus. 'Nobody will do a good deed, as one of my friends, and then quickly insult me. If a man is not our enemy, he is our friend. If anybody gives you a cup of water as a friend of mine, because you are doing God's work, I am very sure he won't miss his place in God's Kingdom.'

ON THE ROAD

Jesus and the 'Twelve' were on the road going up to Jerusalem. Jesus was striding on ahead; his friends were following behind him, alarmed and frightened.

Jesus took them on one side again, and told them what was going to happen to him.

'Look,' he said, 'we're going up to Jerusalem, the capital city. I shall be handed over to the Jewish Leaders, and they will want to put me to death. That means handing me over to the Romans, who won't be very gentle in the way they treat me; they will kill me. But, as I have told you, my death will not be the end. I shall soon "rise".'

'GREAT MEN'

James and John came up to Jesus one day.

'Sir,' they said, 'we're going to ask you for something and we want you to do it for us.'

'What do you want me to do for you?' asked Jesus.

'When you are a real King,' they said, 'make us the chief members of your Government.'

'You don't know what you are talking about,' said Jesus. 'Can you go through what I must go through?'

'Of course we can!' they said.

'You'll go through what I must go through all right,' said Jesus. 'But I can't make anybody "a chief member of my Government". God has marked out my leaders.'

The other ten friends of Jesus were angry with James and John. So Jesus called them all together.

'You know what it is like in the world outside,' he said. 'Those who think of themselves as bosses order their people about, and their great men are bullies. That isn't what you must do. You must turn it all the other way round. Whoever wants to be a "Great Man" among you must be—your servant! Whoever wants to be "Number One" must be—everybody's slave! I didn't come to have servants looking after me. I came to be a servant myself and to give myself to make everybody else free.'

A JERICHO BEGGAR

Jesus and his friends were leaving Jericho by the Jerusalem Road, and there was a large crowd with them. A blind beggar, Bartimaeus, was sitting at the roadside; he heard people saying, 'It's Jesus from Nazareth'.

'Son of David! Jesus!' he shouted. 'Have pity on me!'

The crowd told him to be quiet, but he went on shouting 'Son of David! Have pity on me!'

Jesus stood still.

'Call him over here,' he said.

Everybody then started calling the blind man: 'Cheer up!' 'Get up!' 'He's calling you!'

The beggar threw his cloak off, jumped up and came to Jesus.

'What do you want me to do for you?' asked Jesus.

'Sir,' he said, 'give me my sight back again.'

'Go home,' said Jesus. 'It's your trust in me that has made you better.'

His sight came back, and he followed Jesus along the road.

In Jerusalem

JESUS now told the Good News about God in the villages of Judea in the south and in the villages on the eastern side of Jordan River. In October, he went up to Jerusalem City for the 'Feast of Tents', when pilgrims walked up the Jericho Road and entered Jerusalem City, carrying branches, and remembered the day, 170 years before, when the Jews had recaptured Jerusalem from a foreign king.

Jesus not only told stories to help people to understand God's Way; he acted stories sometimes, as great men of God, like Isaiah and Jeremiah, had done before him. If people forgot the stories he told them, they might remember the stories he acted; for this was a strange thing to do, and people remember strange things. When he rode into the City on a donkey (not a horse, which would look like a war horse) and when he upset the market stalls in the Foreigners' Court and told them God's Temple was for everybody to worship in, he was *acting* God's Way, not just talking about it.

REACHING THE CITY

Jerusalem was at last in sight. Near the Olive Hill, Jesus sent his friends to a village.

'Go into the village facing you,' Jesus said, 'and just as you go in you'll find a donkey. It'll be tied up, and it hasn't been broken in yet. Untie it and bring it; and if anyone asks you why you are doing this, tell them: "The Master needs it, and he'll send it straight back." '

They went off, and found the donkey tied at a door outside in the street. They untied it.

'What are you untying the donkey for?' asked some of the bystanders.

They said what Jesus had told them to say, and the men let them take it away.

They brought the donkey to Jesus and threw their clothes on its back. Jesus sat on it. People spread their clothes on the road, and others cut leafy branches from the fields and spread them out. All the crowd, those in front and those behind, shouted the words from the old Bible hymn:

'They found the donkey tied at a door outside in the street'.

Hurrah!
Happy is he who comes in God's name!
Happy is the Kingdom of King David, our father!
A thousand times—Hurrah!

Jesus· went into the city and into the Temple. He looked all round. Then, since it was getting dark, he went off with his friends out to the village of Bethany.

IN THE FOREIGNERS' COURT

Next day, Jesus walked into the city again and went into the Temple. In the great Foreigners' Court he drove out the shopkeepers who had their stalls there and the people who were buying. He upset the tables of the moneylenders and the chairs of the pigeon-sellers. He wouldn't let anybody take a short cut and carry goods through the Temple.

'Doesn't the Bible say,' he said, ' "My House shall be called the House of Worship for all foreign people"? You have made it a bandits' den.'

The Jewish Leaders heard about all this and tried to find ways of getting rid of Jesus. They were frightened of him, for ordinary people listened to him with amazement.

At the end of the day Jesus and his friends went out of the city.

THE JEWISH LEADERS ASK QUESTIONS

Jesus was in Jerusalem again. As he was walking about the Temple, Jewish Leaders came up to him.

'Who told you to do this sort of thing?' they asked. 'Who gave you the right to act like this?'

'I'll ask you a question first,' said Jesus. 'You answer my question and I'll answer yours. You remember John the Hermit; was he God's messenger, or just another of these mob-leaders? You tell me.'

They didn't know what to say.

'If we say, "He was God's messenger," ' they said to one another, 'he'll say, "Why didn't you join him, then?". If we say, "Oh, just one of these mob-leaders . . .".'

They hardly dared finish the sentence. They were frightened of the crowd, for everybody thought that John was one of God's messengers.

'We don't know,' they said at last.

'Well, I'm not telling you, then, who gave me power to do what I'm doing,' said Jesus. 'But I'll tell you a story.

OUTSIDE THE WALL OF JERUSALEM CITY.

This stone, with its warning to foreigners to keep out, was set in the gates leading from the Foreigners' Court to the Inner Temple. It reads: 'No foreigner must go inside the barrier and wall around the Temple. If any foreigner is caught inside, he will be sentenced to death, and the blame will be entirely his own.'

'Once upon a time a man cleared the ground and made a farm. He let it out to farmers and went off abroad. At harvest-time he sent a slave for his share of the harvest, but the farmers beat the slave and sent him off with empty hands. He sent another slave, but the farmers hit him on the head and insulted him.

'The landowner had an only son; he sent him to the farm.

' "They will respect my son," he said.

'When the farmers saw him, they said to one another: "This is the son himself. Come on, let's kill him and the farm will be ours!"

'They got hold of him, killed him, and threw his body outside the farm.

'What will the landowner do? He will come himself, of course, and destroy those farmers and give the farm to others.'

The Jewish Leaders now made up their minds to get hold of Jesus, for they knew that the story was aimed at them. But they were frightened of the crowd; so they left Jesus and went away.

A TRAP

The Jewish Leaders sent men to catch Jesus off his guard.

'Sir,' they said, 'we know you're straight. You treat everybody alike, you have no favourites and you teach God's Way as it really is.

Tell us the answer to this question: Is it right to pay taxes to the Roman Emperor, or not? Should we pay or shouldn't we?'

Jesus knew that they weren't asking a straightforward question. 'What are you trying me out for?' he said. 'Get me a coin to look at.'

They got one for him.

'Whose face is this?' he asked. 'Whose name is this?'

'The Emperor's,' they said.

'Well, then, give what belongs to the Emperor back to the Emperor,' said Jesus, 'and give what belongs to God back to God.'

That made them speechless.

A Good Question

A teacher heard Jesus talking and knew that he had given some fine answers; so he asked a question himself.

'Which of God's commands,' he asked, 'is more important than all the others?'

'The most important command,' said Jesus, 'is this:

> Listen, O people!
> There is one God only;
> And you must love God with everything you are—
> your heart, your soul, your mind, your body.

'There is another command almost as important:

> You must love the fellow next to you as much as
> you love yourself.

'No other command is more important than these two.'

'Splendid, Sir,' said the teacher. 'You're right when you say that there is one God, and one God only; and that to love God with everything we are, and to love the fellow next to us as we love ourselves, is far more important than all the Temple services.'

Jesus noted his good answer.

'You are not far from being the kind of man God wants you to be,' he said.

ROMAN COINS. These are pictured twice their actual size. The first coin is the silver
denarius used during the reign of Tiberius Caesar (A.D. 14–37). The second coin is the
gold aureus issued in the reign of Nero (A.D. 54–68).

A WOMAN'S EXAMPLE

Jesus was one day sitting in the Temple and watching the crowd
throwing their money into the great Collection Bowl. Many rich
people put in great gifts. A poor widow came along, and threw in
two halfpennies.

Jesus called his friends.

'You see that poor woman,' he said. 'I tell you that she has
thrown more than anybody else into the bowl. All the others had
plenty to give. She had very little money, but she gave everything
she had; she really needed that money to keep alive.'

East of Jordan River

THE Jewish Leaders now knew what Jesus stood for. He had come to the capital city. He had even spoken in the Temple. He had done more: he had upset the market stalls in the Foreigners' Court and said that they, the Leaders, were not using the Temple in God's Way. He was a dangerous man. The Jewish Leaders made up their minds to arrest him and put him to death.

But Jesus had made up *his* mind to speak once again to the Jewish people in the capital city and call them to change their minds. This he decided to do at the Great Feast in the spring next year, the feast the Jewish people called 'The Passover'. At this feast they remembered the day, long ago, when Moses led them out of Egypt.

Jesus knew it would be dangerous to stay in Jerusalem. So he spent the winter in the villages east of Jordan River, where the Jewish Leaders could not get hold of him.

Mark does not tell us anything about what happened during the winter; this is all he tells us:

Jesus went across Jordan River to the villages beyond. Once more the crowds came to hear him, and, as he had done in Galilee, he spent his time telling them the Good News.

The Great Feast

IN the spring, a few days before the Great Feast, Jesus came back to Jerusalem City. On the Wednesday he was in Bethany, a little village not far from the City, where he had friends. On the Thursday evening, Jesus and his friends had supper together in the City itself. Armed men caught Jesus in an orchard as he was on his way back to Bethany. His friends got away. On the Friday, Jesus was brought by the Jewish Leaders before the Roman Governor, Pilate, and Pilate put him to death.

JUDAS

This happened two days before the Great Feast.

The Jewish Leaders were trying to find some way of getting hold of Jesus and killing him. They did not dare to do this openly, or when the Great Feast was on, for they were afraid of a riot.

They were delighted when they heard that one of the 'Twelve', Judas Iscariot, had come and offered to put Jesus into their hands. They promised to pay him, and Judas began to look out for the chance of doing it.

IN BETHANY

Jesus was having dinner with Simon the Leper in Bethany, when a woman came in with a bottle of real Indian ointment that must have cost a lot of money to buy. She broke the bottle and poured the ointment over the head of Jesus. Some of the visitors spoke angrily about it to one another.

'Why should such ointment be thrown away like this!' they muttered. 'It would have made over thirty pounds, and the money could have been given to the poor.'

'Leave her alone,' said Jesus. 'What do you want to upset her for? It's a fine thing she has done for me. There are always poor people among you, and you can help them whenever you want to. But I'm not here for ever. What she could do, she did. She was getting my body ready for burial—before I'm dead! But you may be sure of this: the Good News will be told all over the world, and the story of what this woman has done today will be told with it. Her memory won't die.'

Looking east from the Hill of the Olive Orchard, towards Bethany Village and the mountains east of Jordan River.

FINDING THE HOUSE

'Where do you want us to get the Feast ready?' the friends of Jesus asked him.

'Go into the city,' said Jesus to the two friends he was sending. 'A man carrying a water pot will meet you. Follow him and speak to the owner of the house he goes into. Tell him: "The Teacher says, 'Where is the room where I may eat the Feast with my friends?' " The owner himself will show you a large paved room upstairs. Get ready for us there.'

The men went away into the city and everything went as Jesus said. They got the Feast ready.

SUPPER

It was dark when Jesus and his friends came into the city.

'I tell you,' said Jesus, when they were having supper together, 'that one of you will hand me over to the Jewish Leaders—one who is having supper with me now.'

His friends were hurt at this.

'It can't be me?' they each said to him.

'It's one of the "Twelve",' said Jesus. 'He is sharing this very meal with me. . . . What is going to happen is just what the Bible said would happen. But it will be a terrible thing for the man who hands me over to the Jewish Leaders; it would have been better for him if he had never lived.'

During the supper, Jesus took the loaf, blessed it, broke it, and gave it to his friends.

'Take it,' he said. 'This is my very self.'

He took the cup, said Grace, and gave it to them; they all drank from it.

'This means my death,' he said. 'I am dying to bring all men to God, as the Bible says, "from the least of them to the greatest". I am sure of this: I shall drink no more wine until that day when I drink it fresh in God's Kingdom.'

When supper was over, they sang a hymn; then they walked out to the Olive Hill outside the City, on the road to the village where he was staying.

IN THE STREET

'You will all let me down,' said Jesus, as they walked along. 'The Bible says:

> I will strike the shepherd
> and the sheep will run away.

But after I am "raised", I will go to Galilee before you.'

'Everybody else may let you down,' said Peter, 'but I won't.'

'I tell you, Peter,' said Jesus, 'that this very night, before dawn, you will say more than once that you're no friend of mine.'

'Say I'm no friend of yours?' said Peter hotly. 'I'd die with you first!'

Everybody else said the same.

IN THE ORCHARD

Jesus and his friends came to the Olive Orchard.

'Sit here,' he said to them. 'I am going to pray.'

He took his three friends, Peter, James, and John, with him. He was in very great distress.

'I am broken hearted,' he said. 'This has nearly finished me. Stay here and keep on the alert.'

THE HILL OF THE OLIVE ORCHARD.

He went on a little way, fell on the ground and prayed that, if it could be, the terrible moment that lay ahead of him might pass him by.

'Father,' he prayed. 'You can do anything. Take this suffering away from me. Yet I'll do what You want, not what I want.'

He came back and found them asleep.

'Simon,' he said. 'Are you sleeping? Couldn't you keep awake for an hour? You must keep awake, and keep praying that you may not be put to the test. You are keen enough, but you aren't strong enough.'

He went away again, and prayed as he had done before.

He came back and found them asleep again. They could not keep their eyes open, and they did not know what to say to him.

He came back a third time.

'Are you still sleeping and resting?' he asked. 'He's here! The time's come! I am being handed over to the Romans! Get up! Let us go! Look—my betrayer's here!'

Suddenly, Judas came with a gang armed with swords and clubs. They had been sent by the Jewish Leaders. Judas had arranged a secret signal so that there should be no mistake.

'The man I kiss, that's Jesus,' he told them. 'Get hold of him, and take him away under guard.'

He went straight up to Jesus.

'Sir!' he said, and kissed him—as if he was just meeting him.

The men grabbed Jesus, and put him under guard.

A man standing near drew his sword and struck a Jewish officer and cut off his ear.

'Do you come out armed,' said Jesus to the soldiers, 'to take me like a bandit? I was talking day by day to the people in the Temple; you were there, but you didn't take me then! This, of course, is only what the Bible said would happen!'

Everybody left him and ran away.

There was a young man there with Jesus. He wasn't properly dressed; he had only a linen sheet wrapped round him. The soldiers grabbed him, but he let the sheet go and ran away naked.

BEFORE THE JEWISH LEADERS

The soldiers took Jesus to the High Court.

The Jewish Leaders wanted proof against him so that they could have him put to death. They could find none. Many false reports were given against him, but they were all mixed up.

People got up and told lies about him like this:

'We ourselves heard him say that he would pull down this Temple

THE OLIVE ORCHARD (Gethsemane).

built here in Jerusalem, and without any builders build a new one in no time!'

But they could not make their stories fit together.

At last the Judge stood up and questioned Jesus.

'Have you nothing to say?' he asked. 'Why are these men saying all this against you?'

Jesus gave no answer.

'Are you God's Great Deliverer?' the Judge asked him. 'Are you God's Son?'

'I am,' said Jesus.

The Judge tore his clothes.

'We don't want witnesses any more!' he said. 'You have heard the terrible words. What do you say?'

They all voted for the death of Jesus.

Peter had followed Jesus, a long way behind, right into the courtyard. He sat down there with the servants and was warming himself at a fire.

One of the maids came along. When she saw Peter warming himself she stared at him.

'You, too, were with Jesus, the man from Nazareth,' she said.

'I don't understand you,' said Peter, 'and I don't know what you're talking about!'

He went outside into the yard and the maid saw him.

'This fellow's one of them,' she said again to the people near.

Peter denied it again, but the bystanders soon took him up.

'Of course you're one of them,' they said. 'You come from the north too!'

Peter cursed and swore.

'I don't know the man you're talking about,' he said. A cock crowed a second time, and Peter remembered what Jesus had said to him: 'Before dawn, you will say more than once that you're no friend of mine.'

Peter broke down and cried.

BEFORE THE ROMAN GOVERNOR

Early in the morning, the Council of the Jewish Leaders talked over what they should do with Jesus. They handcuffed him and took him off and handed him over to Pilate, the Roman Governor.

'Are you the Jewish King?' asked Pilate.

'You use the word,' said Jesus.

The Jewish Leaders brought charge after charge against him.

'Haven't you got anything to say?' asked Pilate. 'See the charges they are making against you.'

But Jesus had nothing more to say, and Pilate was very surprised.

At the Feast, Pilate used to set free any prisoner the crowd asked for.

There were some rebels in prison, who had murdered people in the Rebellion, and one of them was Barabbas.

The crowd went up and asked Pilate to do as he had done before.

'Do you want me to set "The King" free for you?' asked Pilate.

He knew that it was for their own ends that the Jewish Leaders had handed Jesus over to him. The Jewish Leaders now stirred up the crowd to get him to set Barabbas free instead.

'What, then, do you want me to do to the man you call "The King"?'

'Hang him on a cross,' they shouted.

'But what's his crime?' asked Pilate.

'Hang him on a cross!' they went on shouting.

Pilate wanted to put the mob in a good mood, so he set Barabbas free and had Jesus flogged. Then he handed him over to the soldiers to be put to death on a cross.

THE SOLDIERS

The guard took Jesus away into the palace and called all the soldiers together. They got hold of a soldier's red cloak and threw it round Jesus and made a crown from a thornbush and put it on his head. They saluted him.

'Hail, your Majesty!' they shouted.

They hit him on the head with a cane and spat on him and went down on their knees and bowed to him.

When they'd finished making fun of him, they took the red cloak off him and dressed him in his own clothes, and led him out to die.

AT SKULL HILL

Simon, whose home was in North Africa, was coming into the city from the country at the time. The soldiers made him carry the wooden cross and marched Jesus to Skull Hill. They gave him drugs to deaden the pain, but he didn't take them.

It was nine o'clock in the morning. They nailed him to the cross and tossed up for his clothes and shared them out among themselves.

The charge against Jesus was fastened on the cross, THE JEWISH KING.

The soldiers put two bandits to death at the same time, one on each side of Jesus.

Passers-by shook their heads and swore at Jesus.

'Aha! You'd pull the Temple down and build it up again in no time! You'd better look after yourself and get down from the cross!'

Some of the Jewish Leaders made fun of him among themselves.

'He looked after other people,' they laughed, 'he can't look after himself! Let the Great Deliverer, the King, get down from the cross now! We'd like to see him do it—we'd believe him then all right!'

The bandits on their crosses insulted him too.

At noon, the sky went dark and the darkness lasted for three hours.

It was now three o'clock in the afternoon.

'My God, my God, why have you left me alone?' Jesus called out loudly. The words are the words of an old Bible hymn.

Some of those standing near heard him call out, but they did not catch the words.

'See,' they said, 'he's calling for Elijah!'

One of them ran and filled a sponge with sour wine and put it on the end of a cane and tried to make Jesus drink it.

'Let's see if Elijah comes to help him down!' they shouted to one another.

Jesus gave a loud cry and died.

The Roman officer in charge of the guard was standing facing Jesus and saw how he died.

'This man was a real king!' he said.

Some of the women were watching him from a distance. They had been with Jesus in Galilee and looked after him there. Among them were Mary from Magdala, Mary the mother of the younger James and of Joses, and Salome, and many other women who had come up to Jerusalem with him.

THE BURIAL

It was now near sunset when the Holy Day of the Jews began, and all preparation for any kind of work had to be finished.

There was a good man called Joseph, a well-known member of the

Jewish Council, from the village of Arimathea. He was brave enough to go to Pilate and ask for the body of Jesus.

Pilate was very surprised to hear that Jesus was already dead. He ordered the Commanding Officer to bring his report; when he heard the report from the officer, he gave the body to Joseph.

Joseph took the body of Jesus down from the cross and wrapped it in a linen sheet which he had brought. He put the body in a cave which had already been cut out of the rock and rolled a stone against the mouth.

Mary from Magdala, and the other Mary, saw where the body of Jesus was buried.

The Story has only begun

YOU will find the earliest account of what happened after the death of Jesus in one of Paul's letters—the first letter he wrote to his friends in the city of Corinth. You can look it up in your Bibles (1 Corinthians, 15. 3–8).

Here is Mark's story.

The last pages of Mark's book have been torn away and lost. The dots show you where it ends. The words in your Bible which follow this sentence were written down much later. We have used some words from Matthew's book so that the story has its proper ending.

JESUS IS RISEN!

When the Holy Day of the Jews was over, three women friends of Jesus—Mary of Magdala, Mary who was James's mother, and Salome—brought sweet-smelling oils to anoint his body.

They got to his grave very early on Sunday, just as the sun was rising.

'Who will roll the stone away from the cave's mouth for us?' they said to one another.

It was a very big stone. They looked up and saw that it had already been rolled away.

They went into the cave and they were amazed to see a young man in white clothes sitting on the right-hand side.

'Don't be frightened,' he said. 'You are looking for Jesus of Nazareth who was put to death. He has risen. You won't find him here; you can see where they put his body. Go and tell his friends that he will be in Galilee before you and you will see him there, as he told you you would. And don't forget Peter.'

They ran out of the cave trembling with terror. They were so frightened that they didn't say a word to anyone . . .

The eleven friends of Jesus went off to the hill in Galilee which Jesus had told them about. They saw him, and worshipped him; but some had their doubts.

'I have been given world-wide power,' said Jesus. 'Go. Help everybody everywhere to follow me. Get them to join my company of friends, and show them how to live as I showed you. Remember, I shall be with you—to the very end.'

BOOK TWO

THE MESSAGE

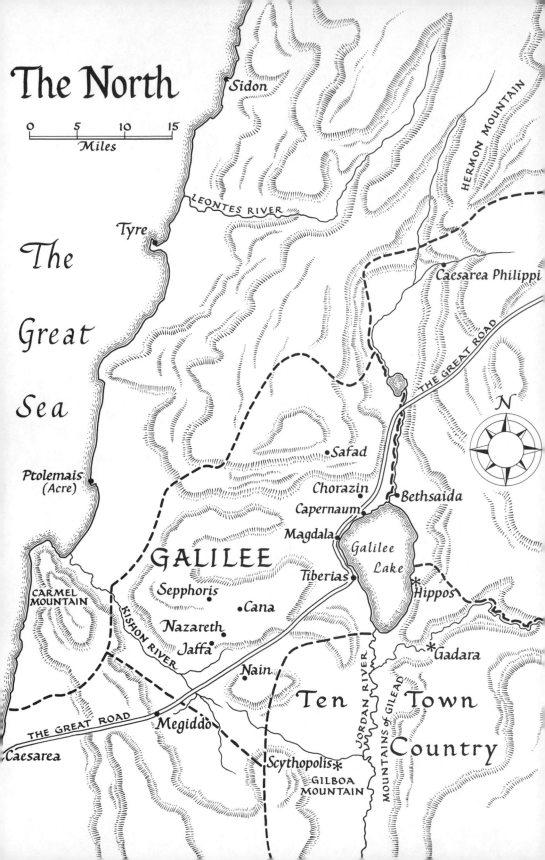

The North

0 5 10 15
Miles

Sidon

LEONTES RIVER

HERMON MOUNTAIN

Tyre

The

Great

Sea

Caesarea Philippi

THE GREAT ROAD

N

Ptolemais
(Acre)

Safad

Chorazin

Bethsaida

Capernaum

Magdala

GALILEE

Galilee
Lake

CARMEL
MOUNTAIN

Sepphoris

Tiberias

Hippos

KISHON RIVER

Cana

Nazareth

Gadara

Jaffa

Jordan River

MOUNTAINS of GILEAD

Nain

Ten

Town

THE GREAT ROAD

Megiddo

Caesarea

Scythopolis

Country

GILBOA
MOUNTAIN

The Conversations of Jesus

The friends of Jesus remembered some of his sayings and just what happened when he said them—where he was, the people he was talking to, and the way the conversation went. These sayings seemed to them very important sayings.

You will find many stories of the conversations of Jesus in *The Beginning*. We have not printed them again here; you can look them up for yourself. Here are other stories of the conversation of Jesus. Notice how each story ends with a saying.

1. In a Meeting House

One Saturday, the Holy Day of the Jews, Jesus was speaking to the people in one of the village Meeting Houses. There was a woman there who had been ill for eighteen years; she was bent double and couldn't stand upright at all. Jesus noticed her and called her over to him.

'My dear,' he said, 'be strong again.'

He touched her with his hands, and there and then she stood straight upright. She was so happy she started to tell everybody how good God was.

The officer in charge of the Meeting House was very angry that Jesus had done this on the Holy Day.

'You've got six week-days for working in,' he kept saying to the crowd in the Meeting House. 'Come along with your troubles then, if you want to be made better. Don't come here with them on the Holy Day.'

'You're only playing at being good,' said Jesus to him. 'Doesn't every one of you untie his ox or his donkey from its stall and take it out to water it on the Holy Day? This woman is as good a Jew as you are. She's been kept bent double, remember, for eighteen years. It's like being chained up day after day. Wasn't it right that she should be set free on God's Holy Day?'

2. *A Voice from the Crowd*

One day a crowd of people were listening to Jesus.

'Sir,' said a man in the crowd, 'when my father died my brother took all he left and kept it. Tell him to share it with me.'

'My good man,' said Jesus, 'this is not a law-court and I'm not a judge. It's not my work to settle questions like this.'

He turned to the crowd.

'Don't get greedy,' he said. 'Being a millionaire isn't the sort of thing that makes life worth living.'

3. *Another Voice*

Jesus was speaking to a crowd of people.

'Your mother must have been a very happy woman!' a woman called out from the crowd.

'No,' said Jesus. 'The really happy people are those who listen to what God says—and then do it.'

4. *Dreadful News*

Pilate, the Roman Governor, had done a dreadful thing. His soldiers had murdered some men from Galilee while they were worshipping God in the Temple in Jerusalem.

Some people came and told Jesus about it.

'Do you think,' said Jesus, 'that their death proves that these men were more wicked than the other people who live in Galilee? I tell you, if you go on doing wicked things, when you know they are wicked, and do not change your ways, you will face something just as terrible.

'Do you remember when the tower near Siloam Pool fell down, and killed eighteen men who were standing there? I tell you, if you go on doing wicked things, when you know they are wicked, and do not change your ways, you will face something just as terrible.'

5. *Meeting a Jewish Leader*

'When shall we really see people living in God's Way?' a Jewish Leader once asked Jesus.

'This isn't the sort of thing that happens all of a sudden,' said Jesus. 'You can't *see* it. Nobody will say, "Ah! Here it is!" or "There it is!" It's here now.'

6. *Going to Dinner*

One Saturday, the Holy Day of the Jews, Jesus went to the home of a Jewish Leader to have dinner with him. The Jewish Leaders themselves were only pretending to be friendly; they were really 'shadowing' him.

There was a very sick man in front of Jesus. Somebody asked a question about him.

'Tell me,' said Jesus to the Leaders there. 'Today is the Holy Day; is making a sick man better *today* right or wrong?'

The Jewish Leaders said nothing.

Jesus took hold of the man, made him better and sent him home.

'Is there any one of you,' asked Jesus, 'who wouldn't pull his son out of the well he'd fallen into, even if it was the Holy Day? Why, he would do that even for his ox!'

That finished the conversation.

7. *Out in the Fields*

One day Jesus saw a man out at work. It was Saturday, the Holy Day of the Jews. Nobody was supposed to do any work on the Holy Day; it was forbidden by Jewish Law.

'Sir,' said Jesus, 'if you know what you are doing, you are a very happy man. If you don't—if you just don't care what you do and when you do it—you are doing a very wrong thing, and you really are breaking the law about the Holy Day.'

8. *Two Messengers*

One day the hermit John, who was in prison, called two of his friends and sent them to Jesus to ask him a question.

'John has sent us to you,' they told Jesus when they met him. 'He wants to know if you are the Great Deliverer God promised to send us, or must we go on waiting for somebody else?'

There was a crowd of people with Jesus that day; he was making many sick people better and giving many blind people the power to see.

THE COUNTRYSIDE OF GALILEE.

'Go back to John,' he said to the two men, 'and tell him what you have seen and heard. You remember what the Bible says?—

> Blind people see again;
>   lame people walk about;
> lepers are made better;
>   deaf people are hearing;
> dead people are alive again;
>   hopeless people are told the Good News.

'The really happy man is the man who isn't shocked at what I am doing.'

9. On a Country Road

Jesus and his friends were walking along a country road. A man joined them.

'I'll go anywhere with you,' he said to Jesus.

'Foxes have dens and wild birds can roost,' said Jesus. 'I and my friends have no home.'

'Come and join my company of friends,' said Jesus to another man.

'I have to go back to my father's funeral,' said the man. 'Let me do that first.'

'There's something more important than a funeral—even your father's funeral,' said Jesus. 'You must come and tell the Good News of God's Way far and wide.'

'I'll come and join your company of friends, sir,' said a third man. 'But let me first of all say good-bye to my family.'

'Nobody who starts ploughing and then keeps looking back at the field behind him,' said Jesus, 'is living in God's Way.'

10. Peter's Question

Peter came to Jesus one day.

'Sir,' he said, 'how often can somebody treat me badly, and I forgive him and be friends with him again? Will seven times be enough?'

'This isn't something you can add up like sums,' said Jesus. 'The answer is—every time.'

EARLY MORNING BY GALILEE LAKE.

STORM BREAKING OVER GALILEE LAKE.

11. In the House

Jesus and his friends one day came back to Capernaum. The tax-collectors stopped Peter.

'Doesn't your master pay taxes?' they asked him.

'Of course,' said Peter.

When Jesus went into the house he was the first to speak.

'What do you think, Peter?' he asked. 'Do the Romans force their own citizens or foreigners to pay taxes?'

'Why, foreigners, of course,' said Peter.

'You see,' said Jesus, 'citizens are free men.'

12. In the Temple

One day Jesus and his friends were coming out of the Temple in Jerusalem.

'Look, sir,' said one of his friends to Jesus. 'What huge stones! What grand buildings!'

'You see these great buildings?' said Jesus. 'None of the walls will be left standing; every stone will be pulled down.'

13. On the Road to Skull Hill

Soldiers were marching Jesus to Skull Hill. There was a great crowd of people following him, and among them were women, very sad indeed and crying.

Jesus turned to them.

'You women of Jerusalem,' he said, 'don't cry for me. You should be crying for yourselves and your children. The time is coming when war will have broken out, and the streets will be full of fighting. People will say, "She's a very happy woman—she's got no children to worry about". Do you remember what the Bible says?—In those days

> They shall say to the mountains,
> "Fall on us!"
> And to the hills,
> "Hide us!"

'If this is how they behave in the springtime, what will they do when autumn comes?'

The Stories of Jesus

1. Boys on a Farm

A FARMER lived on a farm with his two boys.

'Tom,' he said to the first boy, 'give me a hand on the farm today.'

'All right, Dad,' he said.

But he didn't go.

The farmer said exactly the same to his second boy, Bill.

'Not I!' said Bill.

But later on he changed his mind, and went to give his father a hand on the farm.

Did Tom, or Bill, do what his father wanted?

2. Girls at a Wedding

God's Way is like this.

There was a wedding in a village. Ten village girls picked up their torches, and went out to meet the bridegroom.

Five of the girls took no spare oil; the others carried flasks of oil.

The bridegroom was a very long time coming; so long that the girls got drowsy and went to sleep. Suddenly, in the middle of the night, there was a great shouting.

'Look, the bridegroom's coming,' the watchman called out. 'Off you go to meet him.'

All the girls jumped up and trimmed their torches.

'Lend us some oil,' said the girls who had no oil, to the others. 'Our torches are going out.'

'Not likely,' said they. 'There won't be enough for us all. Go to the shops and buy your own.'

Off they went to buy oil; and, while they were away, the bridegroom came.

Everybody who was ready went in with him to the feast; and the door was shut.

It was some time before the girls got back.

'Sir! Sir!' they shouted. 'Open the door for us!'

3. *Playing in the Street*

What are people today like?

They are like children playing games in the street. There they are—sitting on the ground.

'We wanted to play at weddings,' the boys call out to their playmates, 'but you didn't dance.'

'We wanted to play funerals,' the girls call out, 'but you didn't play the part of the mourners.'

John the Hermit starved himself:

'He's mad,' people say.

I go out to dinner with all sorts of people:

'Glutton and drunk,' they say, 'friend of traitors and scoundrels.'

God will be proved right; you see what happens.

4. *The House Door*

Try as hard as you can to go in through the narrow door. Lots of people, I am sure, are trying to get in; but they can't.

5. *The Lamp*

What do you light a lamp for?

To put it out?
To put it under the bed?

Or to put it on the stand
to light the whole house
and all who live in it?

6. *Yeast*

God's Way is like this.

A woman took some yeast and mixed it into a lot of flour; and *all* the flour rose.

7. *Salt*

Salt is good.
But what can you do with salt that is no longer salty?
It's fit neither for food nor for manure.
You can only throw it into the street.

8. Cloth and Wineskins

You don't sew a patch of new cloth
  on an old dress.
If you do, the new patch
  pulls at the old dress.
Then you've got a worse tear.
You don't put new wine
  into old wine-skins.
If you do, the wine bursts the skins
  and wine and skins are lost.
New wine-skins for new wine!

9. Sawdust and Log

Why do you see a little speck of sawdust in your friend's eye, but don't notice the great log of wood in your own eye?

'Tom!' you say to your friend, 'let me take that little speck of sawdust out of your eye.'

But you yourself don't see the great log of wood in your own eye.

When you act like this, you are only pretending to be good. Take the great log of wood out of your own eye first. Then you will be able to see clearly enough to take the little speck of sawdust out of your friend's eye.

10. Where the Wild Birds Roost

How shall I picture God's way of doing things? What story shall I use? It's like this.

When a mustard seed is sown in the soil, it's the smallest seed in the world. But it grows up and becomes the largest plant in the world. Its branches are so big that (you remember what the Bible says?)—

In the shelter of its branches
the wild birds roost.

11. The Fig Tree

The fig tree can teach us something.

Its branch is leafless in the winter. When it begins to bud and the leaves come out, summer is here.

12. *Father on the Farm and Mother at Home*

Is there a farmer with a hundred sheep who wouldn't leave them on the moors—if he had lost just one of them? Wouldn't he go after that lost sheep until he found it?

When he finds it, how happy he is! He puts it on his shoulders and brings it home. He calls his friends and neighbours together.

'I've found the lost sheep,' says he. 'Let's celebrate!'

God is as happy as that, I am sure, if one bad person makes up his mind to be good; happier than he is with ninety-nine 'good' people who (so they say) 'don't need to change their minds'.

Is there a woman with ten shillings who wouldn't light the lamp and sweep the room very, very carefully, and look everywhere—if she had lost just one of them? Wouldn't she go on looking until she found it?

When she finds it, how happy she is! She calls her friends and neighbours together.

'I've found the shilling I lost,' says she. 'Let's celebrate!'

God is as happy as that, I am sure, when one bad person makes up his mind to be good.

13. *Builders*

Everybody who listens to me
   and then does something about it
      is like a sensible builder.

He builds his house—
   and he builds it on rock.

Then winter comes.
   The rain pours down,
   the mountain torrents come tumbling down the hillside,
   the great winds blow
      and batter the house.

But it stands up to it all—
   underneath it is rock.

Everybody who listens to me
   but doesn't do anything about it
      is like a stupid builder.

THUNDERSTORM OVER JERUSALEM CITY.

He builds his house—
  but he builds it on earth.

Then winter comes.
  The rain pours down,
  the mountain torrents come tumbling down the hillside,
  the great winds blow
    and hurl themselves against *his* house.

Down it comes
  with a tremendous crash!

14. Fishermen and their Net

God's Way is like this.

Fishermen throw their dragnet into the sea, and it catches all sorts of fish. When it is full of fish, they pull it up on to the beach.

Then they sit down and sort the fish out: the fish they want to keep go into their baskets; the fish that are no good go back into the sea.

15. The Moneylender

Two men owed a moneylender money.

One owed him £500; the other £50. They hadn't a penny in the world; so the moneylender crossed their debts out.

Which of the two men would most want to say 'Thank you' to him?

16. Getting out of Trouble

Wouldn't *you* say something like this to a man who owed a moneylender a lot of money?—

'While you are going along the road to the court with him, do your best to get things settled up. You know what will happen if you don't. He'll drag you to the judge; the judge will hand you over to the constable; the constable will throw you into jail. There you'll stay until you've paid the last penny of your debt.'

17. The Unexpected Visitor

There's a neighbour who's a friend of yours. One night, about midnight, you go along to his house.

'Fred!' you call out, 'lend me three loaves of bread. A friend of mine's on a journey; he's just turned up at our house, and I haven't a thing to give him.'

'I can't be bothered,' says he from inside the house. 'The door's locked, and we're all in bed. I can't get up to give you anything.'

You know what happens. You stay there knocking on the door, and up your friend gets and gives you whatever you want; not because he's a friend of yours, but because you just wouldn't be put off.

18. Thieves

A thief can't just go in and ransack the house of a very strong man. He goes for the strong man first, and ties him up. Then he sets to and ransacks the house.

You can be sure of this. If the householder knew just when the thief was coming, he wouldn't let his house be broken into. Be ready!

A FARMYARD IN PALESTINE.

THE BIG FARM

19. Brothers' Quarrel

A man and his two sons were farmers.

The younger son came one day to his father.

'Dad,' he said, 'it's time you handed over the farm to the two of us. Give me my share.'

That's what the father did. He divided up the farm between his two sons, and handed it over.

The younger son quickly packed his things and went abroad. There he threw his money away having 'a good time'.

At last, his pockets were empty. Then the harvest failed all over the land. There he was—no money and no food. He took a job with a farmer there, and the farmer sent him off to feed the pigs in the fields. He felt like swallowing the pigs' food himself. Nobody lifted a hand to help him.

Then he knew what a fool he'd been.

'How many of the labourers on my father's farm have more food than they want,' he thought, 'and here I am starving to death! I'm going home to my father. I've wronged God, and I've wronged my father. I'll tell him so. And I'll tell him, too, that I don't deserve to be called a son of his; he can take me on as a labourer.'

He got up and went home.

When he was still quite a long way from his father's farm, his father saw him coming. He felt very sorry for him; and he ran out to meet him, threw his arms round his neck and kissed him.

'Dad,' the boy began to say, 'I've wronged God and I've wronged you. I don't deserve to be called a son of yours . . .'

'Quick!' his father called to the servants, 'go and get his best clothes out. Get a ring and sandals and dress him properly. And kill that calf we've fattened. We'll have a feast and a grand time tonight. My boy was dead and lost; and here he is alive and back home again!'

And they began to celebrate.

Now the older son had been out on the farm. He was coming home and had almost reached the farmhouse when he heard the sound of bagpipes and dancing. He called one of the farmhands out, and asked him what was going on.

'Your brother's back,' said the man. 'Your father's killed the calf because he's safe home again.'

The older son was furious, and he wouldn't even go inside the house. His father came out and begged him to come inside.

'Look,' he answered back, 'I've slaved for you all these years. I did everything you told me to do. But what do I get? Not even a kid to have a good time with my friends. This son of yours can throw his money away on girls, if he likes, and come home again—and you go and kill the calf for him!'

'My dear boy,' said his father. 'We're always together. All the farm is yours—you know that. We had to celebrate tonight. It's your *brother* who was dead and lost; it's your *brother* who's alive and back home again!'

20. *Trouble at Harvest Time*

God's Way is like this.

It was harvest time, and a farmer went out to the market square to hire workmen for his vineyard. He settled with them for the proper wage for the day—a pound—and sent them out to work.

About nine o'clock he went out again. Men were hanging about the square with nothing to do.

'You, too, can go and work in the vineyard,' he said, 'and I'll pay you the proper wage.'

Off they went to work.

At noon and at three o'clock in the afternoon he went out to the market square again, and the same thing happened.

About five o'clock he went out again to the square. Men were still hanging about.

'Why are you hanging about all day doing nothing?' he asked.

'Nobody has taken us on,' they said.

'You can go into the vineyard with the others,' he told them.

By now it was evening. The farmer spoke to his foreman.

'Call the workmen in,' he said, 'and pay them their wages. And start with the last ones we took on.'

Those who started work at five o'clock in the afternoon came up and got a full day's wage—a pound.

Then those who had started work at six o'clock in the morning came up; they expected to get more than that. They, too, got a full day's wage—a pound.

They began to go for the farmer.

'These fellows who started last have only done an hour's work!'

'And you are treating them like us!'

'We've had to do all the hard work!'

'And we've had the scorching sun to put up with as well!'

The farmer tackled their leader.

'My dear man,' he said, 'I'm not treating you badly. Didn't you settle with me for a proper day's wage? Take your money and get out. I'm going to give these fellows who started at five o'clock the same wage I'm giving you. Can't I use my own money as I want to? Does my generosity make you jealous?'

21. *A Clever Rascal*

A rich man had a manager.

One day he was visiting his estates, and this manager was charged with letting them go to rack and ruin.

He called the manager in to see him.

'What's this I hear about you?' he asked. 'You'd better give me an account of how you've been managing things. You can't go on as manager.'

'What shall I do?' the manager thought. 'My master's sacking me. I'm not strong enough for farm work; it would be a disgrace to start begging . . . I know what I'll do; and then, when I'm out of a job, people will open their homes to me.'

He sent word to the wholesale traders who hadn't paid their debts, and asked them to come and see him. He talked to them like this.

'How much do you owe my master?' he asked the first trader.
'Eight hundred gallons of oil,' he said.

'Here's your receipt,' said the manager. 'Sit down; be quick and write four hundred gallons down.'

'You,' said the manager to another trader, 'how much do you owe?'

'Five hundredweight of wheat,' he said.

'Take your receipt,' said the manager. 'Write four hundredweight down.'

(When Jesus told this story, wrote Dr. Luke, he had a good word to say for this clever rascal: he was a shrewd fellow.)

22. *Golden Corn*

Look! A farmer went out sowing.

As he sowed his seed,
   some fell on the path
      and the birds came and gobbled it up.

Some fell on rocky ground
   where it had little soil;
   it grew up quickly
   because the soil was thin.

When the sun was high in the sky
   it was burned up;
   because it had no roots
      it withered away.

Some seed fell among thorn bushes
   which grew up and choked it;
      it never ripened.

Some seed fell into good soil
   and ripened and grew big.
When harvest came—
   some seeds bore up to thirty seeds,
   some up to sixty seeds,
   some up to a hundred seeds.

OLIVE HARVEST.

23. *Out with the Sickle!*

God's Way is like this.

A farmer went out sowing. He scattered the seed on the earth, and then didn't bother about it any more. Every day he got up and went on with his farmwork, and every night he went to bed and slept.

The days went by, and the seeds sprouted and grew tall. The farmer didn't know how it happened, but he knew what the soil itself could do: first there would be the green shoot, then the ear, then the ripe corn. But when the crop was ready (you remember what the Bible says?)—

> He puts in the sickle—
> harvest time's here.

24. *The New Barn*

The farmlands of a rich farmer were bearing wonderful crops.

'What on earth shall I do?' the farmer kept thinking. 'There's no room in the old barn for these grand harvests.

'I know,' he went on. 'I'll tear down my old barns and build bigger ones, big enough to hold all my wheat and wealth. "You've wealth enough for many years. Take it easy, mate," I'll say to myself. "Have a good time. Eat and drink as much as you want."'

That night he died.

What happened to his wheat and his wealth?

25. A Fig Tree but no Figs

A farmer had planted a fig tree in his vineyard. One day he went to look for figs on it; there were none.

'Look,' he said to his gardener. 'I've been coming here, looking for figs on this tree, for three years; I haven't found a single one. Why should it waste good ground?'

'Sir,' said the gardener, 'let it alone for another year. I'll dig the earth round it and put manure on it. If there are figs on the tree next year—that will be fine. If not, you can cut it down.'

26. Farmers' Quarrel

God's Way is like this.

One November, after the early rains, a farmer sowed his fields with corn; and he sowed good seed.

THRESHING WHEAT.

A neighbour of his had a grudge against him. One night, when everybody was asleep, he and his men came over, and sowed weeds all over the newly sown fields; and off they went.

Nobody noticed anything. The first green shoots of corn and weed all looked alike. But when the corn began to grow tall, everybody could see what had happened—everywhere weeds were growing among the corn.

'Sir,' said the farmer's slaves, 'the seed we sowed was good seed, wasn't it? Where have all the weeds come from?'

'I think I know,' said the farmer. 'Somebody has got a grudge against me; this is his work.'

'What do you want us to do, then?' they asked. 'Go out and pull the weeds up?'

'No,' he said, 'we won't do that. We might pull up the corn as well. I'll let the fields lie, corn and weeds together. I'll deal with them at harvest time. "Get the corn into the barns," I'll tell the harvesters, "and tie up the weeds in bundles; we'll use them for the winter fires." '

SIFTING WHEAT.

STORIES OF SLAVES

27. Three Slaves

God's Way is like this.

A rich man was about to go abroad. He called his slaves and handed over his property to their keeping. To three of his slaves he gave £5 each and went abroad.

The first slave did some business with his money and doubled it. The second slave did the same. The third slave went off and dug a hole in the ground and buried his master's money.

The rich man was abroad for a long time. At last he came back and settled accounts with his slaves.

The first slave came and brought his £10.

'Sir,' he said, 'you handed £5 to me. Look, I've made it into £10.'

'Fine!' said his master. 'You're a good slave. You can be relied on. You've proved yourself with a small sum of money. I'll put you in charge of something much more important.'

The second slave came to him.

'Sir,' he said, 'you handed £5 to me. Look, I've made it into £10.'

'Fine!' said his master. 'You're a good slave. You can be relied on. You've proved yourself with a small sum of money. I'll put you in charge of something much more important.'

The third slave came along.

'Sir,' he said, 'I know the sort of man you are. You're a hard man. All you think of is making money; you get rich while other men do the work. I lost my nerve. I buried the £5 in the ground; I didn't want it stolen. Here's your money back.'

'You're a bad lazy slave,' said his master. 'You knew I get rich while other men work, did you? You should have taken my money to the bankers; then, at least, I should have got some interest on it when I came back. Take the money from him, and throw him into prison.'

28. Master and Slave

What would you do?

Suppose you were a farmer and you had a slave out ploughing or looking after the sheep. How would you talk to him when he comes in from the field?

Winnowing Grain.

Something like this?

'Come along in and get on with your supper.'

I know what you'd say.

'Get my supper ready,' you'd say, 'and tidy yourself, and wait on me while I have it. You can get your own supper when I've had mine.'

Would you thank him for doing what you told him to?

29. Slave Law

If a slave knows exactly what his master wants him to do, but doesn't get things ready and do what he's told, he gets a good flogging.

If a slave gets into trouble because he doesn't really know what his master wants, he gets off lightly.

30. Testing a Slave

How can a man tell if a slave is sensible and can be trusted? He is going away on business, and here's his chance: he puts him in charge of the other slaves and their rations. If the slave gets on with his job and his master finds him doing everything he was told to do when he comes home, he's a happy man. His master, no doubt, makes him his manager.

But suppose this happens.

'My master's a long time coming home,' the slave thinks. So he starts bullying the other slaves; he spends his time gorging himself and getting drunk. Then, suddenly, back comes his master— just when he's not expecting him. His master will give him the flogging he deserves; he knows he's a slave who can't be trusted.

31. Waiting for the Master

The master of the house is away at a wedding feast. The slaves are waiting for him to come home, ready to open the gates as soon as he knocks. They are happy slaves if their master finds them awake. They don't mind when he comes—before midnight or after midnight—so long as he finds them on the watch.

You must be like them—your belts fastened and your lamps alight.

A CARPENTER.

32. The Gatekeeper

God's Way is like this.

A man left home and went abroad. He put his slaves in charge of everything; each had his own job.

'Keep a sharp look out,' he said to the gatekeeper.

OUT ON THE ROAD

33. Bandits

A man was going down the road from Jerusalem to Jericho, and fell into the hands of bandits. They tore his clothes off him and beat him up. Then off they went, and left him lying half-dead on the road.

Quite by accident, a priest was going down the same road. He saw the man lying there, but he didn't stop. He went on past him—on the other side of the road. It was just the same with a Temple caretaker. He, too, came to the spot and saw the man lying there; he, too, didn't stop—he went on past him on the other side of the road.

Then a foreigner, who was on a journey across the country, came upon the man. He saw him lying there, and felt very sorry for him. He went across to him, put ointment on his wounds and bandaged them up. He lifted him up on to the horse he had been riding, and brought him to an inn and looked after him.

Next morning, he took a pound out of his purse and gave it to the inn-keeper.

'Look after him,' he said. 'If it costs more than a pound, I'll put it right with you on my way back.'

34. Farm Worker and Pearl Merchant

God's Way is like this.

Money had been buried in a field. One day, a man working in the field found it, and covered it up again. Wasn't he happy! Off he went and sold everything he had, and bought the field.

Or God's Way is like this.

A merchant was travelling from town to town, looking for beautiful pearls. One day, he found a wonderful pearl. Off he went, and sold everything he had and bought it.

35. Blind Men

Can a blind man lead another blind man along the village street? Won't they both fall into the ditch?

VILLAGE STORIES

36. King and Governor

God's Way is like this.

Once upon a time there was a foreign king who wanted to settle accounts with his high officers. One officer, a governor of a province, was brought to him who owed a million pounds, and he hadn't a penny left. The king ordered him to be sold—and his wife and children and whatever property he had.

The governor fell down on the ground before the king in great fear.

'Give me time,' he begged, 'and I'll pay everything back to you.'

The king felt sorry for him. So he set him free, and crossed out the whole debt.

The governor went off. On the way home he met one of his fellow officers who owed him £5. He got hold of him and nearly throttled him.

'Pay me the money you owe me,' he said.

His fellow officer fell down on the ground in front of him.

'Give me time,' he begged, 'and I'll pay everything back to you.'

But he wouldn't listen to him; he threw him into prison, to stay there until he had paid everything back.

The other officers saw what was happening. They were very angry indeed, and they told the king everything that had happened.

The king called the governor into his presence.

'You're an utter scoundrel,' he said angrily. 'I crossed out your huge debt when you begged for time to pay. Ought you not to have treated your fellow officer as I treated you, and shown him some pity?'

He handed him over to the jailors—to stay in prison until he had paid every penny back.

37. Farmer and King

What does a farmer do when he wants to build a watch-tower in his vineyard?

Doesn't he first sit down, and work out what it's going to cost? He wants to make sure he's got enough money. He knows what would happen if he laid the foundations of the tower, and then couldn't finish it—all the passers-by would make fun of him.

'This fellow started building,' they'd laugh, 'and couldn't finish it.'

What does a king do when he is going to meet another king in battle?

Doesn't he first sit down and work it all out: 'How can I, with 10,000 soldiers, meet my enemy who is coming against me with 20,000 soldiers?'

If he thinks he can't win, he sends officers, while his enemy is still a long way off, to ask for peace.

38. A Royal Wedding

A king gave a wedding feast for his son. He came in to see the wedding guests, and saw a guest who wasn't correctly dressed.

'My dear sir,' he said, 'how did you get in here without the correct dress?'

The man couldn't think of anything to say.

The king called his bodyguard.

'Tie him hand and foot,' he said, 'and throw him out into the night.'

39. Rich Man, Beggarman

Once upon a time there was a very rich man who lived in a palace.

He wore rich, purple clothes and ate the most wonderful food every day.

Lazarus, a lame beggar, lay outside his palace gate. He was covered with sores, and the street-dogs came and licked him. He used to dream of gorging himself with the bread that was left from the rich man's meals.

One day, the beggar died and the angels carried him away to heaven to live with Abraham. The rich man died and was buried.

Everything was now changed.

The rich man was very miserable. He looked from where he was, and there, a long way off, he saw Abraham and Lazarus having supper together.

'Father Abraham,' he called out, 'have pity on me. Send Lazarus to dip his finger-tips in water and cool my tongue. This heat is torture!'

A SHEPHERD.

'Son,' said Abraham, 'you've got a short memory. On earth you had your good time; Lazarus had a very bad time. Here it's all the other way round. Anyhow, there's a great gulf between us; nobody can cross it, either from us to you or from you to us.'

'Father,' he said, 'then I have one thing to ask you. Send him to my old home on earth to warn my five brothers. I don't want them to come here where I am, and be miserable like me.'

'They can read the Bible,' said Abraham, 'and do what it says.'

'That isn't enough, Father Abraham,' said he. 'But if someone like Lazarus went back from heaven and told them, they would change their minds.'

'They wouldn't,' said Abraham. 'If they won't read the Bible and do what it says, they won't listen to someone like Lazarus, even if he did go back from heaven.'

40. *Rude Guests*

Once upon a time a rich man was giving a great feast, and he invited many guests.

When the feast was ready, he sent his slave to all who were invited: 'Come along: it's all ready.'

And they all alike made excuses.

'I've bought some land,' said the first. 'I must go out and look at it. Please excuse me.'

'I've bought ten animals,' said another, 'and I'm going to test them. Please excuse me.'

'I've just got married,' said another. 'I can't come.'

The slave went back and told his master what they said. The master was angry.

'Go out into the town at once,' he told his slave. 'Bring in the beggars and the cripples and the blind people and the lame people from the streets and alleyways.'

41. *A Wicked Judge*

Once upon a time, in a certain town, there lived a judge who was a really bad man. He didn't care about God and he didn't care about men and women and what happened to them. In the same town there lived a widow. She kept coming to him to get a money matter settled.

'I want justice,' she kept saying, 'I want justice. I've been wronged.'

The judge took no notice of her for a long time.

'I couldn't care less for God or men,' he thought at last. 'But this widow is a regular nuisance. I'd better see that she gets justice. One of these days she'll be giving me a black eye!'

42. *Nobleman and Rebels*

Once upon a time a nobleman set off on a journey across the sea to the Emperor in Rome. He wanted the Emperor to make him a king.

His countrymen hated him. Some of them went to Rome themselves to tell the Emperor what they thought.

'We don't want this man to be our king,' they told him.

The Emperor wouldn't listen to them; and home the nobleman came—a king.

'Where are these enemies of mine?' he asked. 'They didn't want me to be king, eh? Drag them here to my palace, and kill them in front of me!'

43. A Ghost Story

Once upon a time a ghost lived in a haunted house. At last he was driven out. He wandered through the dry desert looking for somewhere to make his home. He had no luck.

'I'm going back to the old house,' said he.

So he went back, and there was the old house, swept clean and freshly decorated—and empty!

Off he went again, and brought seven other ghosts, much worse than himself, to live with him. They all settled down there together. Things in that house were far worse than they had ever been before.

This can happen to us.

44. Two Men

Once upon a time two men went up from the city streets into the Men's Court of the Temple to say their prayers.

The first man was a 'good' man; every Saturday, the Holy Day of the Jews, he went to the Meeting House to worship God.

The other man was a tax-collector; he worked for the foreign government, and, because he did that, 'good' people thought he was a 'bad' man.

The good man stood straight up and prayed aloud for everybody to hear:

'My God, I thank Thee that I was not born a foreigner but a Jew; not a slave but a freeman; not a woman but a man.'

While he was praying, he was thinking like this:

'O God, I thank Thee that I am not like other people, greedy, dishonest, wicked, or even like this tax-collector here. I fast twice each week; I give one-tenth of everything I earn to the Temple.'

The tax-collector stood a long way off. He wouldn't even look up; he was so sorry for all the wrong things he had done that he beat his chest with his hands.

'O God,' he kept saying, 'have mercy on me, vile wretch that I am!'

It was the tax-collector, believe me, not the 'good' man, who went home forgiven.

45. *Going to a Wedding Party*

When you are invited to a wedding,
  at the party afterwards
    don't sit down in the place of honour.
Somebody more important than you
  may have been invited.
Your host will come and say
  'Go lower down the table!'
What a fool you'll feel
  doing that!

When you are invited to a wedding,
  at the party afterwards
    take the least important seat.
Your host will say
  'Sir, come higher up the table!'
What honour you will have
  doing that!

The Poetry of Jesus

HOW GOD CARES FOR EVERYBODY

1. God looks after Us

This is what I want you to know:

Don't worry about what you are going to eat
   or what sort of clothes you are going to wear;
what you are is more important that what you eat,
   what you are is more important than what you wear.

Look at the wild birds:
   they don't go out farming;
   they have no store-house or barn;
God feeds them.
   How much more than wild birds you mean to God!

Look at the wild flowers:
   they don't work like mothers at home.
Yet, believe me, King Solomon wasn't robed as gloriously
                         as a wild flower.

God dresses the wild grass—
   blowing in the field today,
   a bonfire on the farm tomorrow.

How much more will God look after you!
   You don't trust him enough.

2. Sparrows

You can buy sparrows five a penny;
   Yet God keeps his eye on every sparrow.
He counts every hair of your head.
   There's nothing to fear:
   you mean more to him than a flock of sparrows.

3. Asking, Looking, Knocking

Keep asking—it will be given you;
   keep looking—you will find;
      keep knocking—the door will be opened.
Everyone who keeps asking, gets;

everyone who keeps looking, finds;
to everyone who keeps knocking, the door opens.

What father will give a stone to his boy
   if he asks for bread?
What father will give him a snake
   if he asks for fish?
Fathers are not all they should be,
   but they know how to give the very best to their children.
God is far better than our fathers;
   of course he will give the very best to those who ask him.

HOW JESUS WAS DOING GOD'S WORK

4. These are Wonderful Days

What happy people you are
   to see what you are seeing!
I tell you this:
   Kings and great men of old longed to see what you are seeing,
      but did not see it;
   they longed to hear what you are hearing,
      but did not hear it.

5. A Prayer of Jesus

I praise You, Father,
   Lord of the world—
very clever people have missed the secret of your heart,
   simple people have found it.
   Yes, Father, I give glory to you;
      this is your way.

6. Jesus makes God Known as Father

My Father has made everything clear to me:
   my Father alone knows who I am,
and I alone know him as the Father he is,
   I—and those I want to learn the secret from me.

7. *Come Here to Me!*

Come here to me
  all you who are tired with hard work,
    I. will put new life into you.
Let me give you a hand and show you how to live.
  I'll go your pace and see you through—
    and I'll give you the secret of the quiet mind.

Pulling with me is easy,
  the load with my help is light.

8. *God is Here Among You*

(For people who said that Jesus made mad people better, not with God's
help, but with the Devil's)

Civil war makes a country a desert—
  house crashes on house;
if there is civil war in the Devil's country,
  how can he stay king?
I make mad people better (you say) with the Devil's help.
If I make mad people better with the Devil's help,
  with whose help do *your* friends make mad people better?
  They shall be your judges.
But if I make mad people better with God's help,
  then God himself is here among you!

9. *Friend of Jesus, Jesus, and God*

He who says Yes to you says Yes to me;
  he who says Yes to me says Yes to God.
He who says No to you says No to me;
  he who says No to me says No to God.

10. *Helping the Least of my Brothers*

I was hungry and you gave me food;
  I was thirsty and you gave me drink;
I was a foreigner and you took me home with you;
  I was in rags and you gave me clothes;
I fell ill and you looked after me;
  I was in prison and you came to see me.

Believe me—
   when you helped the least of my brothers,
     you helped me.

I was hungry and you gave me no food;
   I was thirsty and you gave me no drink;
I was a foreigner and you didn't take me home with you
   I was in rags and you gave me no clothes;
I fell ill and you didn't look after me;
   I was in prison and you never came to see me.
Believe me—
   When you didn't help the least of my brothers,
     you didn't help me.

11. First Things First

He who puts his father and mother before me,
   is no real friend of mine;
he who puts his children before me
   is no real friend of mine;
he who isn't ready to face anything and follow me
   is no real friend of mine.

12. A World on Fire

I came to set the world on fire—
   how I wish the fire were burning now!
Mine is a dangerous life;
   how hard it will be for me until my work is done!
Do you think it is 'peace' I have come to give the world?
   I tell you No—the very opposite of 'peace'!

This is what will happen
(do you remember what the Bible says?):
   a home of five people will be divided,
     three on one side and two on the other—
       father against son and son against father,
       mother against daughter and daughter against mother,
       mother against son's wife and son's wife against his mother.

How the Friends of Jesus must Live

13. The Happy People

Who are the happy people?
You poor people,
   you belong to God;
you who are hungry now,
   you shall have food;
you who are worried now,
   you shall laugh.

Who are the unhappy people?
you rich people,
   you have had your good time;
you who have plenty to eat now,
   you shall be hungry;
you who are laughing now,
   you shall be worried and sad.

14. Heart and Treasure

Do not store up for yourself treasure on earth,
   where moth and worm eat things up,
     where thieves break into houses and steal.
Store up for yourself treasure in heaven,
   where no moth or worm eats things up,
     where no thieves break into houses and steal.
For heart and treasure
   go together.

15. Bandits, Beggars, and Thieves

To the man who hits you on the cheek
   give the other cheek to hit;
let the man who grabs your coat
   take your shirt as well.

Give to every beggar.

Don't ask for your things back
   from the man who steals them.

FISHERMEN and their drag-net on Galilee Lake.

16. Use Plain Words

You know the law that was given in days of old:
  'If you swear "By God . . . ," you must do what you say.'
I say to you:
  'Don't use language like that at all;
    it only spoils words.
Let your words be plain words, "Yes" and "No";
  when you swear, you are not really telling the truth.'

17. Be Clear-eyed

Your eye is the lamp of your body.
  If your eyesight is good,
    you can see the whole world clearly;
  if your eyesight is bad,
    you can't see anything clearly;
  if you are really blind,
    how dark it is!

18. Do Everything Well

The man who can be trusted with a small job
   can be trusted with a big one;
the man who can't be trusted in 'things that don't matter'
   can't be trusted in things that really matter.

If you can't be trusted with money,
   who will trust you with real wealth?
If you can't be trusted in ordinary business,
   who will give you a place in God's great work?

19. Use your Wits

When you see a cloud coming up in the western sky,
   you say at once 'There's a thunderstorm coming',
     and the storm comes.
When you see the south wind blowing,
   you say 'It's going to be scorching hot',
     and scorching hot it is!

You know how to tell the weather;
   why don't you know how to tell what is happening in
              the world of men?
   You are only playing at being good.

20. Be Genuine

No healthy tree
   grows rotten fruit;
no rotten tree
   grows healthy fruit.
You can tell every tree by its fruit:
   from a thorn-bush you don't get figs;
   from a bramble-bush you don't get grapes.

The good man out of the richness of a good heart
   grows goodness;
the evil man out of an evil heart
   grows evil.

A FISHERMAN casting his net on the beach of Galilee Lake.

21. Don't show off

When you help people,
    don't 'blow your own trumpet' like people who are only
                pretending to be good;
    they want people to say 'He's a good fellow!'
    Very good. They get what *they* want.

When you help people,
    don't let your right hand know what your left hand
                is doing;
    help people without others noticing it.
    Your Father will notice, and give you what *you* want.
When you pray,
    don't make a show of it, like people who are only
                pretending to be good;

they want people to say 'He's a good fellow!'
Very good. They get what *they* want.

When you pray,
   go into your own room and shut the door,
     and say your prayers to God your Father alone.
     Your Father will notice and give you what *you* want.

When you fast,
   don't look sad and make your face gloomy, like people
            who are only pretending to be good;
     they want people to say 'He's a good fellow!'
     Very good. They get what *they* want.

When you fast,
   brush your hair and wash your face;
     don't let anybody but God your Father see that you
            are fasting.
     Your Father will notice and give you what *you* want.

22. *Don't be Underhand*

   There's nothing hidden
     that won't be brought into the light;
   there's nothing secret
     that won't be openly known.
   Whatever you've said in the darkness
     will be heard in the light;
   whatever you've whispered in the house
     will be shouted in the streets.

23. *The World will be Full of Light*

The time is coming when you will long to see God's new world
   and you will not see it.
'Here it is!' somebody will say, or 'There it is!'
   Don't run after them.

For as the lightning lights up the whole sky
   God himself will light up the whole world.

LEADERS

24. *John the Hermit*

What did you go out on the moors to see?
 Grass blown by the wind?
But what did you go out to see?
 Somebody clothed in silk?
 You must look in palaces for splendour and luxury!
But what did you go out to see?
 One of God's great men?

Yes! I tell you—
 Somebody greater than God's great men of old.

25. *Leaders should set an Example*

What bad leaders you are!
 You don't forget about the collection,
 but you forget about God's justice and his love.
 You like front seats in the Meeting House;
 and everybody touching their hats to you in the street.
 You're like gravestones that look like a pavement:
 people walk on them without knowing what's underneath.
What bad leaders you are!
 You make ordinary people carry heavy loads;
 but you don't lift a finger to help them.
 You build monuments to God's great men of old,
 but you are like your fathers who murdered them.
 You have taken away the key to the door of knowledge;
 you don't want to go in yourselves, and you won't let
       anybody else go in.
Alas for you leaders of the people:
 you clean the outside of a cup and a dish,
  but inside they are full of greed and violence.
 How blind you are!

Make the inside of the cup clean first,
 then the outside may be clean too.

HOW WE CAN LEARN FROM WHAT HAPPENED LONG AGO

We have many stories about things that happened and about people who lived in our own country long ago. Some are happy stories; some are very unhappy stories. Jesus had many stories like our stories; stories about his own country and about his own people. We can read them in the *Old Testament*, which was his Bible.

Here are some of his poems that tell us of places and people famous long ago in the history of his people. When Jesus made these poems, everybody who heard them knew these old stories; if you don't know them, look them up in your Bible.

Here are a few words about the places and the people in his poems.

The Places

Jesus uses stories about five famous cities—all foreign cities, famous in their time. Sodom was an old city which, people believed, stood where now the Salt Sea (or Dead Sea) lies; it was destroyed in a great earthquake. Nineveh and Babylon were the capital cities of the great enemy nations; both were destroyed in war. Tyre and Sidon were famous cities on the coast—ports from which sailors took their cargo ships across the seas to Africa and Spain; their great days were long past, and now they were only small towns.

FAMOUS PLACES: the Salt Sea (The Dead Sea) where 'the earthquake happened'.

The People

You will have heard stories of the people Jesus speaks about. The Queen of Sheba came from a distant country to see the glory of Solomon the King. Jonah was sent by God to call the people of the great enemy city of Nineveh to change their minds and live good lives.[1] Elijah and Elisha were great men of God; the people they went to were all foreigners. Two old legends told about Noah who built the Ark at the time of the Great Flood, and Lot who escaped just before the earthquake destroyed Sodom.

  Chorazin, Bethsaida, and Capernaum are three cities where Jesus himself had told the Good News about God and made many sick people better. Capernaum was his home after he left his native village of Nazareth; Bethsaida was Peter's home town; we do not know anything about Chorazin.

26. The Flood and the Earthquake
('Business as usual'—and everybody taken by surprise)

As it was in the days before the Flood,
so will it be when God's Great Day comes:
    everything was just like an ordinary day—
    breakfast, dinner, tea, supper,
    mother, father, boys and girls—
until (as the Bible says) 'Noah went into the Ark'.
Then came the Flood, and the old world was destroyed.

As it was in the days of Lot:
    everything was just like an ordinary day—
    breakfast, dinner, tea, supper,
    all the shops open,
    farmers out in the fields, builders building houses—
until Lot went out of the city of Sodom.
'Then the earthquake happened' (as the Bible says), and the
                              old world was destroyed.
So will it be when God's Great Day comes.

----

[1] This did not actually happen; it is an Old Testament story (or parable) like the stories of Jesus.

27. Six Cities

Alas for you, Chorazin! Alas for you, Bethsaida!
  If Tyre and Sidon had seen the great things you have seen,
    they would have long ago changed their ways.
Believe me—
  Tyre and Sidon will do better than you in God's Great Day.

Alas for you, Capernaum!
  Do you remember what the Bible says about Babylon city?
    'These were your proud thoughts:
    "The skies I'll climb;
    "up above the highest stars
    "I will set my throne;
    "I will climb past the tallest clouds:
    "I will be like God himself!"
    How low you have been brought!
    How far you have fallen!'
  So far will you fall from your pride!
  If Sodom had seen the great things you have seen,
    it would still have been a great city today.
Believe me—
  Sodom will do better than you in God's Great Day!

FAMOUS PLACES: the Seaport of Tyre 'from which sailors took their cargo-ships across the seas to Africa and Spain'.

FAMOUS PLACES: a Monument from Assyria (Nineveh was its capital city), once the enemy of the Jewish people. The picture celebrates the defeat of a king of Israel, 'Jehu, son of Omri'.

28. Foreign Queen and Foreign City

The Queen of Sheba will stand up in God's Great Day
   and show how blind people today are:
she came from a far-off country to hear King Solomon the Wise.
   Look! Something much more important than Solomon is here.

The people of Nineveh will stand up in God's Great Day
   and show how blind people today are:
when they heard Jonah, they listened and changed their ways.
   Look! Something much more important than Jonah is here.

29. The 'Proof'

People today do not really love and trust God;
   they keep looking for a 'proof' that I am doing God's work.

No 'proof' will be given to them—
   only the 'proof' that Jonah was:
Jonah and what he said were the only 'proof' the people of
                   Nineveh had;
   I myself today am the only 'proof' that I am doing God's work.

30. Foreign Widow and Foreign Soldier

There were many widows in our own country when Elijah was
                           living.
   No rain fell for three long years and more,
   famine walked through town and village;
but God sent Elijah to nobody in our own country,
   but only (says the Bible) 'to a widow in a foreign city'.

There were lepers in our own country when Elisha was living.
   But God made nobody in our own country better,
      only a foreign soldier.

THE DOOMED CITY

Jesus lived in an occupied country. These poems deal with the war the
'Resistance Movement' was planning to fight against the Romans; they are
a warning to all who thought that hatred and fighting was God's Way and
that foreign people were God's enemies.

31. Jerusalem

Jerusalem, Jerusalem, killer of God's great men,
   murderer of God's messengers,
how many times have I longed to gather your people together
                 as a family,
   like a bird gathering her brood under her wings;
   you would not have it so.
Look! You've made the Temple your kind of Temple, not God's.

32. How Blind the City is!

If only today you knew how to live for peace instead of war!
   You cannot see what you are doing.
The time will come when
   your enemies will throw up a palisade round you,
   besiege and attack you on all sides,
   dash down your buildings and your people,
   leave not a wall upstanding:
all because you did not see that God had already come to you
   in love, not war.

33. How Terrible it will be!

When you see the city besieged by armies,
   be sure the last days of the city have come.

Let those inside her walls escape
   and those in the villages stay in the villages.
These are the days of punishment,
   the words of the Bible are coming true.
There will be great distress among men
   and a terrible time for this people.
They will fall at the point of the sword
   and be scattered as captives throughout the world.
Foreign soldiers will tramp the city's streets
   until the world is really God's world.

THE JEWISH WAR: the sculpture is part of the Arch of the Emperor Titus in Rome, and celebrates the capture of Jerusalem City by Roman soldiers. It shows loot they took from the Temple.

34. *A Time of Sudden Violence*

I warn you—
  two men will be sleeping in the same bed,
  one will be caught, one escape;

  two women will be grinding at the same farm,
  one will be caught, one escape;

  two men will be working out in the fields,
  one will be caught, one escape.

35. *The Only Hope*

The man resting on the roof must not stop to go indoors
  to pick up anything in the house;
the man working in the fields must not go home
  to get his clothes.

Forty years after Jesus made these poems, the Great Rebellion of the Jewish people broke out. Villages were burned, very many people were killed, and the city of Jerusalem was burned and captured by Roman soldiers.

Sayings without Stories

The friends of Jesus remembered many of his sayings without always remembering just what happened—where he was, when he said them, the people he was talking to. But they didn't forget the sayings themselves. They wrote them down, collected them together and arranged them as they thought best. That is why you will sometimes find that Mark puts a saying in one place, Matthew in another place, and Luke in a different place still.

Here are some of these sayings of Jesus which his friends remembered and wrote down.

About the Work of Jesus

1. God has given me world-wide power. Go. Help everybody everywhere to follow me. Get them to join my company of friends, and show them how to live as I showed you. Remember, I shall always be with you—to the very end.

2. Don't think I have come to pull the Bible to pieces. I haven't come to get rid of it; I have come to help men to see what God is really doing and to live in his way.

3. He who is not my friend is my enemy; he who does not help me to get people everywhere to live together as God's Family, sets people against one another.

4. He who is not our enemy is our friend.

5. Nobody knows the date when everybody everywhere throughout the world will be living in God's Way. Angels don't know and I don't know. Only God himself knows that.

6. See, I am standing outside the door and knocking. If you hear the sound of my knocking and open the door, I'll come into your home, and we'll have dinner together.

7. My words will outlive the world itself.

How the Friends of Jesus must live

1. God is your Father, and you must live in his Way. He cares for everybody everywhere—bad people and good people, honest people and dishonest people. See how the sun shines and the rain falls on all their farms alike.

2. You, who are my friends, must be like salt; you must make the whole life of the world worth living.

3. You, who are my friends, are like daylight; you must help people to see everything clearly.

4. Everybody can see a town on a hilltop. You must be like that.

5. If you've got ears, use them.

6. When you listen, you must really listen.

7. If there is something you can really do, what a lot of other things you can learn to do too! If you don't try to do something, you won't be able to do anything!

8. If you want to help me you must give all your heart to it. You must put yourself last. You must be ready to let people do their worst to you. And you must keep your eyes on me.

9. Nobody can work for two masters. He will think less of one than he does of the other; or he will be devoted to one, and have no use for the other. Either God is your master—or money is.

10. Living in God's Way sometimes takes all the courage you've got. You'll be all right—if you never give in.

11. If you are always thinking of saving your skins, that's just what you won't do. But, if you forget all about yourself because you are keen on helping me, even if you lose your life, you will be all right. You will really be yourself.

How the Friends of Jesus must worship God

1. You are my friends, and this is what I want to say to you: you must never worship men—not even men like the Roman Emperor; the worst they can do is to take your life away from you. You must worship God alone—both life and death are in *his* hands.

2. When you are saying your prayers, you must really forgive anybody who has done you a wrong—so that God your Father may forgive you the wrong things you have done.

3. When you say your prayers, don't babble away without thinking about what you are saying. That is what they are doing in temples all over the world; people think God listens to you if you just go on talking and talking. Don't do that sort of thing. You know what God is like: he is your Father, and he knows just what you need before you begin to ask him for it.

5. You musn't keep on saying 'What shall we eat?', 'What shall we drink?', 'What clothes shall we wear?'. You mustn't worry like that. People who don't know what God is like worry about food and drink and clothes. Your Father knows that you need all these things. You must make God's Way your aim, and God will give you all these things as well.

5. Can anybody add one hour to his life—by worrying?

6. Believe me: if two of you meet together as my friends and are sure about what you are asking, my Father will do what you ask; for, if two or three people meet together as my friends, I am with them too.

7. Trusting in God—even though it is as small as a small mustard seed—can move mountains or pull up a mulberry bush with its long roots.

How the Friends of Jesus must behave

1. Treat everybody you meet in the same way as you would like them to treat you.

2. Be wise like serpents and innocent like doves.

3. If somebody treats you badly, this is what you must do. Tell him plainly what he has done. If he says he is really sorry, be friends with him again. If he treats you badly again and again in one day, and every time comes to you and says he is really sorry, be friends with him again. It won't be easy—so watch yourself.

4. If a Roman soldier forces you to carry his baggage for a mile along the road, go two miles along the road with him.

A ROMAN MILESTONE on a road in Palestine.

5. Give
to the man who asks you;
don't turn your back
on the man who wants to borrow from you.

6. You should never think anything is impossible.

7. Why don't you make up your own minds about what is right and what is wrong?

8. You'll get as good as you give—and more.

9. How much better off would you be if you won all the money in the world and lost—*yourself*? What would you give in exchange for —*yourself*?

10. It's a good thing to be healthy. But we may have to risk the loss of an eye or a hand sometimes; God's Way must always come first.

11. God will put the boaster in his place—down at the bottom; he will put the humble man, who never boasts about himself, in *his* place—at the top.

12. Don't forget this: some of those at the bottom of the class will find themselves at the top of the class; and some of those at the top will find themselves at the bottom.

13. You know what climbing a steep hill is like: if you slip on a stone, you can fall to your death; if you send a stone rolling down the hillside, it can kill the man following you.

14. When you have a party, don't always invite friends, cousins, relatives, and well-to-do neighbours; they will invite you back to *their* party, and all of you will be just having a good time together. When you have a party, give it freely; invite poor people, cripples, lame people, blind people; they can't invite you back. That's the way you'll find happiness. That's what heaven is like.

15. Giving makes us really happy, not getting.

16. Worldly people deal with one another much more intelligently than religious people do.

There must be New Standards

1. You have often heard, in the Meeting House, the law about murder read aloud: 'You shall not kill'. You know that a murderer will be arrested and tried before a judge. Believe me: God judges a man who is even *angry* with his brother man.

2. You have often heard, in the Meeting House, the law about revenge read aloud: 'An eye for an eye, a tooth for a tooth'. Believe me: there must be no fighting back—that's not the way to deal with enemies.

3. You have often heard, in the Meeting House, the law about fellow-citizens read aloud: 'Love your fellow-citizen'. My command is: 'Love your enemies'.

4. There are religious leaders who like 'showing off'. They walk about in fine clothes. They like people to say 'Sir' when they pass them in the street. Whey they go to the Meeting House, they sit in the best seats. When they go out to dinner, they like to sit next to their host. They buy up the houses of widows and make them homeless. Yet, to look like 'good' people, they go to the Meeting House and make their prayers very long. God will judge them more severely than other people. Keep away from them.

5. Don't you see or understand? Are you still so dull? Don't you remember what the Bible says?—

      Listen, you foolish and thoughtless people:
        you've eyes, but you won't look;
        you've ears, but you won't listen.

6. Why do you say 'Sir, Sir' when you speak to me, but don't carry out my teaching?

7. If only you understood the Bible when you read it! There God says:

      It is your affection I delight in,
        not your Temple services.

  If you had understood that saying, you wouldn't have got things all mixed up, and called innocent people wicked.

8. Believe me: unless your goodness is very different from the 'goodness' of the Jewish Leaders, you won't even begin to live in God's Way.

9. Alas for you, Jewish Leaders! You are only pretending to be good. You travel all over the world to make one foreigner a Jew; when he becomes a Jew, you make him twice as bad as yourselves.

The Heart of the Matter

Jesus has been talking about many things.

We have read his conversations, the stories he told in the villages, the poems he gave to his friends, the sayings people remembered. We know why he said all this: he was helping people to understand what God was like and what he was doing; who we are and how we should live; what the world in which we live is really like and what it will be like when everybody lives in God's Way.

Jesus put the meaning of all he had been saying in two short poems, and we have called them 'The Heart of the Matter.' The two poems are 'God's Way must be our Way' and 'The Prayer of the Friends of Jesus'.

God's Way must be Our Way

By the side of this poem we have put some words to guide you as you read it. Here Jesus is showing us in simple words what God's Way is really like and how we must try to live in God's Way.

GOD'S WAY MUST BE OUR WAY

THESE ARE
OUR
ORDERS
	Love your enemies,
	    do good to those who hate you,
	    bless those who curse you,
	      pray for those who treat you badly.

LIVING IN
GOD'S WAY
MAKES A
DIFFERENCE
	If you love those who love you,
	    what is there special about that?
	Everybody does that sort of thing.
	If you favour those who favour you,
	    what is there special about that?
	    Everybody does that sort of thing.
	If you lend money to those you hope
	                    will help you,
	    what is there special about that?
	    Everybody does that sort of thing.

WE MUST DO
MORE THAN
OTHERS
	Love your enemies;
	    do good and lend,
	      expecting nothing back.

IT IS REALLY   You *will* get something back:
WORTH WHILE   you will be living in God's Way—
                              he is kind to those who never say
                                                'Thank you',
                              and to those who are selfishness itself.

IT CAN BE PUT   Be merciful
QUITE SIMPLY   as God your Father is merciful.

SO WE MUST   Don't judge and you won't be judged;
SET THE   don't condemn and you won't be condemned;
PACE   forgive and you will be forgiven;
                          give and you will be given;
                              good measure,
                              pressed down,
                              shaken together,
                              running over,
                              will be poured into your lap.

IT AMOUNTS   The measure you give
TO THIS   will be the measure you get.

The Prayer of the Friends of Jesus

We call this 'The Lord's Prayer', but this is shorter than the prayer we use
in school and at home and in church or chapel. The shorter form (which
we give here) is the way Jesus first put it; this is easy to say when we are
alone or with one or two people. When the friends of Jesus began to use
the prayer in their worship they used the longer form. Instead of saying
'Father', they used the longer saying from their Jewish prayers—'Our
Father who is in Heaven'. And at the end they added words of praise to
God. If you look it up in your Bibles, you will find that Luke gives us the
shorter prayer, and Matthew gives us the longer one.

Here, then, is the heart of the matter. Here Jesus tells us what he
wants us to do and how he wants us to live.

THE PRAYER OF THE FRIENDS OF JESUS

Father,
    may your name be used with reverence,
    may everybody live in your way.
        Give us today our bread for tomorrow.
    Forgive us as we forgive others;
    do not put us to the test.

BOOK THREE

FROM GALILEE TO ROME

Part One—The Pioneer

A LETTER TO HIS EXCELLENCY THEOPHILUS

We do not know who Theophilus was, except what we can learn from this letter. He seems to have been an important person; Roman governors were addressed as 'Your Excellency'. He may have been a Christian.

Many people have tried to write the story of what has happened among those of us who are the friends of Jesus; they used the reports which those who met Jesus face to face have handed down to us.

I thought that I too, Your Excellency, would try to write the story down. For some time now I have been trying to find out what actually happened, and I will put it down in its proper order. I want you to know the truth of what has been told to you.

Luke

The story of Jesus that Dr. Luke tells us is the same story that Mark told. But he tells it in a different way; he wants us to see from the very beginning *why* Jesus lived as he did, something his friends were very slow to learn. Indeed, he wants us to see *how* his friends came at last to understand what he wanted them to do.

He wants us to see that Jesus is Lord as well as Leader, one to whom we can give our whole hearts and the service of our lives, and who gives us God's power—God's Spirit in our hearts—so that we can live in God's Way. Jesus is everybody's Lord.

Dr. Luke was not born in Palestine and he was not a Jew, as we have seen; he came from one of the great cities of the Roman Empire. It was an amazing thing, he felt, that Jesus cared for *him*—and people like him—as well as for his own fellow-countrymen like Peter. And it was not just that Jesus cared for everybody everywhere, whatever their race or the colour of their skin; what amazed Dr. Luke was the way Jesus cared especially for people nobody else bothered with.

How could he, then, tell the story of Jesus as if it was just a story of something that happened in Palestine? It was a story for the whole world about the whole world.

This is just where the friends of Jesus come in. His Galilean friends were only the first members of a great company of friends who were to spread all over the world. They did not realize this at first; but Dr. Luke wants us to see that this was why Jesus called them—and why he calls us to be his friends today.

What Dr. Luke also could not forget was what the love of Jesus cost Jesus himself. He faced death itself because he cared for everybody everywhere. Those last few days show us how great his love was.

The story begins by Jordan River, and Part One of his book ends in a capital city—Jerusalem. But this is not the end of the story (as the friends of Jesus thought at the time); it is only the beginning. So Part One of Dr. Luke's story is only the story of what Jesus *began* to do and to teach, as he told His Excellency Theophilus.

THE BEGINNING OF THE VENTURE

Dr. Luke's story begins, as Mark's did, with the story of John the Hermit and the Call of Jesus by Jordan River. It is the year A.D. 27, and the Emperor Tiberius had been ruling the Roman Empire for fourteen years.

Dr. Luke tells us more about John the Hermit than Mark did. He describes the sort of man he was and what he said to the people.

Most of all Dr. Luke wants us to see what his Call meant to Jesus. Jesus had come to join John's company of friends to get ready for the coming of God's Chosen Leader. Jesus now knew that God had called *him* to be the Chosen Leader. He had to think through again what sort of Leader God wanted him to be. He made his great decision and left the moorlands to be a wandering teacher, talking to people in their villages and meeting them as equals.

John the Hermit

In the year A.D. 27—the fifteenth year of the reign of the Emperor Tiberius—Pilate was the Governor of Judea; King Herod and his brother Philip and King Lysanius were ruling princes in the countries to the north and east; and Annas and Caiaphas the High Priests were the Leaders of the Jewish people. However, it was to John the Hermit, out on the moorlands, that God spoke.

Now John had gone out to the banks of Jordan River and was calling people to change their ways so that God might forgive them.

He was like the man in the old poem in the Bible—

> The voice of a man
> Shouting in the lonely desert—
> 'Get God's road ready,
> Make his paths straight.'
> Every valley shall be filled up,
> Every mountain and hill be levelled out,
> Winding roads made straight,
> Rough roads made easy.
> Everybody shall see God coming to our help.

Crowds went out to be baptized by John in Jordan River as a sign that they had changed their ways.

'You are like poisonous snakes,' John told them. 'Who told you to escape from the terrible times that are coming? If you've really changed your ways, you must show it in the way you live. You mustn't say "Oh—we are God's chosen people; we are all right." Believe me, God can make anybody his "chosen people"—even these rocks here. He's like a farmer with his axe. He's already put it at the root of the trees; and he will chop down every fruitless tree for the winter fires.'

'What must we do?' people asked him.

'The man with two coats,' said John, 'must share them with the man who has none. The man with food must share it with those who are hungry.'

'Sir, what must we do?' asked the tax collectors who came to be baptized in Jordan River.

'Collect the tax,' said John, 'and nothing more than the tax.'

'What must fellows like us do?' asked some soldiers.

'No beating up people for their money,' said John, 'and no telling lies about people. Live on your soldiers' pay.'

There was great excitement in all the towns and villages.

'Is John God's Chosen Leader?' people were asking.

'I have used water as a sign that your hearts shall be made clean,' said John. 'A Stronger One than I is coming; I am not good enough to bend down and untie his shoelaces. He will really give you God's power. He'll be like fire. He'll be like a farmer at harvest when, shovel in hand, he's cleaning out his threshing floor—storing the wheat in the barn and making a bonfire of the straw.'

This was what John told the people, day in, day out.

He was not even afraid of King Herod himself. He told him that he had done wrong to marry Queen Herodias—she was not his wife but his brother's wife. He charged him with doing many other wicked things. So King Herod did a still more wicked thing—he had John thrown into prison.

Jesus hears God's Call

Crowds came to John to be baptized in the water of Jordan River. And among them came Jesus.

He had been baptized and he was standing on the bank of the river, praying.

Then it happened. From the open heavens, God's Spirit came down on him, like a dove.

'You are my only Son,' said a voice from heaven. 'With you I am very well pleased.'

Which Way?

Jesus went away from Jordan River, his heart filled with God's Spirit. And God led him out on to the lonely moorlands.

He was there many a long day. He was being tested; he had to think things out; what did God want him to do? All this time he had nothing to eat, and at the end he was very hungry indeed.

This conversation took place in his mind: Jesus imagined himself to be sometimes on the moorlands themselves, sometimes on the top of a very high mountain, sometimes standing on top of the Temple Gate in Jerusalem.

On the moorlands:

Voice: If you are God's Son, tell this stone here to become a loaf of bread.

Jesus: The Bible says: Bread is not the only thing a man needs to live on.

On the top of a very high mountain, where he could see so far that all the world seemed to lie at his feet:

Voice: I will give you all the power of these great countries and their royal splendour. It is all mine—mine to give to anybody I want to. It can all be yours—on one condition: you must take me for your King—not God.

Jesus: The Bible says: God himself must be your King; you must be his servant and his servant only.

Jerusalem, on the top of the Temple Gate, looking down on all the people gathered in the Court below:

Voice: If you are God's Son, jump down from this high place. The Bible says: God will command his angels to look after you. And again the Bible says: Their hands will hold you fast— you won't even stub your toe on a stone.

Jesus: The Bible also says: You must not put God to the test.

The testing time of Jesus was over   but it was not the last test he had to face.

DANGERS AHEAD

Jesus knew that his work would be dangerous work. We know, from Mark's story, how, at the end, Jesus would meet a lonely death on a cross. But the danger was there all the time.

For Jesus came to change the way we live, and we do not like changing our way of life. He came to call us to live in God's Way; and that calls for courage and unselfishness. We must be ready for anything, and, if we meet opposition and danger, we must not give in. Jesus knew what it was to live dangerously.

So Dr. Luke now goes on to tell us what happened at the village where Jesus had grown up and where everybody knew him. We have also put here two other stories about the dangers Jesus faced.

His Own Village is Unfriendly

Jesus went back to Galilee, made strong by God's Spirit in his heart.

Everybody everywhere was talking about him. He told the people the Good News in their Meeting Houses, and everybody had a good word to say for him.

He came at last to Nazareth where he had grown up.

On the Saturday, the Holy Day of the Jews, he went along to the Meeting House there, and the leader of the Meeting House asked him to read the Bible to the people. The reading was from the book of Isaiah, one of God's great men of old. He stood up, opened the book and found these words—

> God's Spirit is in my heart;
> he has called me to my great work.
> This is what I have to do—
> give the Good News to the poor;
> tell prisoners that they are prisoners no longer,
> and blind people that they can see;
> set conquered people free,
> and tell everybody God's Great Day has come.

Jesus closed the book, gave it back to the leader of the Meeting House and sat down. Everybody was staring at him.

'You have been listening to the words of the Bible,' said Jesus. 'Today what God said would happen has happened.'

Everybody spoke well of him; they were astonished and charmed by the way he talked.

'Isn't he Joseph's son?' they were asking one another.

'I know what you will say to me—"Doctor, cure yourself",' said Jesus. ' "We've heard all about what you did down at Capernaum. Do it here in your own village." '

'No Man of God is liked by his own home-folk,' Jesus went on.

> 'There were many widows in our own country
> when Elijah was living.
> No rain fell for three long years and more,
> people starved in town and village;
> yet God sent him to none of our own countrymen,
> but only (says the Bible) "to a widow in a foreign city".

'There were lepers in our own country
when Elisha was living.
Yet God made none of our own countrymen better,
only a foreign soldier.'

The people in the Meeting House were very angry when they heard him talk like this. They got up and took him outside the village to the edge of the cliff to throw him over it.

But Jesus walked through the village crowd and went on his way.

The Government is Unfriendly

One day, in Galilee, some Jewish Leaders came to Jesus.

'You'd better get out of here,' they said. 'King Herod's after you.'

'This is what I've got to say to that "fox", and you can tell him,' said Jesus. 'I shall go on doing what I have been doing, healing people who are sick in mind or body—today and tomorrow and the day after. I shall finish the work God has given me to do. A man of God is in no danger—outside Jerusalem City.'

A Foreign Village is Unfriendly

This happened in Samaria. Jesus was on his way south to Jerusalem City.

He sent friends on ahead to find somewhere to spend the night. They came to a village, but the villagers turned them out, for one reason only—Jesus and his friends, it was obvious, were on their way to Jerusalem, the Holy City of their hated enemies.

'Sir,' said James and John, when they heard this, 'you remember what happened when Elijah was turned away from a village—fire came down from the sky and burned the villagers up. Do you want us to ask God to burn these villagers up?'

Jesus turned round and stopped such talk; and they went on to another village.

The Plan of the Venture: His Friends

Jesus himself could tell the Good News to only a few people, and they were his own countrymen. Time was short, and this was the work he believed God had given him to do.

But the Good News was for the whole world. So he gathered friends round him to learn to live in God's Way and to help him. After his death it would be *their* work to take the Good News 'to the ends of the earth'.

This is what happened. When Dr. Luke was writing his book, there were friends of Jesus in many great cities of the Roman Empire. He wanted His Excellency Theophilus to see that this was what Jesus had planned from the beginning.

In the second part of his book, Dr. Luke is going to tell how the friends of Jesus learned to follow him and carry on his work; here he tells us how they helped him in Galilee and Judea.

Peter

Jesus was one day standing right on the edge of Galilee Lake; the crowd of people, listening to the Good News about God, was pressing round him and pushing him into the water.

He noticed two boats lying just off-shore—the fishermen had landed and were washing their nets. He climbed into one of the boats—it was Peter's—and asked him to anchor it a little way out. He sat down and talked to the crowd from the boat.

At last he finished talking to them.

'Take the boat into deep water,' he said to Peter. 'Out with your nets and let's catch some fish.'

'Sir,' said Peter, 'we were out all night, hard at it, and we didn't catch one fish. But I'll get the nets out, of course, if you want me to.'

They got out the nets—and made a tremendous catch. The nets began to break, and they had to signal to their friends in the other boats to come and give them a hand. Over they came, and together they filled the two boats with so many fish that they were dangerously overloaded.

When Peter saw what had happened, he fell down in front of Jesus.

'Leave me alone,' he said, 'I'm not good enough to be a friend of yours.'

GALILEE LAKE, near Magdala, looking south.

He was amazed at the catch of fish, and so were James and John his fishing partners and all the men in the boat with him.

'Don't be afraid,' said Jesus to Peter. 'From now on, you will be fishing for men instead of for fish.'

They beached their boats, gave up their fishing and went along with Jesus as his comrades and friends.

The 'Twelve'

This happened in Galilee.

One day Jesus went out to 'The Hill' to pray. He spent all night thinking things out in prayer.

At daybreak he called his friends to him, and from them he chose the 'Twelve', and gave them the name 'Messengers' as well. Here is the list of the 'Twelve':

Simon   'Rock' (we say 'Peter')
Andrew, Simon's brother
James and John
Philip
Bartholomew
Matthew
Thomas
James, the son of Alphaeus
Simon   'Rebel'
Judas, the son of James
Judas (who later handed Jesus over to the Jewish Leaders).

The Seventy-two

One day Jesus gave some special work to seventy-two of his friends. He was going through Galilee, telling people the Good News about God. He wanted them as his 'advance party'—to go ahead of him, two together, to any town or village he was going to visit.

This is what Jesus told them.

'There's a wonderful harvest; but there aren't enough harvesters. God is the owner of the harvest fields. Ask him to send harvesters out into the fields.

'Go; remember it's dangerous work; I am sending you like lambs to a pack of wolves.

'Here are your orders: no money-bag, no knapsack, no sandals, no greetings on the road.

'The first words you must say when you enter a house are— "Peace to this house". If a man who cares for peace lives there, your greeting will do his heart good. If he's not that sort of man, your greeting will at least do your own heart good.

'Make one house your home, and share meals with the people who live there—a workman should be paid. But don't go changing homes.

'If you come to a town and the townspeople are friendly, eat whatever they give you. Heal the sick people there and tell them— "God himself, in all his power, is here among you".

'If you come to a town, and the townspeople are unfriendly, go out into the streets. Tell them—"The dust of your town is sticking to our feet; we wipe it off to show you what sort of people you are. Yet your unfriendliness makes no difference to this: God himself, in all his power, is here among you". Believe me, the old foreign city of Sodom, wicked as it was, will do better than that town in God's Great Day.'[1]

Martha and Mary

One day, on his travels, Jesus came to a village. A woman called Martha welcomed him into her home. She had a sister called Mary.

Mary used to sit beside Jesus, listening to him talking; Martha went hurrying about the house, doing this and that and the other.

Suddenly, she stopped in front of Jesus.

'Sir,' she said, 'doesn't it matter to you that my sister leaves me to do all the housework by myself? Tell her to give me a hand.'

'Martha, Martha,' said Jesus, 'what a lot of things you worry and fuss about! There's only one thing that matters. Mary's choice is better; nobody can ever take it away from her.'

Women who helped

Jesus and the 'Twelve' were going about the countryside, visiting towns and villages, telling the people the Good News about God.

Some women went along with them too—women who had been

---

[1] See the poem of Jesus, 'Six Cities', *The Message*, p. 95.

ill and whom Jesus had cured. One of them was Mary from the village of Magdala—she had been very ill indeed. Another was Joanna; she was the wife of one of the great officers of the court of King Herod. Another was Susanna. There were many others too. They used their own money to look after Jesus and his friends.

THE PURPOSE OF THE VENTURE:
BREAKING DOWN ALL BARRIERS

Jesus believed that God's will is that the world should be his Family and live in his Way.

Men and women were not living together as a Family. They were divided from one another by all sorts of barriers. There were barriers between rich and poor. People hated other people, as the Jewish people of his day hated the Roman soldiers. There were barriers, too, between individual people.

We must learn, Jesus believed, to break all these barriers down if we are to live in God's Way. There will always be differences between people; but we must not let them become barriers separating us from one another. We must use our differences to make our lives richer and wider.

Dr. Luke was amazed at the way Jesus cared for people, especially for those whom nobody else cared for. He has told us many stories about the way Jesus took no notice of what people thought about him, but treated everybody he met, even if they were lepers or outcasts, as persons and equals.

A Roman Officer

Jesus was in Capernaum; a detachment of Roman soldiers was stationed there.

One of the captain's slaves, a man of whom he was very fond, was dangerously ill. The captain heard that Jesus was in town, and he sent a message to him by some Jewish Leaders, who were friends of his, to ask him to come and cure his slave.

They found Jesus; they were very keen to get him to help the captain.

'He deserves help like this,' they said. 'He's a friend of all Jewish people. It was he who built our Meeting House for us.'

Jesus went along with them.

He had almost reached the house, when the captain again sent some of his friends to meet him.

The Gravestone of a Roman soldier who died on active service in Palestine: 'In memory of L. Magnius Felix, a soldier of the Tenth Legion, the Fretensis, orderly to the Colonel, 19 years in the army, 39 years of age'.

'Sir,' he sent word, 'don't go to any more trouble. It wouldn't be fitting for you to come inside my house; that's why I didn't think it was right for me to come to meet you myself. Give the word of command, and my boy will be well. I am an officer in the army; there are generals over me and soldiers under me, and I know what orders are. I tell this soldier to go, and he goes; I tell that soldier to come, and he comes; I tell my slave to do this, and he does it.'

Jesus was filled with admiration for this Roman captain.

He turned to the crowd.

'Believe me,' he said, 'I haven't found a Jew who trusted me like this.'

The captain's friends went back to the house, and they found the slave fit and well.

A Widow

On another day Jesus came to the village of Nain. His friends and a lot of other people were walking along the road with him.

At the town gate, there was a large crowd of people coming out. It was the funeral of the only son of a widow.

Jesus saw her and felt very sorry for her.

'Don't cry,' he said to her.

He went up to the coffin and touched it; the bearers stood still.

'Young man,' he said, 'get up.'

The dead man sat up and spoke.

Like Elijah in the old Bible story, Jesus gave him back to his mother.

Everybody felt that God himself was with them.

'Praise be to God!' they said.

'A great man has come among us!'

'God cares for his people.'

News of this spread throughout the whole of Palestine and beyond its borders.

A Woman who was 'a Bad Lot'

One day a Jewish Leader, Simon by name, asked Jesus out to dinner. So they went along together to his home and sat down to dinner.

Now there was a woman in the town who, in the eyes of religious people, was 'a bad lot'; the people who went to the Meeting House wouldn't have anything to do with her. She heard that Jesus was having dinner in Simon's house, and this is what she did. She got hold of a bottle of real Indian ointment. She went and stood behind the couch on which Jesus was reclining. She was crying, and her tears fell on his feet. She wiped them dry with her hair, kissing them and putting ointment on them again and again.

Simon noticed all this.

'If this man was really a Man of God,' he thought, 'he'd know who was touching him like this, and what kind of woman she was. He'd know she was "a bad lot".'

Jesus was in no doubt about what Simon was thinking.

'Simon,' he said. 'I've something to say to you.'

'Go ahead,' said Simon.

Jesus turned to the woman.

'You see this woman,' he said. 'I came home with you, but

you didn't give me any water to wash my feet; this woman wet my feet with her tears and dried them with her hair. You didn't greet me with a kiss; this woman has kissed my feet again and again ever since she came in. You didn't give me any perfume to put on my head; she's put ointment on my feet.

'Listen: because of her great love, all the wrong things she's done—and they are many—are forgiven. You don't show much love for me, do you? But then, you don't feel you need to be forgiven.'

Jesus turned to the woman.

'All the wrong things you've done are already forgiven,' he said.

The guests started whispering to one another.

'Who's this? He's even forgiving people's sins!'

'It's your trust in me that's saved you,' said Jesus to the woman. 'Go home and don't worry.'

Lepers

Jesus was on his way to Jerusalem. He was passing through the border country of Samaria and Galilee, and he went into one of the villages. On the road into the village, ten men met him—all lepers. But they kept their distance.

'Jesus! Sir!' they shouted to him. 'Take pity on us!'

Jesus saw them.

'You know the law for lepers who are cured,' he called back. 'Go and show yourself to the priest.'

Off the lepers went; and as they walked along the road they found they were lepers no longer—they were cured.

One of the men turned back to say 'Thank you'.

'Praise be to God!' he kept shouting loudly. He fell down on his face at the feet of Jesus and thanked him. He was the only one who wasn't a Jew; he was a 'foreigner' from Samaria.

'There were ten lepers cured, weren't there?' asked Jesus. 'What's happened to the other nine? Was this "foreigner" the only one who could come back and say "Thank you" to God?'

'Get up and go home,' he said to him. 'It's your trust in me that's made you well.'

A Chief Tax Collector

One day Jesus was going through Jericho City.

Now there lived in Jericho a very rich man called Zacchaeus, manager of the Tax Office there. He was very keen to see what sort of person Jesus was; but he was a little man and he couldn't see over the heads of the crowds. So he ran on ahead along the road Jesus was taking; and to get a good view of him he climbed into a fig tree.

Jesus came along the road and looked up at Zacchaeus in the tree.

'Zacchaeus,' he said, 'you'd better be quick and get down—I must stay with you today.'

He was down in a moment, thrilled to have Jesus as his guest.

The crowd didn't like it.

'**He's staying with that scoundrel of a fellow,**' they muttered.

Zacchaeus stopped.

'I'm not the man they think I am, Sir,' he said to Jesus. 'Look, I give half my income to people in need; and if I've taken more than I ought from anybody, I give four times as much back.'

'God himself has come to this home today,' said Jesus. 'This man belongs to God's family too. You know what God said in the Bible—"I will seek the lost". That's what I and my friends are doing.'

THE COST OF THE VENTURE

Dr. Luke has already told us about the dangers Jesus faced. Now he faces the greatest danger of all.

Jesus has told the Good News in Galilee. He must also tell the Good News in the capital city of his country. At the Great Feast, Jewish pilgrims from all over the world would be in Jerusalem City. Jesus would have the chance of speaking to as many of his countrymen as possible.

What drove Jesus forward was his love for people. He loved them because God his Father loved them. He knew the danger he would face in Jerusalem. His going to Jerusalem shows how great his love was, and what it cost him.

Reaching the City

Jesus had climbed the mountain road from Jericho and had almost reached Jerusalem City. He had come to the spot where the road begins to drop down from the top of the Olive Hill into the valley. Crowds of pilgrims were going along the road. All his friends were very happy and were singing hymns of praise to God for all they had seen Jesus do. The words came from an old Jewish hymn—

> Praise to the King
>   who comes in God's name!
> Peace in heaven!
>   Glory in heaven!

There were some Jewish Leaders among the crowd.

'Sir,' they said, 'tell your friends to stop singing.'

'Believe me,' said Jesus, 'if my friends were to stop singing, the rocks would shout out!'

As Jesus went on down the road, he saw Jerusalem City across the valley. His eyes filled with tears.

'If only today you knew how to live for peace instead of war! [he said]

> You cannot see what you are doing.
> The time will come when
> your enemies will throw up a palisade round you,
> besiege and attack you on all sides,
> dash down your buildings and your people,
> leave not a wall upstanding:
> all because you did not see that God had already come to
> you in love, not war.'

Every day Jesus went into the Temple to tell the people the Good News about God. The Jewish Leaders had made up their minds to get rid of him, but they couldn't do anything about it. The crowds listened to him, spell-bound.

The Supper

It was near the time for The Great Feast to begin, when all Jews remember together how God rescued them from Egypt and sent Moses to lead them to their homeland.

Jesus and his friends sat down at supper together.

'I have looked forward eagerly to sharing this Great Feast with you before I die,' he said. 'I shall never share it with you again until all it means has come true and God's Great Day has come.'

He took the cup in his hands and said Grace.

'Take this cup,' he said, 'and share it among yourselves. Believe me, I shall drink no more wine like this until God's Great Day comes.'

His friends started quarrelling about who was the most important person among them.

'Foreign kings,' said Jesus to them, 'are dictators to the people of their country; and powerful governors are called "Father and Friend" of their people. You—my friends—must turn it all the other way round. The "most important person" among you must live just as if he was the youngest among you. The "Leader" of my friends must live as the servant of all the others. Who is "the most important person"—the man who's having supper or the waiter who's looking after him? I know what you'll say—the man who's having supper, of course. Yet I have lived among you like the waiter who looks after the needs of other people.   •

'You are the ones who have stood by me, all through the hard times I have had,' Jesus went on. 'I will give you real "royalty"— the kind of "royalty" my Father has given me; you will have supper with me, as we are having supper together tonight, at *my* "Royal Court" and you'll be the real "Leaders" of God's People.'

Jesus turned to Simon Peter.

'Simon, Simon,' he said, 'Satan's after you to see the kind of man you are—like a farmer shaking and sifting wheat at harvest. But I have asked my Father that your trust in me may not break down. When you've won through, stand by my other friends—your brothers in God's Family.'

'Sir,' said Peter, 'I'd face prison and death with you—now.'

'When I sent you out to tell people the Good News about God,' said Jesus, 'you went without purse or bag or sandals. Did you find you were ever in real need?'

'No,' they said.

'Now it's very different,' said Jesus. 'You'll need everything you've got—purse and bag and sword; if you haven't a sword, you'd better sell your coat and buy one! You remember what the Bible says—"God's Servant was treated like a criminal"?—that's what I've got to face. It will all happen as the Bible has made clear.'

'Sir,' they said, 'see—here are two swords.'

'Enough of this,' said Jesus.

In the Orchard

Jesus set off for the Olive Hill—a spot he was very fond of—and his friends went along with him.

'The real test is coming,' said Jesus when they got there. 'You'd better pray that you won't have to face it.'

He went off a little way by himself.

He knelt down on the ground.

'Father,' he prayed. 'Take this suffering away from me. Yet I will do what you want, not what I want.'

God gave him the strength he needed. He was in very great distress, and he prayed with all his heart. Sweat fell from him on to the ground like drops of blood.

He finished praying and stood up. He went over to his friends and found them asleep, tired out by sadness.

'Why are you sleeping like this?' he said to them. 'Get up and pray that you won't have to face the real test that's coming!'

Before he had finished speaking a crowd of men rushed on them; and there, at their head, was the man called Judas, one of his close friends. He went right up to Jesus to greet him with a kiss, as if he was just meeting him.

'Judas,' said Jesus, 'is it with a kiss that you are handing me and my friends over to these men?'

His friends saw what was going to happen.

'Sir,' they said, 'shall we draw our swords?'

One of them hit out with his sword at one of the Temple police.

'Stop!' said Jesus. 'Let them have their way.'

He touched the man's ear and healed him.

'This is your hour indeed, the night and all its darkness,' said Jesus to the officers of the Temple guard.

The men arrested Jesus and marched him off to the High Court.

The soldiers guarding Jesus made fun of him and beat him up. They covered his face with a cloth.

'Be a real Man of God now,' they said, 'and tell us who struck you!'

And they swore at him again and again.

JERUSALEM CITY—the Damascus Gate.

Jesus on Trial

When it was daybreak, the Jewish Leaders had Jesus brought before their Council.

'Are you God's Chosen Leader?' they said. 'Tell us.'

'You won't believe me if I tell you,' said Jesus. 'You won't answer any questions I ask you. Do you remember the dream Daniel saw at night?—

> In the cloudy heavens
>   I saw the figure of a man
> coming into God's presence
>   and being presented to him.
>
> God gave him power and honour
>   and made him king.
> His power shall last
>   for ever;
> his kingly rule
>   shall never be overthrown.

'This will all come true—from this very moment.'

'You are God's Son then?' they all called out.

'It's you who use the words,' said Jesus.

'What are we bothering about evidence for?' they said. 'We've heard it for ourselves from his own lips!'

The whole Council got up and took him to Pilate, the Roman Governor.

These were the charges brought against him.

'This fellow calls himself a king,' they said. 'We've found him raising rebellion and telling citizens not to pay their taxes to the Emperor.'

'Are you the Jewish King?' Pilate asked Jesus.

'It's you who use the word,' he said.

'My judgment,' Pilate told the Jewish Leaders and the crowds, 'is that the man's innocent.'

They wouldn't have that.

'He's a mob leader,' they said. 'All over the south he's spreading his ideas. He started in the north, in Galilee, and now he's here in the capital city!'

'Is the fellow a Galilean?' Pilate asked, when he heard the word 'Galilee'.

When he found out that Jesus belonged to the country Herod ruled, Pilate sent Jesus off to him for trial, for he was in the city for the Feast.

Herod was very glad to see Jesus. He had heard many stories about him, and for a very long time had wanted to see him—he wanted to see him do a miracle. He asked him all sorts of questions, but Jesus made no reply.

The Jewish Leaders were standing near Jesus, loudly telling Herod all the crimes they said he was guilty of. Herod and his soldiers insulted him and made fun of him. At last, Herod dressed him like a real king and sent him back to Pilate.

Pilate and Herod had been enemies, but on this day they became good friends.

Pilate sent for the Jewish Leaders.

'You brought this man before me as a mob-leader,' he said. 'You were here when I examined him. I found nothing in what you had to say against him. Nor did Herod—he just sent him back to this court. He hasn't done anything that deserves the death sentence. I'll flog him and set him free.'

'Take him away!' the crowd shouted all together. 'Set Barabbas free for us!' (Barabbas had been thrown into prison as a murderer and a leader of a rebellion in the city.)

Pilate wanted to set Jesus free; so he called out to the crowd again. But they kept on shouting—

'Hang him on a cross! Hang him on a cross!'

Pilate spoke a third time to the crowd.

'But what's he done wrong? I find him innocent of anything that deserves the death sentence. I'll flog him and set him free.'

The crowd went on yelling, demanding the death sentence. The shouting of the crowd won the day, and Pilate gave orders that they should have their way.

He set free the man who had been imprisoned for rebellion and murder—the man they were asking for; and he handed Jesus over to them—they could do what they liked with him.

At Skull Hill

Jesus was not alone when he died; two other men, both bandits, were marched off with him to be put to death on Skull Hill. They hung all three on crosses; Jesus hung between the other two.

'Father,' Jesus kept on praying, 'forgive them. They don't know what they are doing.'

The soldiers went on tossing up for his clothes and then shared them out. The crowds stood by, watching.

The Jewish Leaders just laughed at him.

'He could save other people all right!' they sneered. 'Let him save himself now—if he really is God's Chosen Leader!'

The soldiers also joined in the foolery. They marched up to him and presented him with their sour wine.

'Get yourself out of this—if you are the Jewish King!' they called out.

Above the head of Jesus was the notice: THE JEWISH KING.

One of the bandits hanging alongside him cursed him too.

'You're God's Chosen Leader, are you?' he shouted. 'Get yourself and us out of this, then!'

The other bandit told him to be quiet.

'Aren't you afraid even of God?' he said. 'You've been given the same sentence as he has. We deserve it; we're guilty. This man hasn't done anything wrong.'

He turned to Jesus.

'Don't forget me,' he said, 'when you are King.'

'Believe me,' said Jesus, 'you'll be with me in heaven itself— today.'

Then Jesus raised his voice.

'Father,' he prayed (in the words of an old hymn), 'I put my whole life in your hands.'

With these words he died.

The officer in charge of the guard was watching.

'This man was innocent,' he said.

The crowds who had come out to see the three men die were staring at everything that happened. They went home, horrified at what they had seen.

The friends of Jesus watched all this from a distance.

The women who had come with Jesus from Galilee were among them. When his body was taken down from the cross they followed, and found out where the grave was and how his body was placed in it. Then they went home to get perfumes ready.

Not the End but the Beginning

When Jesus had been arrested and executed, his friends thought everything was over.

They had not really understood Jesus. They thought he would be the great deliverer of his people from their enemies. But he was not this sort of deliverer. Now he was dead, there was nothing more that they could do. Dr. Luke wants us to see how certain they were that the story was finished.

But it certainly was not finished. To their great surprise, they found that the story had only just begun. This is his account of what happened.

We shall not discuss this important story here. But in *Paul the Explorer*, we shall see what this story meant to Paul, and, in *Jesus Leader and Lord*, what he and John, who wrote the Fourth Gospel, had to say about it.

The Women at the Grave

The women rested on the Saturday—work of all kinds on the Holy Day was forbidden by Jewish law.

At dawn, on Sunday morning, they went to the grave and took the perfumes that they had got ready. They found that someone had already rolled away the great stone from the mouth of the cave. They went inside but found it empty.

They didn't know what to do. Suddenly two men in shining clothes came right up to them. The women were very frightened—they didn't dare even to look up at them.

'Why are you looking for someone who is alive—in a graveyard where there are only dead people?' the men asked. 'Remember what he told you when he was still in Galilee—that he must be handed over to men who didn't live in God's way and face death itself, but that his death would not be the end.'

Then they remembered that Jesus had told them this. They left the grave and went back to report everything that had happened to the eleven close friends of Jesus and all the others. But their story seemed to the others a lot of nonsense; nobody believed a word of it.

On a Country Road

That same Sunday two friends of Jesus—one of them was Cleopas—were walking back to a village, the village of Emmaus, about seven miles away. They were discussing what had happened on the Friday.

As they talked and argued, Jesus himself joined them and walked along the road with them. They looked at him, but he didn't seem to be anybody they knew.

'What's all the talk about?' he asked.

They stopped, looking completely downcast.

'Are you the only visitor in the city who doesn't know what's been going on this last day or two?' said Cleopas.

'What?' he asked.

'Why,' they said, 'all this about Jesus from Nazareth. He was a Man of God indeed—you could tell that from the way he talked and what he did. He made God real—and everybody knew it. Our Leaders handed him over to the Roman Government to sentence to death, and they hung him on a cross. He'd made us all feel that he was the man to set our people free; but he wasn't.

'The story's three days old now,' they added. 'Some of our own women, though, gave us a shock this morning. They were at his grave at dawn; but it was empty, they said, and they came back with a story, if you please, about seeing angels—angels who talked about his being alive. Some of us went off to the grave there and then. The women's story about the body was true all right, but they didn't see anything of Jesus himself.'

'How dull you are!' said Jesus. 'How slow you are to see what the Bible's all about! Hadn't God's Chosen Leader got to face death like this? Wasn't this his only way to triumph?'

He told them the whole Bible story again. He began with Moses who led the people out of Egypt and went on to talk about the great Men of God like Isaiah and Jeremiah. He showed them what *they* had to say about God's Chosen Leader.

By this time they had reached the village and the end of their journey. Jesus was going on along the road beyond the village, and they had some trouble in persuading him to stop there.

'Come in and stay with us,' they said. 'It's getting dark and daylight will soon be gone.'

So he went home with them.

It was supper time, and he sat down at the table with them.

He picked up a loaf, said grace, broke it and gave it to them to eat. They were looking at him, and suddenly they knew who he was—and he was gone!

'Wasn't it thrilling to listen to him as we walked along the road,' they said to one another, 'and didn't he make the Bible come alive?'

THE VILLAGE OF EMMAUS

They got up at once and were off back to the city. They found the eleven close friends and other friends in the room together.

'He's really alive again,' the men in the room told them. 'Peter's seen him!'

The two of them reported what had happened as they were walking along the road, and how they'd realized who he was when he broke the loaf at supper.

In the House

The friends of Jesus went on talking together. Suddenly Jesus himself stood there in the room with them. They were scared and terrified; they thought they were seeing a ghost.

'What are you troubled about?' asked Jesus. 'Why are you so full of doubts? Look at my hands and my feet—it's me. Touch me and look at me—you can't touch a ghost as you can touch me.'

They couldn't believe what they saw, for joy and astonishment.

'Have you anything to eat?' he asked.

They gave him a piece of cooked fish, and they watched him take it and eat it.

He went on to make the story of the Bible plain to them so that they could see what it was really about.

'I told you all this when we were in Galilee together,' he said. 'What the Bible says about the work I've been doing must come true. You know what it says—God's Chosen Leader must face death, but his death isn't the end of everything; he will soon rise to life again. This must be told to everybody everywhere, all over the world, starting from this city. People must be told that if they change their ways God will forgive them for all the wrong things they have done. You know this is true—you have seen it all with your own eyes.

'Look, I shall give you what God my Father promised—his own power in your hearts. But you must stay here in this city until you are given it.'

At Bethany

Jesus took his friends out of the city, almost as far as Bethany Village.

He lifted his hands up in prayer and asked God to be with them. And while he was praying he left them.

They went back to the city as happy as could be; they almost lived in the Temple, thanking God for all he had done.

Part Two—Across the World

In the first part of my work, Your Excellency, I have told the story of Jesus—all he began to do and say. I bring this to an end by telling you what orders he gave to his friends on the day when he was taken up from us.

After his death, for a month or more, he showed himself alive again to his friends and talked to them about God's Way. While he was with them, he told them not to leave the city.

'You must wait here,' he said, 'until God gives you his power, as he has promised to do and as I have told you. John the Hermit baptized people with water; before long God will give you his own power in your hearts.'

The second part of my work tells you what happened then.

Luke

The story now begins again. Jesus is alive again! That makes all the difference.

God's raising Jesus to life again is the part of the story that many people find very difficult to believe. 'We can believe', they say, 'that Jesus was a good and great man; but how can we believe that such an improbable and amazing thing as this happened?'

We shall come back to this in our last book, *Jesus Leader and Lord*, where we shall see what Paul and John had to say about it. For they found it just as improbable and amazing as we do; and yet they were sure it happened.

The first Friends[1] of Jesus did not agree among themselves just how it happened. After all, they never expected it to happen and they were taken by surprise; they had thought, when they saw Jesus executed, that it was all over and finished. (Look up 'On a Country Road', p. 132.)

But now they knew that the death of Jesus was by no means the end of the story. They gave as honest an account as they could of what happened; they knew that Jesus was their Friend for ever, and now they were ready to die for him, if need be. Four of them—and these were not all—did die for him: Stephen, James (John's brother), Peter and Paul. Knowing that Jesus was alive for ever made them new men and gave them their courage.

The World Adventure had now clearly begun. Four men took a leading part in it.

Stephen was the first to see that Palestine was too small for Jesus; only the world itself was big enough, for God's love is for everybody. He was the first man to die for Jesus.

Philip went to Samaria; he was also the first man to win an Egyptian as a Friend of Jesus.

Peter and Paul were the great leaders.

Dr. Luke tells us, in a very vivid story, how Peter came to see that 'God has no favourites'. He welcomed a Roman officer as a Friend of Jesus, and told the Friends of Jesus in Jerusalem City that they must be much bolder than they had been.

But Paul was the man who saw clearly what Jesus wanted his Friends to do—the man who, when the story begins, was his bitter enemy. He knew that the Good News must be told to Jew and foreigner alike. We shall tell Paul's story in *Paul the Explorer*. Here we have chosen six stories from Dr. Luke's notebook to show how the Good News was taken to Cyprus, Anatolia, Asia and Greece until at last it reached Rome itself. Dr. Luke must have been very proud that it was the Friends of Jesus in his own city of Antioch who took the lead in this world adventure.

---

[1] We shall print 'Friends of Jesus' with a capital letter in this part. This was one of the names Christians used for themselves in the earliest days (look up Acts 27. 3, John 14. 14–15).

We do not know who first told the Good News in Rome; there were Friends of Jesus in the city and in other Italian towns, as you will see, when Paul got there. Perhaps Italian Jewish merchants heard the Good News when they were pilgrims in Jerusalem, and took it home with them. When Dr. Luke tells us how Paul came as a prisoner to Rome, he wants us to see him as the representative of all the Friends of Jesus who took the Good News 'to the ends of the earth'.

THE VENTURE BEGINS AGAIN

You will notice, as the story begins again, how far the Friends of Jesus were from understanding him. They still thought he was going to be the deliverer of his people from their enemies.

So, at the beginning of the second part of the story, Dr. Luke tells us what orders Jesus gave his Friends. They were to tell the Good News in Jerusalem City, but they were not to stop there. They were to go out all over the world.

They would need God's own power to do God's work. So Dr. Luke goes on to tell us how, a few weeks later, God's power was given to them.

The Last Words of Jesus

Jesus and his Friends were together on the hill called 'Olive Orchard'.

'Lord,' they asked him, 'will you now make the Jewish people a free nation again?'

'That's God's business!' said Jesus. 'It's not your business to ask "How long are we going to be an occupied country?" or "When shall we be free?" You will be given God's own power when his spirit comes into your hearts; and then *your* business will be to go all over the world to tell everybody what you know about me. You must start here in this city first of all, go out into your own homeland, and then right to the very ends of the earth.'

With these words, Jesus was hidden by a cloud and they saw him no more.

His Friends went back to the city and to the room where they were staying. They were all there—Peter, John, James, Andrew, Philip, Thomas, Bartholomew, Matthew, James (whose father was Alphaeus), Simon (who had been a member of the Resistance Movement) and Judas (the one whose father was James). They spent their time together in prayer. The women Friends of Jesus were there too—and his mother, Mary, and his brothers.

The Great Day

It was now the time of the Feast, 'The Fiftieth Day' (Pentecost), when Jewish people remembered how Moses gave them God's Law on Mount Sinai.

The Friends of Jesus were all together in the house where they were staying. Then it happened. Suddenly—as if a storm of wind and fire burst upon them—they were all filled with God's own power and they began to talk in many strange ways. God gave them the power to speak out boldly.

Jewish pilgrims from lands all over the world were staying in Jerusalem City; they came from Mesopotamia in the east, from the shores of the Black Sea in the north, from Egypt in the south, and even from Rome in the west.

A great crowd gathered, talking excitedly; they were amazed and didn't know what to think.

'What's all this about?' they were asking.

Others thought it was all very queer.

'They're all drunk,' they said.

Peter stood up, and the other close Friends of Jesus stood up with him. He shouted over the noise of the crowd.

'Men of the South! Citizens of this city!' he called out. 'This is something you all ought to know about—so listen to me. You've got it all wrong. These men aren't drunk—after all, it's only nine o'clock in the morning. What's happened is something you'll find in your Bibles. Do you remember these words?—

> In the days that are to be
>   I will give my Spirit to everybody;
> Your people shall understand me—
>   Your old men shall dream dreams
>   Your young men shall see visions.
> Even to slaves
>   I will give my Spirit.

'My fellow countrymen, listen to me.

'You yourselves know all about Jesus of Nazareth. He lived and worked among you. All he did was proof enough that God sent him and that God was with him. He cured sick people; that was a

Roman Empire

Miles
0 100 200 300 400 500

N

Black Sea

GAUL

SPAIN

ITALY

Rome
APPIAN WAY

Puteoli

SICILY

Syracuse

Rhegium

Malta

Carthage

AFRICA

MACEDONIA
IGNATIAN WAY

Troas
Assos

GREECE

Athens
Corinth

Crete

ANATOLIA

ASIA

Ephesus
Miletus

Rhodes

Attalia
Perga

Myra

Cyprus

Cyrene

Alexandria

EGYPT

UPPER
EGYPT

Tarsus

Antioch
Seleucia

PHOENICIA

Damascus

Samaria

PALESTINE
Caesarea

Jerusalem

ARABIA

Babylon

Boundary of the
Roman Empire

Boundary of the Roman Empire

sign of God's power. You handed him over to the Romans and killed him. This, indeed, was all part of God's plan, for God raised him to life again; death could not be the end of his work. All of us here have met him and been with him since his death and know he is alive. God has given him high honour. Long ago God promised to give us his own power in our hearts; he has kept his promise and through Jesus he has given us his power. These are not idle words; you can see and hear for yourselves. Let all the Jewish people be in no doubt that God has made the man you killed Leader and Lord.'

They were very troubled when Peter spoke like this.

'Brother men,' they said, 'what shall we do?'

'You must change your ways,' said Peter, 'join the company of the Friends of Jesus as a sign that you are really sorry, and know that God has forgiven you. God will give you the power of his Spirit in your hearts. His promise is for all the Jewish people— you and your descendants; and it's not only for Jewish people; it is, as the Bible says, "for all those who live in far-off lands", everybody everywhere. What matters is not who we are but whom God calls.'

Peter told them the story of Jesus again and again and called them to make up their minds.

'This is a dishonest world today,' he said. 'Have nothing to do with its dishonesty.'

About three thousand people accepted what Peter said, and joined the company of the Friends of Jesus.

JERUSALEM CITY

Many of the Friends of Jesus still did not understand what he wanted them to do. They told the Good News in Jerusalem City, as he had told them to do; but it looks as if they thought that this was *all* he wanted them to do.

They were certainly changed men and women, very different people from what they had been before. They were brave, and they lived together as members of God's Family. They faced the anger of the people and of the Jewish Leaders with courage, and they told the Good News fearlessly.

But they were soon to learn how much more Jesus wanted them to do.

How the Friends of Jesus lived

The Friends of Jesus made a great stir in the city.

They lived day by day in God's Way as Jesus had shown them; Peter and James and John explained it to them.

They lived together like members of one family.

When they had supper together, they broke the loaf, shared it as Jesus had done at the last supper on the night before he died, and remembered what Jesus had done for everybody everywhere.

They spent much time in prayer.

They lived together and shared everything with one another. They sold their property and possessions and shared the money out so that nobody went without anything he needed. Every day they went to Temple worship, and met at home to 'break the loaf' together. They shared their meals together with real happiness. All this was their way of thanking God for all he had done for them. The people in the city thought well of them. Day by day, with God's help, their numbers grew.

They were one in heart and mind, and none of them thought that his own things were just for his own use—they were for everybody to share. So the close Friends of Jesus, like Peter, made it very clear what 'Jesus being alive again' really meant.

They were a happy company. Nobody went without what he needed. The rich people among them sold their lands and houses, and brought the money they got to their leaders. It was then shared out as each had need.

Here is an example. One of them, Joseph, was a rich man (Peter and his friends called him Barnabas). He was born in the island of Cyprus but he worked in the Temple, helping in the services there. He owned a field. He went and sold it and brought the money to the leaders.

More and more people, crowds of men and women, believed in Jesus and joined his company of Friends. Just as Jesus healed those who were ill, so did his Friends. People brought sick people on beds and mats out into the streets.

'Peter's shadow will fall on them as he walks along,' they said.

They brought the sick from villages outside the city, too.

Clash with the Jewish Leaders
How the Trouble began

Peter and John were walking one day up to the Temple. It was three o'clock in the afternoon, and people were gathering there for prayer.

In those days, a cripple whom everybody knew used to sit at one of the Temple gates—the 'Beautiful Gate'. He had been a cripple all his life, and his family put him there to beg from people as they were going into the Temple. This afternoon he was being carried to his pitch just as Peter and John came along. He caught sight of them and asked them for money.

They stopped.

'Look at us,' said Peter, watching him closely.

He stared back at them both; he thought he was going to get something.

'I've no money,' said Peter, 'but I'll give you what I have: In the name of Jesus of Nazareth, get up and walk.'

He got hold of the man's hand and pulled him up. His feet and ankles became strong at once; he jumped about, stood still and walked round. Then he went into the Temple with Peter and John, now walking, now jumping, and thanking God all the time.

The crowd saw him walking round and thanking God. One after another they realized who he was—he was the beggar at the Temple Gate! They were amazed at what had happened to him. He kept holding on to Peter and John, and the people came crowding round them.

By now they had got as far as Solomon's Porch; and, when Peter saw what a crowd there was, he stood and faced them.

'Fellow countrymen,' he said, 'why does this surprise you? Why do you stare at us? There's nothing special about *us*; we didn't make this man walk about like this. Remember what the Bible says—"The God of our fathers, who has cared for us from the beginning of our history . . . has given great honour to his Servant"; the words "his Servant" there mean Jesus.'

He went on to tell them again the story of Jesus, how he died and how he was alive again.

'It was his trust in Jesus,' he said, 'that has made a healthy man of this beggar you all know so well. I know that you didn't really know what you were doing when you treated Jesus as you did.

But he is God's Servant, and God raised him to life for your good, to get you to change your ways.'

At this moment the chief of police and some priests pushed their way in. They didn't want the Friends of Jesus to talk to the people like this and tell them that Jesus was alive. They arrested Peter and John and took them off to prison for the night, for it was now getting dark.

The fact was that many of the people had taken Peter at his word—the number was reckoned at about five thousand.

Next Day

Next morning, the Council of the Jewish Leaders were called together—the judges who had sentenced Jesus to death were among them. Peter and John were put in the dock.

'By what right did you do this?' the judges asked. 'Who are you?'

Peter spoke out—a man inspired.

'My lords,' he said, 'are we being questioned about a good deed done to a lame man? I can tell you the answer—and the whole country ought to know: in the name of Jesus of Nazareth, dead on a cross, raised by God to life again, this man stands before you in good health. We know what you think of Jesus—but do you remember the words of the Bible—

> The stone the builders would not use
> has become the key stone?

'There's no other way to put things right—only by the way Jesus made plain. One man, and one man only, matters for everybody everywhere—and that man is Jesus.'

The members of the Council stared at the boldness of Peter and John. They knew that they were laymen without any proper education, and they were amazed. And they knew, too, that they had been in the company of Jesus. But there was the beggar himself standing in the court, as healthy as any of them; how could they say nothing had happened?

They had the men taken out of court. They had to talk this matter over together.

'What are we going to do with these men?'

That was the question.

'Everybody in the city knows what these men have done.'

'We can't say it didn't happen.'

'We don't want the report to spread far and wide.'

'We'd better just let them off with a warning and tell them not to talk about Jesus any more.'

They decided just to warn them.

They called Peter and John back, and told them what the judgment of the court was: no more public speaking of any kind anywhere about Jesus of Nazareth; all this must stop.

'Well,' the two men said, 'you must make up your own minds whom we ought to obey—you or God—when we are doing God's work. Our duty is plain—we can't stop talking about what we ourselves have seen and heard.'

The Council repeated its warning and then set them free. They couldn't think of any way of punishing them. The crowds made that impossible; all over the city they were saying that God was behind it all.

'After all, the beggar was over forty years old,' the people said.

Peter and John went back to their friends, free men, and told them what the Council had said.

Prison Again

Peter and John and the other Friends of Jesus went on telling the Good News. They met together in the Temple. Many people joined their company, and many sick people were cured.

The Jewish Leaders were very angry about all this. So they arrested the Friends of Jesus again and put them in the common prison. But they escaped during the night, and by dawn they were back in the Temple, telling the Good News again to the people there.

While this was happening, the High Priest and the Jewish Leaders called the Council together, and sent for the prisoners. The police officers went to the prison, but the prisoners were no longer there. They went back without them.

'We found the prison safely locked all right,' they reported. 'The warders were on guard at the doors. When we unlocked the doors, we found nobody inside.'

When the Chief Constable and the members of the Council heard this report, they had no idea what to do or what would happen next. Then someone came in with a report.

'The prisoners are back in the Temple, talking to the crowds,' he said.

The Chief Constable himself went to the Temple with police officers and brought them back to the court. They were very careful not to use any violence; they were afraid the crowd might start stoning them.

The Friends of Jesus faced the judges, and it was the High Priest who spoke.

'We gave you strict orders to stop talking about Jesus,' he said. 'Now everybody in the city is talking about him, and you're trying to make it look as if we were the people who killed him.'

'It's God's orders we must obey,' said Peter, 'not yours. The story we are telling is the plain truth. We are only talking about what we've seen for ourselves. God's power in us is proof of it too, the power he gives to all those who obey him.'

These words made them very angry and they wanted to pass the death sentence.

But one of the members of the Council stood up—Gamaliel, a lawyer who was deeply respected by the people of the city. He ordered the prisoners out of the courtroom for a few minutes.

'My fellow-countrymen,' he said, 'be careful what you are about to do with these men. We've had people like them before. There was Theudas; he set himself up as a leader of the people. Four hundred men joined him. But he got killed, and all his followers were scattered. The whole affair came to nothing. Then there was Judas—he came from Galilee too. He raised a rebellion, when the Romans were carrying out a census of the population here. He died, and all his followers were scattered. The point is this: keep your hands off these men and leave them alone. If this affair is just another popular uprising, it will come to nothing. If God is at the back of it, you can't stop these men—you'll be fighting against God himself!'

The Council agreed with him. They fetched the Friends of Jesus back into court and had them flogged. They ordered them to stop talking about Jesus, and then set them free again.

The Friends of Jesus left the court happy men, happy because it was for telling the story of Jesus that they had been treated so shamefully. But they didn't stop telling the people about him, either in the Temple or at home.

PALESTINE

About this time one of the Friends of Jesus, Stephen (whose story we shall tell later) told the Good News boldly in one of the city Meeting Houses. He could see what a different world Jesus wanted it to be, and he boldly said that all Jewish people must now change their way of life and begin to live in God's Way. Everything must be changed.

The Jewish Leaders arrested him and had him put to death. Other Friends of Jesus, who shared Stephen's point of view, were now also marked men and their lives too were in danger. So they escaped from the city, and went off to other towns and villages, some in Palestine itself, and some beyond its frontiers to other lands.

In this wider world they began to understand Jesus much more clearly.

We begin with those who went to other towns and villages in Palestine. Dr. Luke tells us two stories of a Friend of Jesus called Philip, to show us something of what happened there.

In Samaria

Philip escaped north to a city in Samaria and told the crowds there the story of Jesus.

They listened to him and watched his good deeds—sick people were cured and cripples walked again. Everybody felt that Philip was telling them the truth about God, and the city was a very happy city.

There was a magician, Simon, living there. For many years his magic had amazed everybody, in the city and far beyond it. He called himself 'The Great Magician'. Members of the Government as well as the citizens were taken in by him.

'This man is indeed the Great Servant of God,' they said.

Now everything was changed. The people listened to Philip as he told them the Good News about God and the story of Jesus; many men and women became Friends of Jesus. Even Simon the magician became a Friend of Jesus and stayed with Philip. Philip's good deeds amazed even him.

News about all this came at last to the Christian Leaders in Jerusalem City.

They sent Peter and John to find out what was happening.

Nobody in Samaria had yet learned all that it meant to be a Friend of Jesus. So Peter and John held meetings for prayer, and asked God to give them his power. They put their hands on those

THE COUNTRYSIDE OF SAMARIA.

who had become the Friends of Jesus—as a sign that God would give them his power—and God gave them his power.

Simon the magician was there and saw what happened. He brought some money and gave it to Peter and John.

'Show me how to do this,' he asked, 'so that I can put my hands on people too and get God to give them his power.'

'Take your money away!' said Peter. 'Do you think you can buy God's gift as you can buy magic—with money? You're no real Friend of Jesus; you haven't changed your heart at all. And what you've just done is a terrible thing. You must change the whole way you think and live, and you must ask God to forgive the thoughts that are in your heart, if possible. I can see how much of a magician you are still!'

'Pray to God for me,' said Simon, 'so that all the terrible things you've been talking about don't happen to me.'

Peter and John told the people again the story of Jesus and explained the Good News to them. Then they went home to Jerusalem City; and on their way they told the Good News in many of the villages of Samaria.

On the Desert Road

The Desert Road goes down from Jerusalem City to the plain and then on to Egypt.

One day, a high officer of the Queen of Upper Egypt, her Chief Treasurer, was riding in his carriage along the Desert Road. He had come all the way to Jerusalem City on pilgrimage, and was now going home. He was sitting in his carriage and reading the Bible aloud.

God had already spoken to Philip.

'At midday,' God had told him, 'be on the Desert Road.'

So Philip was on the road as the Chief Treasurer's carriage came along.

'Go up to this carriage,' said God, 'and join the traveller.'

Philip ran up to the carriage and heard the officer reading the Bible.

'Do you know what it all means?' he asked.

'How can I?' he said. 'I need someone to explain it to me.'

He invited Philip to climb up into the carriage and sit beside him.

The officer was reading the great poem in the Bible about God's Servant. Here is a verse of the poem:

> As sheep on the way to the butcher
> and lambs in the hands of a shearer make no noise;
> So God's Servant keeps quiet.
> He was badly and unfairly treated,
> Who will be able to talk about his descendants?
> for at last they killed him.

'My question is this,' said the officer. 'Who is he talking about? Is he talking about himself? Or is he talking about somebody else?'

This gave Philip his chance. He began by explaining the poem to the officer and went on to tell him the Good News of Jesus.

As they were going along the road, they came to some water.

'Look—there's water here,' said the officer. 'What's to stop me from joining the company of the Friends of Jesus here and now?'

He told the driver to stop the carriage. Both of them, Philip and the officer, went down to the water. Philip baptized him there and then; and the officer joined the company of the Friends of Jesus.

They came up out of the water. God had other work for Philip to do. The officer lost sight of him, but went on to Egypt a very happy man.

Philip turned up at a nearby town, Azotus, and then went on from town to town telling people the Good News. At last he came to the port of Caesarea, the headquarters of the Roman Army.

WORLD ADVENTURE:
EVERYBODY EVERYWHERE MATTERS

So far the Friends of Jesus have stayed in Palestine. They have been telling the Good News to the Jewish people, as Jesus did.

They now begin to realize that the Good News is for the whole world, not just for their own countrymen. Three men—Stephen, Peter and Paul— helped them to see how wide was the work that Jesus wanted them to do. The adventure Jesus called them to was a world adventure.

The Man who died for it : Stephen

We wish we knew more about Stephen, the first man to see that the Good News was for everybody everywhere and the first man to die, as a Friend of Jesus, in the world adventure. But all we know about him is what Dr. Luke tells us in the story which follows.

His Arrest

There were many Jewish people in Jerusalem City who had not been born in Palestine. They had come from their homes in such far away places as North Africa and Asia. They spoke Greek and read the Bible in Greek. Many were freed slaves or the sons of freed slaves. They had their own Meeting House in the city where they met together to worship God—the Freedmen's Meeting House. Most of them had come on pilgrimage. Some of these Jewish people had joined the company of the Friends of Jesus; and their leader was Stephen, a man who spoke, as Jesus had spoken, with such charm and power that people felt they had to listen.

Stephen told the Good News to these Jewish people from over-seas in their Meeting House. Many of them got up and argued with him, but they could not answer *his* arguments. He spoke sensibly and with God's power.

So they made secret plans. They spread rumours about him.

'We've heard him say terrible things about Moses who led us out of Egypt,' they whispered, 'and even about God himself!'

This made the Jewish people and their Leaders very angry indeed; and they arrested Stephen and dragged him off to the Jewish Council.

'This fellow never stops insulting the holy Temple and our religion,' they got men to lie. 'Why, we've even heard him say that this Jesus of Nazareth will knock this Temple down and change the way in which Moses taught us to live.'

All this time Stephen stood there, and members of the Council were sitting and staring at him, for there was an angelic look on his face.

'Is all this true?' asked the High Priest.

Stephen then spoke to the Council, and he had a lot to say.

His Defence

He told them their national story, how they became 'the People of God' in the days of Abraham and Joseph and Moses. He tried to make clear to them what God had really wanted them to be.

'Our ancestors,' he said, 'always worshipped God in a *tent*. God told Moses to set up a *tent* in the camp on the march across the desert, and they took it with them wherever they went. They set it up here in Palestine, and here it stayed until David became King. It was only then we began to think about a *building* for God. It was King David who wanted to build a Temple for God. He didn't build it, you know; it was his son Solomon who built it.

'But you see what this means: God doesn't really live in buildings. The Bible puts it plainly—

> Heaven is my throne;
> earth is my footstool.
> What kind of house will you build for me,
>   says God,
> or where can I stay?
> Haven't I made everything in heaven and earth?

'Only the world is big enough for God, and we must live in his Way. But you Jewish people are always the same, as the Bible makes clear—you will never listen to God. You are just the same as your ancestors. Is there any Man of God your ancestors did not treat badly? They even killed the Men of God, although they were explaining God's Way and telling them how one day he would send his Chosen Leader. In our own day God *has* sent his Chosen Leader, and all you could do was to hand him over to the Romans and have him killed—you whom God himself has taught but who never did what he told you!'

They had listened quietly to him so far, but these last words made them wild with anger and they hissed at him. Stephen himself was filled with God's power and gazed over their heads. All he was thinking about and all he could see was—Jesus, full of God's glory and full of God's power.

'I see God's throne in heaven,' he said, 'and Jesus at God's right hand!'

His Death

The whole crowd broke into a great roar. They pressed their hands to their ears to shut out the sound of his voice; and in one great rush they tumbled over one another to get at him. They dragged him outside the city to stone him to death.

The men whose duty it was to see that he was really dead brought their clothes and put them down before a young officer of the court called Saul.

'Lord Jesus, receive me,' Stephen kept praying, even while they were throwing the stones at him.

He knelt down on the ground.

'O God,' he called out, 'forgive them this great wrong they are doing.'

It was all over. Saul was quite sure the right thing had been done.

That wasn't all that happened on that day, either. The crowds went off to get hold of other Friends of Jesus like Stephen, but they escaped into the country districts of Judea and Samaria. The close Friends of Jesus like Peter and John were left alone.

But Saul wanted more than the death of one man; he wanted to get rid of all the Friends of Jesus. He went from house to house, and dragged men and women off to prison.

The Man who began it : Peter

We have already seen how brave a man Peter was. He was not afraid of government or people, and he knew how dangerous it was to stand up in the Temple and tell the crowds the Good News about God 'in the name of Jesus'.

Yet he had not seen how wide God's love was and how big was the adventure Jesus had called him to. But one day he came to Caesarea, the headquarters of the Roman Army, and met a Roman Officer—a foreigner, not a Jew like himself. The officer, Captain Cornelius, was a good man who loved God and became a Friend of Jesus. It was then that Peter realized what Jesus had really cared for—the whole world, not just his own country of Palestine.

Lydda

Peter was going about the country visiting the Friends of Jesus. One day he went down from Jerusalem City to visit those who lived in the town of Lydda.

There he met a man called Aeneas, a cripple who had been in bed for eight long years.

'Aeneas,' said Peter, 'Jesus cures you. Get up and make your bed yourself.'

He stood straight up there and then.

All the people who lived in Lydda and the nearby town of Sharon saw for themselves that the man was strong and well again. That made them think seriously about the story of Jesus.

Joppa

In Joppa, a seaside town not far from Lydda, there lived a Friend of Jesus called Tabitha. She spent her time helping people in every way she could. She fell ill and died, and was laid in the room on the flat roof of the house.

The Friends of Jesus heard that Peter was at Lydda and they sent two men to tell him what had happened.

'Come across to us,' they said, 'and come quickly.'

Peter got up and went back with them; and when he got there they took him straight away up to the room on the roof. The widows whom Tabitha had helped crowded round him, with tears in their eyes, and showed him the coats and clothes which she had made when she was alive.

Peter had them all taken outside. He then knelt down and prayed. He turned toward the body.

'Tabitha, get up,' he said.

She opened her eyes. Then she saw Peter and sat up, and he gave her his hand and helped her to her feet. He called all the others into the room and showed them Tabitha—alive.

The news spread all over Joppa, and many people became Friends of Jesus. Peter stayed for quite a long time there, and made his home with Simon, a tanner.

Captain Cornelius

1. The Dream

Caesarea was the Headquarters of the Roman Army in Palestine, and among the officers there was a man called Cornelius, a captain of the Italian Regiment. He was a good man who, with all his family, loved God. He was always ready to help anybody in need and prayed to God every day.

One day, about three o'clock in the afternoon, he had a dream. Everything was very clear and he saw an angel of God coming towards him.

'Cornelius,' the angel called.

He stared at his visitor in terror.

'What's the matter, sir?' he asked.

'God knows all about you, your prayers and your good deeds,' he said. 'Send to Joppa and fetch a man called Simon—he's also known as Peter. He is staying with Simon the tanner; his house faces the sea.'

The angel left him.

Cornelius, without wasting a minute, called two of his slaves and one of his soldiers who loved God as he did, told them all about the dream and sent them off to Joppa.

2. Next Day

About noon next day, the three men were well on their way and had almost reached Joppa.

And it was about noon that Peter went up on to the flat roof of the house to pray. He suddenly felt hungry and wanted his dinner, but while the servants were getting it ready he fell asleep and started to dream.

It was a strange dream.

He saw something dropping down out of the open sky—something like a great sheet, tied at the four corners and being lowered to the earth. All sorts of animals and reptiles and wild birds were inside, including things no Jew, by Jewish law, was allowed to eat.

He heard a Voice speaking.

'Get up, Peter,' it said, 'kill them and eat them.'

'Never, sir,' said Peter. 'I've never eaten any forbidden food.'

'What God calls good food,' said the Voice, 'you mustn't call forbidden food.'

This happened three times. Then the thing was suddenly drawn up into the sky.

While Peter was wondering what the dream could mean, the messengers of Cornelius stood outside the gate; all this time they had been asking people the way to Simon's house.

'Is Simon, called Peter, staying here?' they called out.

Peter was still up on the roof, wondering about the dream.

'There are three men looking for you,' God told him. 'Get up and go down to them and go along with them. There's nothing to worry about; I've sent them.'

Peter went down to the men.

'I am the man you are looking for,' he said. 'What have you come for?'

'We come from Captain Cornelius, a good man who loves God— all the Jews in Caesarea will tell you that. He was told by God to invite you to his house, and to listen to what you have to say.'

Peter asked them to stay with him. Next morning, he got up and went off with them; and some of the Friends of Jesus in Joppa went along with him.

THE PORT OF CAESAREA, the headquarters of the Roman Governor.

3. At Caesarea

They got to Caesarea the next day.

Captain Cornelius had asked his relatives and close friends to come along, and was looking out for Peter and the three men. He met Peter as he was entering the house, and fell down on the ground in front of him; he thought Peter must be no ordinary man.

Peter pulled him to his feet.

'Stand up,' he said, 'I'm an ordinary man like yourself.'

Talking with Cornelius, he went on into the crowded house.

'You all know about Jewish Law,' he said. 'You know it forbids a Jew to have anything to do with a foreigner—even to visit him. But I now know better, for God has made it quite clear to me that I must not call anybody at all, whoever he is, "foreigner". I couldn't say No when you sent for me. Tell me why you wanted me to come.'

Captain Cornelius told him about his dream.

'So, you see,' he said, 'I sent at once to invite you and you have kindly come along. All of us in this room know God is here, and we want to listen to what God has told you to tell us.'

'It's as clear as daylight to me now', said Peter, 'that God has no favourites. It doesn't matter what race or nation you belong to; if you love God and do what is right, God welcomes you.

'You know what the Bible says—

He sent out his word and healed them.

and

How lovely on the hills
    are the footsteps of the man who brings the Good News
    and calls all the world to be at peace.

'All this is really about Jesus.

'He is God's Chosen Leader; all the world is his Kingdom, and he has brought the Good News of peace.

'You yourselves, too, know something about what has happened in Palestine in our own time—the events that began in Galilee after John the Hermit had been preaching in Jordan Valley, and the story of Jesus from Nazareth Village.

'Let me tell you what really happened.

'God called Jesus to his great work, and gave him his Spirit and power. He went from village to village doing good and healing sick people; for God was with him. We saw with our own eyes all he did in Palestine and in Jerusalem City.

'He died on a Roman cross; but God soon raised him from the dead—the same Jesus we had known in Galilee. The crowds didn't see him; only those whom God had chosen saw him—we who had dinner with him when he was alive again. He told us what to do: to tell the Good News to everybody, and to make it quite clear that, in all he said and did, God has shown us what is right and what is wrong. Jesus, not Caesar or Moses, is the judge of all men everywhere. Everybody who trusts in Jesus is forgiven for all the wrong things he has done—because he was what he was. This is surely what the Bible tells us.'

Peter was still speaking when God's power was given to everybody who had been listening to him. The Jewish Friends of Jesus

THE ROMAN THEATRE AT CAESAREA. It is used today, and the photograph shows a play being performed there.

who had come along with Peter were amazed—fancy God giving his power even to *foreigners*! They themselves heard them, there in the room, singing God's praises!

'God has given his power to these foreigners just as he gave it to us Jews,' said Peter. 'Can anybody say they ought not to join the company of the Friends of Jesus?'

He gave orders for them to be baptized 'in the name of Jesus'.

Afterwards they all wanted Peter to stay a few days in Caesarea.

4. Back in Jerusalem

News about what had happened in Caesarea reached the Jewish Friends of Jesus in Jerusalem and the south—foreigners had become Friends of Jesus!

Some of them thought this was wrong. Only Jews, they thought, could become Friends of Jesus; if foreigners wanted to, they should become Jews first. So when Peter went up to Jerusalem City, they took the matter up with him.

'Why did you meet foreigners,' they said bitterly, 'and share their home-life?'

Peter told them the whole story—his dream at Joppa and what happened in the home of Captain Cornelius.

'Then I remembered the words of Jesus,' he went on. 'He said, you remember, "John the Hermit used water as a sign; God will give you, my Friends, his own power in your hearts". God gave these foreigners in Caesarea his own power in their hearts. If God gave to them, foreigners though they were, the same gift that he gave to us when *we* became the Friends of Jesus, who was I to say No to God himself?'

When they heard Peter talk like this, they had nothing more to say.

'Foreigners also can change their ways,' they said, 'and live in God's Way!'

And they praised God.

Trouble Again

Herod again arrested some of the Friends of Jesus. He had James, the brother of John, beheaded. This made him popular. So he looked round for others, and, during the Great Feast, arrested Peter as well. After his arrest, he put him in prison with sixteen soldiers on guard. He planned to parade him before the people when the Feast was over. All the Friends of Jesus could do was to pray for him, and this they did day and night.

The Feast was over and the very next day Herod had planned to bring Peter out and show him to the crowds. It was late at night. Peter was asleep. Two soldiers lay on either side of him and he was handcuffed to them. Outside the prison door, sentries stood on guard.

A light shone in the cell and a messenger from God stood there. He tapped Peter on his side and woke him up.

'Get up quickly,' he said.

The handcuffs fell from his wrists.

'Fasten your belt,' he said, 'and put your sandals on.

Peter did what he was told.

'Put your cloak on and follow me.'

Peter followed him out. It was like a dream; it didn't seem real.

They passed the first sentry, then the second sentry, and came to the great iron gate. Beyond the gate lay the city. Nobody was there, but the gate swung open. They went through, and along the narrow street. The messenger vanished.

By this time Peter was wide awake.

'Now I know God has rescued me,' he said to himself, 'rescued me from Herod and the show the crowds were looking forward to.'

He realised what had happened, and off he went to the house of Mary, John Mark's mother, where many Friends of Jesus were meeting to pray for him.

He knocked on the door of the outer gate, and Rhoda, a maid, came to see who it was. She knew at once it was Peter's voice. Back she ran to tell everybody—she didn't stop to open the door, she was so happy.

'Peter's outside the door,' she burst out.

'You're mad,' they told her.

'It *is* Peter!' said Rhoda.

'It's his ghost,' they said.

Peter went on knocking.

At last they opened the door, and, to their amazement, there was Peter himself!

With a wave of his hand, he got them to be quiet, and told them how God had rescued him from prison.

'Tell James and the other Friends of Jesus,' he said.

Then he left them and went away.

There was great alarm among the soldiers when daylight came. They hadn't any idea what had become of Peter. Herod ordered a search for him, but he was nowhere to be found. He had the guards examined and ordered them to be executed. Then he went down from Jerusalem to his palace at Caesarea.

The Man who led the Adventure : Paul

When Dr. Luke was telling us about Stephen and how he died, he gave the name of the 'young officer of the court' who was in charge of the execution. His name was Saul, and he hated all the Friends of Jesus. It is this man who is going to be the hero of Dr. Luke's book. For, not long after, he himself became a Friend of Jesus.

This is the story of how it happened near the city of Damascus.

Saul is a Jewish name. It was the name of the first Hebrew King, and boys of the Benjamin Clan would be proud to be called Saul. Saul was born a Roman citizen, so he had a Roman name, Paul, as well as his Jewish name. Perhaps his full name was Gaius Julius Paulus. Later in the book Dr. Luke uses his Roman name, and this Roman name, Paul, is the one by which he is best known.

On the Road

Saul was hot on the trail of the Friends of Jesus, thirsting for their blood. He went to the High Priest and asked him for warrants to search the Meeting Houses in Damascus, to arrest all 'the People of God's Way'—as the Friends of Jesus called themselves—and to bring them, men and women alike, as prisoners to Jerusalem City.

He set off along the Damascus Road.

He had almost reached his journey's end when, suddenly, a light from the sky burst on him and he fell down on the road. He heard a Voice.

'Saul! Saul!' the Voice called. 'Why do you treat me like an enemy?'

'Who are you?' asked Saul.

'I am Jesus—and you are treating me like an enemy! But get up and go on into Damascus City. You'll get your orders there.'

His fellow-travellers stood speechless with fright; they heard the Voice, but they saw nobody.

Saul got up. When he tried to see where he was, he found he was blind; they had to lead him by the hand into the city. For three days he was blind and had nothing to eat or drink.

In Damascus

A Friend of Jesus, Ananias, was living in Damascus City. He had a dream, and in the dream he saw Jesus.

'Ananias!' said Jesus.

'I'm here, Lord,' he answered.

'Get up,' said Jesus, 'and go to Straight Street. Find the house where Judas lives, and ask for Saul, a citizen of Tarsus City. You'll find him praying. He's had a dream, and in his dream he has seen a man called Ananias enter the house and put his hands on his eyes and give him his sight back again.'

'Lord,' said Ananias, 'I've heard all sorts of stories about this man; he's here with a warrant to arrest all your Friends in the city.'

'Off you go,' said Jesus. 'I've marked him out as my messenger. His orders are to tell the whole world the Good News—foreigners and their governments as well as Jewish people. And I'll not hide from him the dangers he'll have to face as a Friend of mine.'

Ananias went off and found the house and put his hands on Saul.

'Brother Saul,' he said, 'It was the Lord Jesus you saw on the road outside the city. He has sent me to you. May you have your sight back again, and may you be filled with God's power!'

His sight came back—as suddenly as he had lost it—and he could see quite clearly.

He got up, and Ananias baptized him and received him into the company of the Friends of Jesus. He had a good meal and felt quite well again.

He stayed with the Friends of Jesus for a few days. The first thing he did was to go along to the Meeting House—and tell them the story of Jesus!

'He *is* God's Son,' he said.

Everybody, listening to him talk, was amazed.

'Isn't this the man who tried to wipe out the Friends of Jesus in Jerusalem City?' they asked. 'Why, he came here with a warrant for the arrest of those who live here, to take them back as prisoners to our Leaders.'

This didn't stop Saul. He spoke all the more powerfully in the Meeting Houses. He shocked the Jewish people in the city—they didn't know how to answer his arguments. He had only one thing to say—Jesus is God's Chosen Leader.

This went on for quite a time. At last the Jewish people plotted to murder him, and they picketed the city gates the whole twenty-four hours of the day. Somebody told Saul about the plot; and one night his friends took him to the city wall, and lowered him over the wall in a basket.

To Jerusalem and Tarsus

Saul went back to Jerusalem. He tried to get in touch with the Friends of Jesus there; but they were afraid of him. They thought he was just pretending to be a Friend of Jesus.

DAMASCUS CITY—the Gateway leading to Straight Street.

But Barnabas introduced him to the Christian Leaders. He told them how Saul had seen Jesus on the Damascus Road and been given his orders, and how he had told the Good News boldly in the Meeting Houses of Damascus City.

That settled it, and he was welcomed into all their homes. He showed the same boldness in talking about Jesus in Jerusalem City as he had in Damascus City. His chief aim was to meet the Jews from overseas and argue with them; but they, like the Damascus Jews, made up their minds to murder him.

Somebody told the Friends of Jesus about the plot, and they took him down to the port of Caesarea and sent him off home to Tarsus City.

The Great Plan

Dr. Luke now leaves Palestine and takes us to Antioch City in the north. This was a large and famous city, and roads from north, south, east and west met there. It was not an old city; it had been built, two hundred or more years before, in honour of King Antiochus.

After the death of Stephen, some of his friends escaped to Antioch, and, later, Friends of Jesus from other lands came to live there. All these men believed that Jesus cared for everybody, not just for Jewish people. Antioch was crowded with people from many lands, and these Friends of Jesus began to tell the Good News to anybody who would listen, without bothering whether they were Jews or not.

Then one day, in a prayer meeting, they were sure that God wanted them to begin to take the Good News all over the world. They made up their minds to plan this great work. This is the story of what happened, and how Paul comes into it.

The *first* great day in the story of the Friends of Jesus was the day when, in Jerusalem City, they received God's power to live in his Way (p. 163); this is the *second* great day in their story—and, it is important to note, it takes place on foreign soil.

How the Good News came to Antioch City

After the death of Stephen, many of the Friends of Jesus were scattered, as we have seen. Some of them went to Phoenicia, where ships set sail for Africa and Italy and Spain. Some went to the Island of Cyprus, the homeland of Barnabas. Some went to Antioch City in the north, the third greatest city of the Empire, where the

ANTIOCH CITY.

great roads from Europe and Egypt and Babylon met. It was in this city that the Friends of Jesus made the great plan to take the Good News all over the world, to foreigners and Jewish people alike. This is how it happened.

At first, the Friends of Jesus in Antioch City told the Good News to Jewish people only. But Friends of Jesus from the island of Cyprus and from North Africa came to live there; and *they* began to tell the story of Jesus to Greek people, foreigners, not Jews. This was clearly what God wanted them to do, for many of the Greek foreigners believed the Good News and became Friends of Jesus.

News of all this reached Jerusalem City, and the Leaders of the Friends of Jesus there sent Barnabas off to Antioch to find out what was happening. When he got there, he saw what a difference God's love had made to them all; and he was very glad.

'You've made up your minds to be Friends of Jesus,' he told them. 'Stick to it, and don't let Jesus down.'

He was a good man, full of God's power, and he trusted God with his whole heart.

The company of the Friends of Jesus grew. So Barnabas set off for Tarsus City to find Saul, and brought him back with him to Antioch. For a whole year they met the Friends of Jesus there in their meetings together, and explained the story of Jesus to a large company of people. It was in this city that the Friends of Jesus were first nicknamed 'Christians'—'Christ's Men'.

The Great Decision

Now in the company of the Friends of Jesus, there were leaders who explained the meaning of the Bible and leaders who explained the meaning of all that Jesus said and did. These are their names: Barnabas, Simon the 'Black', Luke from North Africa, Manaen who had been the close friend of King Herod, and Saul. One day they were meeting for prayer and fasting.

'I have called Barnabas and Saul to a great work,' God said to them. 'Give them this work to do.'

They went on with their prayers and fasting, asking God to guide them. Then they sent Barnabas and Saul to tell the Good News to the people of the Empire.

THE ISLAND OF CYPRUS. Here Barnabas and Paul began 'the great adventure' of taking
the Good News to the whole world. It was where Barnabas had grown up as a boy and he
would know it well.

From East to West

The Friends of Jesus in Antioch City did not know what a great adventure they were beginning, an adventure which was to spread all over the world and go on all down the centuries. It is going on still today.

Two men started out from Antioch, Barnabas and Saul. Saul was the great leader.

Dr. Luke now begins the story of Saul and his journeys across the world. (From now on we will use his Roman name—Paul.) We shall tell this story in our next book, *Paul the Explorer.* Here we tell six of Dr. Luke's stories to show how the Good News was taken all over the world, until at last, one spring day, Paul walked into the capital city of the Roman Empire, Rome itself.

As the Friends of Jesus walked along the roads of the Empire, climbed the mountains and sailed the seas, they began at last to understand Jesus. As they told the Good News to everybody they met, and men and women everywhere listened to it and became Friends of Jesus, they knew why Jesus had lived and died and been raised to life again. They remembered his words, and they followed his example.

So we shall find ourselves in Greek and 'barbarian' islands, in famous cities and country towns high in the mountains, and at last we shall enter the gates of Rome itself. Everybody everywhere matters.

How the Good News came to a Greek Island

Barnabas and Paul set off. They were now sure that this was the work God had given them to do.

They went down to the port of Seleucia, took ship for Cyprus and landed at Salamis Town, in the eastern part of the island. John Mark went along with them to help them.

They told the story of Jesus in the Jewish Meeting Houses, and in this way they went through the whole island.

They came at last to Paphos on the west coast, where the Roman Governor, Sergius Paul, had his headquarters. Here they met a Jewish magician, called Bar Jesus, who was friendly with the Governor.

The Governor was a thoughtful man, and when he heard about Barnabas and Paul, he asked them to come to see him. He wanted to hear the story of Jesus. Bar Jesus the magician was there, and tried to prove to the Governor that they were wrong; he didn't want to lose his job.

Paul (his Roman name was the same as the Governor's) was filled with God's power and looked straight at the magician.

'There isn't a trick or a lie in your trade you don't know,' he said. 'You're a bad man. You'd twist anything for gain—even religion! But you're dealing with God not men; you shall be blind for a time —you won't even see the brightness of the sun!'

Suddenly, the magician's world went misty and dark, and he had to feel his way about and get people to lead him by the hand.

The Governor watched all this, and became a Friend of Jesus. But what amazed him was the story of Jesus.

How the Good News came to the Highlands of Anatolia

Barnabas and Paul came one day to the old town of Lystra, high up in the highlands of Anatolia, where people, though they could speak Greek, usually spoke their own strange language which Paul and Barnabas couldn't understand.

There was a man here who had been a cripple all his life and had never been able to walk.

Paul was talking to the crowd near the town gates and the cripple sat there on the roadside listening to him. Paul looked straight at him and saw the man believed he could cure him.

'Get up on your feet!' said Paul, loudly enough for everybody to hear. 'Stand up straight!'

The cripple jumped up and walked about.

The crowd saw what Paul had done, and they started shouting in their own strange language.

'The gods have come down like men and here they are in our city!' they said.

They thought Barnabas was the great god Zeus, and Paul the messenger of the gods, Hermes—because he did all the talking!

The priest of Zeus, who looked after the nearby temple called 'The Temple of Zeus-outside-the-Town', brought bulls wreathed with flowers to the town gates, to sacrifice to Barnabas and Paul as gods.

Barnabas and Paul couldn't help but hear all this noise. When they saw what it all meant, they tore their clothes and ran among the crowd.

THE HIGHLANDS OF ANATOLIA.

'Sirs!' they shouted. 'What's all this for? We are just ordinary men like you, and all we're doing is bringing you Good News. Stop all this nonsense and learn what God is really like. He's the Living God; he made the sky and land and seas. He made the whole world. Until now God let people everywhere do what they thought best. Yet even then he showed you what he was like. He looked after you all. He gave you rain from the sky and harvest time. He saw that you had food to eat. All your happiness comes from him.'

Even words like this hardly stopped the crowd from going on with their sacrifice.

Then Jews from the towns where Paul and Barnabas had already been came along and told the crowd what *they* thought about them. That turned the crowd against Paul and Barnabas, and they started throwing stones at Paul. They thought they had killed him, and dragged him outside the town.

Paul's friends stood round him; they, too, thought he was dead. But he got up and went back into the town.

How the Good News came to a Jewish Meeting House

Paul and his friend Silas came one day to the town of Beroea in northern Greece. They had been travelling through the night, and when they reached the town they went into the Jewish Meeting House.

The Jewish people here were better mannered than those in other towns they had visited. They listened to the story of Jesus gladly, and every day they read the Bible carefully to see if what Paul said was true. Many became Friends of Jesus, and among them were well-known Greek women and quite a number of men. But the Jewish people in the city from which Paul had come heard that he was now telling the Good News in Beroea, and they came across to cause trouble and set the mob against him.

The Friends of Jesus there at once got Paul off on his way to the sea. Silas and Timothy stayed behind, and Paul's guides took him by boat as far as the city of Athens.

How the Good News came
to the Most Famous Greek City of all

Paul came to Athens by boat, and he was waiting there for Silas and Timothy.

He wandered through the streets; everywhere there were temples and images of the Greek gods. This made Paul very unhappy. He had to talk to somebody about it. He went to the Jewish Meeting House and argued there; he went to the Market Place and argued with anybody who happened to be there. There were many lecturers in the city, for its university was very famous; some of them met Paul, and he argued with them.

'What's this chatterer talking about?' sneered some.

'It's some foreign fellow talking about his gods, it seems,' said others.[1]

The City Council was called 'Mars Hill', after the name of the hill where it used to meet in earlier times. This Council was specially interested in all new speakers who came to teach in Athens. The

---

[1] Paul had been talking, of course, about Jesus and how he was risen from the dead. The word he used here was 'Anastasis' which simply means 'rising from the dead'; the lecturers thought it was the name of another foreign god!

citizens of Athens and their foreign visitors always had time to talk about or listen to anything strange and new; they seemed to do nothing else.

The lecturers got hold of Paul and took him before the Council.

'Tell us, if you please, something more about this "News" of yours,' they said. 'What you've been talking about sounds very strange to us. We'd like to know what it's all about.'

Paul stood before the Council.

'Citizens of Athens,' he said, 'by just wandering around your streets, I can see that religion matters very much to you. I had a good look at your temples and the images of your gods. And I noticed one altar that had these words on it "To an Unknown God". You do not know him; I will tell you about him.

'The God who made the world and all that's in it by that very fact is the Master of the whole world. His home can't be a temple in a street that you can build with your own hands.[1] He can't need temple servants, as though he had to have somebody looking after him. He gave us the very lives we live and everything we have. We may belong to different nations now, but at the beginning God made us all one people and gave us the whole world for our home. All things are in his hands—the rise and fall of nations and the boundaries of their territories. He did all this for one purpose only— that men and women might look for him and find him.

'Yet he is very near every one of us. Your own poets have said this very thing—

In God we live and move and exist,

and

We, too, belong to his family.

'If, therefore, we belong to God, we can't possibly think that gold and silver and stone are good enough to show us what he is like. No artist can paint God's picture, however clever or thoughtful he may be.

'What, then, has God done? He takes no notice of the past, when we didn't know what he is like. But today, in our own time, he calls all people to change their ways. We can no longer say we do not know; Jesus has made him plain. The day is fixed when everybody everywhere will be judged by this man he has chosen—

[1] See the speech of Stephen (p. 151).

'THE MOST FAMOUS GREEK CITY OF ALL'—ATHENS. The photograph shows the great temple on the high hill called the Acropolis.

and truly judged. The proof of this he has given to all men—he has raised him from the dead.'

Some of them laughed out loud at Paul when they heard him talk like this—about God 'raising Jesus from the dead'. But there were others.

'We'll hear you again about all this,' they said.

So Paul left them.

But there were some who went along with Paul and became Friends of Jesus. Among them were Dionysius, a member of the City Council itself, and a woman whose name was Damaris.

How the Good News came to a 'Barbarian' Island
(The Diary)

Sailing to Rome

This story begins in Palestine, and in the port of Caesarea, the headquarters of the Roman army.

The Roman Governor decided to send us by ship to Italy. He put Paul and some other prisoners in the care of Captain Julius of the Imperial Regiment whose officers served as messengers between the Emperor and his armies. There was a boat in harbour which came from a port near Troas; it was about to sail home, calling at places along the coast on the way. We went on board and set sail.

Next day we called at Sidon. Captain Julius was very good to Paul and let him visit the Friends of Jesus there and be cared for.

We put to sea again and sailed under the shelter of the island of Cyprus, for the north-west winds were blowing against us. We left the shelter of the island and sailed across the open sea to the mainland, and came to the port of Myra. There Captain Julius found an Egyptian grain-ship bound for Italy and put us on board. There were two hundred and seventy-six passengers.

For many days we sailed slowly westward, and it took us all our time to get as far as Cnidus. The wind was too strong to let us go on across the open sea; so we sailed southward round the island of Crete, where we were sheltered from the wind. It was hard enough sailing along the coast of the island, but we came at last to a small bay called Fair Havens, not far from a city. There we dropped anchor.

We had wasted a lot of time, and the dangerous season for ships had begun, when great storms blow up. Even the Jewish Feast, which took place on October 5th, was over.

Paul spoke to Captain Julius and the pilot and the ship-owner.

'Gentlemen,' he said, 'if we put to sea again now, I can see we shall run into great danger; we shall lose not only the cargo and the ship but our own lives as well.'

But Captain Julius listened more to the pilot and the ship-owner than to Paul.

The harbour at Fair Havens, it was true, was not a good place to spend the winter in. Most of the officers on board were for putting to sea and trying to get to the port of Phoenix to spend the winter there. (This was the only safe harbour, in all winds, on the south coast of Crete; it faces away from the winds, north-east and south-east.)

The Great Storm

One day the wind blew gently from the south-west. Now was their chance. They weighed anchor and sailed close along the coast of Crete. Suddenly a gale, called 'The Northeaster', blew down from the land. The ship was caught and could not face the wind.

So we ran before it and were driven out to sea. We ran under the shelter of the small island of Cauda, and even then had a hard job to get the ship's boat safely tied up on deck. The sailors fastened ropes over and under the ship to stop her from breaking up. They were frightened that they might be driven southward on to the African quicksands; they put out a sea anchor, but were still swept along.

We were tossed so violently about by the storm that next day the sailors began to throw the cargo overboard. On the third day, they threw away with their own hands everything they could. For many days we saw neither sun nor stars; we were at the mercy of the storm. At last we gave up hope of ever being saved.

All this time crew and passengers hadn't bothered to eat. So Paul stood up and spoke to them all.

'Gentlemen,' he said, 'you should have listened to me. You shouldn't have sailed from Crete; you wouldn't, then, have had such damage and lost so much. But now I'm going to tell you something to cheer you up.

'You'll lose the ship, but none of you will lose your lives. I had a dream last night. A messenger of the God to whom I belong and whom I serve stood by me. "Don't be frightened, Paul," he said. "You must stand before the Emperor. God has saved the lives of all those who are sailing with you." So cheer up, my friends. I trust God that it will all happen just as I've been told. But we shall be ship-wrecked on some island.'

Shipwreck

A fortnight passed, and all the time we were drifting across the open sea.

One night—it was about midnight—the sailors guessed that we were getting near land. They dropped the lead overboard and found we were in twenty fathoms of water. When we had sailed a little farther, they dropped the lead again—this time it was fifteen fathoms. They were now frightened that we might run on to the rocks; so they threw out four anchors from the stern, and prayed for daylight.

The sailors wanted to abandon ship, and lowered the small boat into the sea.

'We only want to let the anchors down from the bow,' they lied.
Paul spoke to Captain Julius and the soldiers.

'If these men don't stay on board,' he said, 'none of you will get ashore.'

The soldiers cut the boat's ropes and let it fall into the sea.

Just before dawn, Paul told them all to get a good meal.

'For a fortnight you've been so scared you haven't bothered to eat anything. You're starving. If you'll listen to me, you'll get something inside you—you'll need it if you're going to get ashore safely. I've told you—you'll not lose a hair of your head.'

With these words, he picked up a loaf, said Grace over it while they all watched, broke it and began to eat it. They all cheered up and had a good breakfast. When everybody had eaten enough, they threw the cargo of wheat into the sea to make the ship ride lighter.

Daylight came, but they couldn't tell where they were; they could see a small bay with a sandy beach—just the place, if they could get to it, to run the ship ashore. They let the anchors go and left them in the sea; and loosed the ropes that held the rudders fast. A breeze was blowing. They set the foresail, and made for the shore.

They ran into rough water where two strong currents met and drove the ship aground. The bow stuck fast and nothing could move it; while the stern, beaten by the great seas, began to break up. The soldiers were for killing the prisoners—they thought they might swim off and escape Captain Julius stopped that; Paul was an important prisoner and he didn't want him killed. He told those who could swim to jump into the sea first and get ashore, and the others, on cargo boards or bits of wreckage, to get there as best as they could. So it was that everybody got safely to the beach.

On the Island of Malta

When we had all reached the beach, we found out where we were —the island of Malta. The natives didn't treat us as we expected, but showed us every kindness. It was beginning to rain and everybody was very cold; so they lit a bonfire and made us all feel at home.

Paul picked up a bundle of brushwood to put on the fire. There was a viper in it and the heat woke it up; it got hold of his hand and was hanging from it. The natives were watching.

MOUNT IDA IN THE ISLAND OF CRETE. It was here that the sailors on Paul's ship wanted to spend the winter.

'The fellow's a murderer,' they said to one another. 'He may have escaped drowning, but the Goddess of Justice has seen to it that he won't get away with it.'

Paul shook the viper off into the fire. The natives waited—surely he would swell up or suddenly fall down dead. Nothing happened. They went on waiting and watching; and still nothing happened. That changed their minds.

'He's a god himself,' they said.

The Chief of the island, a man called Publius, owned all the lands round about the bay. He welcomed us and looked after us for three days in a most friendly way. His father was very ill with fever at the time. Paul went to see him, prayed for him, put his hands on him and cured him. Then everybody else who was ill came along, and Paul cured them too. Nothing was too much for the people to do for us. And when we went on board ship to leave the island, they gave us everything we needed.

How the Good News came to the Capital of the Empire

It was three months before we left.

In February we went on board another Egyptian ship which had spent the winter at the island; she had 'The Heavenly Twins' as her figure-head. We put in at the port of Syracuse. The wind dropped and we had to spend three days there. We weighed anchor at last, and made for the port of Rhegium. The south wind started blowing next day, and it took us only two days to get to Puteoli, one of the ports for Rome.

We looked up the Friends of Jesus in the town, and they asked us to spend a week with them. Then we set off for Rome.

The Friends of Jesus in the city had heard we were coming and came out to meet us—more than forty miles, as far as the Market Town of Appius and The Three Inns.

When Paul saw them he thanked God and felt ready for anything.

We came at last into Rome itself.

Paul was allowed to hire a house outside the barracks and live there by himself with a soldier on guard.

He had been there only three days when he asked the Jewish Leaders in the city to meet him, and they came along.

'I want to tell you about myself, brothers,' he said. 'I have done nothing against the Jewish people or the customs of our

THE ISLAND OF MALTA—the bay where Paul was shipwrecked.

ancestors. Yet I was handed over as a prisoner to the Romans. This happened in Jerusalem. The Romans, after a long trial, wanted to set me free—I had done nothing, they found, to deserve the death sentence. The Jews wouldn't have it. So there was only one thing to do—appeal to the Emperor. But I have no complaint to make against my own people.

'That is why I asked you to come to see me and let me talk to you. It is because of the hope my people have held for hundreds of years that I am wearing these handcuffs.'

'We haven't had any letters from Palestine about you,' they said, 'and nobody who has come here has said anything against you. We would like to hear what you've got to say. All we know about the Friends of Jesus is that everybody says they're a bad lot.'

They fixed on a day for meeting Paul, and a great crowd came to his house. He talked about God's Way. He told them the story of Jesus and tried to show them that this is what the Bible was about. He went on talking all day.

Some of them thought he was right, and some of them thought he was wrong. They couldn't agree with one another and that ended the meeting. Paul had the last word.

'You are doing just what our people have done all down the centuries. We will not listen to what God has got to say. Well, be quite sure of this: it is to foreigners everywhere the Good News about God has been sent—they will listen.'

Paul stayed for two whole years in the house he had rented. He let anybody come to see him who wanted to. He spent his time telling the Good News and explaining the story of Jesus. He did this quite openly; nobody stopped him.

THE APPIAN WAY, the ancient road to Rome. This was the road along which Paul travelled from the port of Puteoli to Rome.

BOOK FOUR

PAUL THE EXPLORER

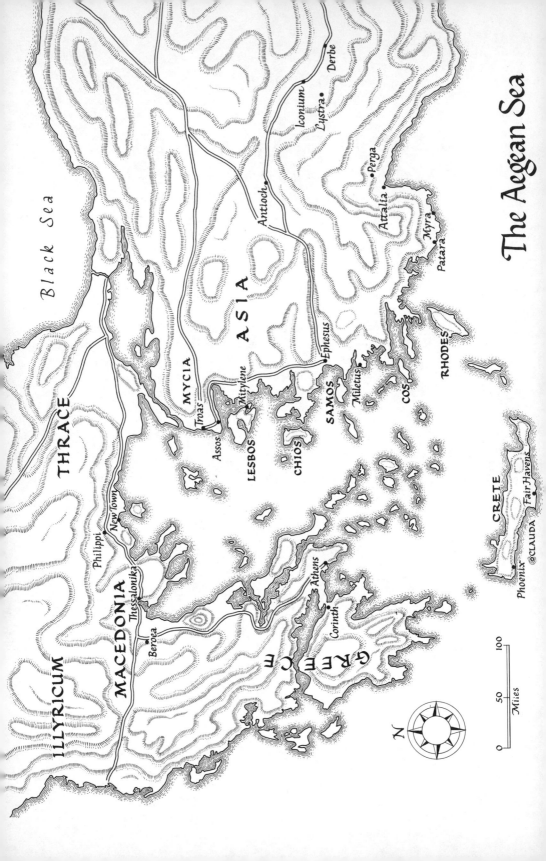

The Aegean Sea

Black Sea

THRACE

ILLYRICUM

MACEDONIA

Philippi
New Town
Thessalonika
Beroea

GREECE

Athens
Corinth

MYCIA

Troas
Assos
Mitylene
LESBOS
CHIOS
SAMOS
Miletus
Ephesus

ASIA

Antioch

Iconium
Lystra
Derbe

Perga
Attalia
Myra
Patara

COS

RHODES

CRETE
Phoenix
CLAUDA
Fair Havens

100

50

Miles

0

N

Paul's Own Story

Paul never wrote his own life story; but he has told us a lot about himself in his letters. He often writes about himself—what he is doing, what he is planning.

Private letters are not easy for other people to follow. In letters to friends, we do not always set things out in order as we do in an essay. We write about this, and then about that, and then something else comes into our minds and we write about *that*; just as we do when we are chatting with them. Paul's letters are a little like that, for they are real letters.

So I have gathered together the passages where Paul talks about himself and his friends, and put them together, so that you can see what he had to say about himself.

I do not think Paul *talked* about himself very much to his friends; he does not seem to have said very much about himself to his good friend Dr. Luke. But Paul had to *write* a lot about himself in his letters. He was bitterly attacked because of his attitude, as a Jew, to foreigners. Jewish Christians felt he was a traitor to his own country and that he had got the Good News all wrong. In defending himself he was really defending the Good News and the freedom of the friends of Jesus everywhere.

In arranging 'Paul's own Story', one passage,[1] in his letter to the friends of Jesus in Anatolia, has been very helpful. People had been attacking Paul and saying that he was the kind of man who would do anything. They quoted—and quoted wrongly—incidents from his past life. He could not be trusted, they said, and he was no true friend of Jesus. To answer them, Paul tells his friends what had happened during the last twenty years of his life: he had not been the kind of man his enemies said he was—'Here,' he says, 'is my record'. He lists the main events carefully one after another. This has given me a framework for all the other passages about himself. I have arranged them in chapters. The chapters and chapter headings are mine; the words are Paul's. I have translated them as if he were writing to us.

---

[1] Gal. 1.11–2.21

How I became a Friend of Jesus

I am a Jew. I belong to the Benjamin clan, King Saul's clan. I grew up in a good Jewish home, and I was very patriotic.

When I grew up, I joined a very strict religious party, the Pharisees, and I did everything I could to become a good man; I kept every rule there was to keep. I was much more serious than many of those who grew up with me; I had a passion for all the age-old customs of my people.

But I didn't find what I was looking for. It seemed as if trying to be good made me take notice of all the bad things men do. For example, I shouldn't have known what 'envying' people was if the Bible hadn't said, 'You mustn't envy anybody'. It looked as if reading the Bible made me worse than I was!

Let me be quite clear. The Bible is a good book, and what it tells us to do is good and right—it's what God wants us to do. But why should a good book not help me to be good?

I was a real puzzle to myself: I didn't do what in my heart I really wanted to do, and I hated myself for doing what I did. All this made me most unhappy. I didn't know who could help me. And then, thank God, I found the secret of being really myself; it was Jesus who showed me God's Way and helped me to live in it.

This is indeed Good News, and I have told everybody I could about it. It's Good News about *how God helps us*; it's Good News *for everybody*, foreigner and Jew alike; and all anybody need do is to *take God at his word*. I didn't make all this up, and I certainly didn't get it from any teacher. I got it straight from Jesus himself. Haven't I myself seen him?

It happened like this.

You know what I was like in my old Jewish days. I was the bitter enemy of the friends of Jesus, and I tried as hard as I could to wipe them out. But God, who made this bright world, filled my heart with light, the light which shines when we know what he really is like. And I saw this light shining from the face of Jesus—Jesus who died, was buried and rose again to life. He was seen by Peter (you remember), by the 'Twelve', and by more than five hundred friends together. (Most of these are still alive, but some, of course, have since died.) He was seen by his brother James; then by all his close friends; and last of all, long after anybody could have hoped, he was seen by me, as I have said.

ARABIA. This was the country Paul went to after he became a Christian in Damascus. Petra was its capital city. Its temples and buildings were cut out of the red rock. This is the road that leads into the city.

God had marked me out for my great work before I was born, and now, in his love, he had called me to it. He had shown me his Son; and my business now was to tell the story of Jesus to everybody all over the world. I come at the bottom of the list of his friends, far below men like Peter; I don't deserve to be called a friend of his, because I was once his enemy. I owe everything I am to God's love.

I did not talk about this to anybody. I didn't even go up to Jerusalem City to see those who had been friends of Jesus long before I was.

I went off into Arabia, and then came back to Damascus City. King Aretas told the Governor of the city to guard the gates and arrest me. But I was lowered in a rope basket through an opening in the city wall and got away.

Three years went by before I went up to Jerusalem to see Peter and stayed a fortnight with him. I didn't meet any of the other close friends of Jesus, except his brother James.

No other of the friends of Jesus there had ever met me face to face. They had only heard what others said—'Our bitter enemy is telling everybody the Good News himself! And to think he once tried to stop it being told!' They thanked God for me.

THE CROWDED YEARS

I'm proud of what I've been able to do to make God's Way known throughout the world. But it's only through Jesus that I've been able to do what I have done.

There is one thing—and one thing only—I care to talk about: how Jesus has used me to help people of many lands to live in God's Way.

From Jerusalem in Palestine all round the world as far as Illyricum in Europe, I have made the Good News of Jesus sound like the Good News it is—Good News for everybody. For I have had one ambition: to tell the story of Jesus where his name had never been heard. I didn't want to go where others had already told the Good News. You remember what the Bible says—

> They shall see
>   who had never been told about him;
>   those who have never heard
> shall know all about him.

SELEUCIA. This is the port of Antioch City in Syria. When Barnabas and Paul went to take the Good News to the island of Cyprus, they went on board ship here. These are the ruins of a Christian church built here many years later.

And wherever I've been they don't just talk about it either—they live it.

Let me tell you what I've had to face. I know it's silly for me to talk like this, but here's the list, for I know what it is to work hard and live dangerously.

I've been beaten up more times than I can remember, been in more than one prison, and faced death itself more than once. Five times I've been thrashed by a Jewish court to within an inch of my life; three times I've been beaten with rods by city magistrates; and once I was nearly stoned to death.

I've been shipwrecked three times; and once, I was adrift, out of sight of land, for twenty-four hours.

I don't know how many roads I've tramped. I've faced bandits; I've been attacked by fellow-countrymen and by foreigners. I've met danger in city streets and on lonely country roads and out in the open sea.

I know what it is to have false friends.

I've been so tired out that I haven't been able to sleep at night. Many a time I've been hungry and thirsty through sheer lack of food. I know what it is to be nearly frozen to death and to have only rags on my back.

I could tell you many a story.

And, as if this wasn't enough, I've had another heavy load to carry day by day—looking after and caring for the Christian churches.

I've been in some tight corners—but never cornered; I've lost my way—but never my courage; I've been on the run—but never left to my fate; I've been knocked down—but never knocked out.

I know what people have thought of me—a feeble fool not worth bothering about. What else, indeed, could they think of a man who goes about starving and in rags, gets beaten up, lives like a vagabond, works like a common labourer? They've cursed me, made my life a misery, told lies about me. I've tried to speak kindly to them, let them do what they want and told them the Good News. But they treated me like dirt.

Yet look at the friends Jesus has given me!

Whenever I think about them, I thank God for them—at Philippi and Thessalonica, in Anatolia, Greece and Asia. Praying for them fills me with happiness. I remember how, from the earliest days, we worked together in spreading the Good News. It's only right I should think like this about them—I am always in *their* thoughts. Whenever I was in prison or facing the judge in the defence of the Good News, I felt as if they were with me, and that we were all sharing God's love together.

I pray that they may always be happy people, held together by their love of men and God, and sure of the Good News in all its richness because they know what they believe. I want them to know the secret of it all—God's secret—Jesus himself.

With such a story to tell, I've learned how to stand on my own feet, wherever I am. I know how to do without things, and I know how to live when I've got more than I need. It doesn't matter now what happens—I can face plenty and poverty, I can enjoy wealth and want. I've learned God's secret. There isn't anything I can't face; but I know where my strength comes from—it comes from Jesus.

Getting the Good News Clear

At Jerusalem

Fourteen years after the fortnight I spent with Peter in Jerusalem, I went there again with Barnabas, and I took Titus, a foreign friend, with me. I felt it was God's will for me to go there, to put the plain story of how I told the Good News to everybody, foreigner and Jew alike, before the Christian leaders in Palestine.

I met them face to face in a private meeting. I didn't want all my work—what I had done and what I was still doing—to come to nothing.

It wasn't the leaders themselves who insisted that Titus, because he was a foreigner, should become a Jew. *That* was the idea of some so-called friends of Jesus who had slipped into the meeting. They had no right whatever to be there; they came just to put an end to the freedom I have claimed for people of all nations and races to become friends of Jesus, just as they are. These people wanted all friends of Jesus to become Jewish nationals first. I wasn't having that sort of slavery for a single minute.

The very heart of the Good News is that it is Good News for everybody everywhere, no matter what their nationality—and it was going to stay like that.

I needn't have taken the trouble, of course, to put the matter to the Christian leaders in Jerusalem. The Bible says that God doesn't take any notice of a man's rank—and it doesn't count much with me. Still, those whom everybody accepts as the chief Christian leaders—men like Peter—had nothing to add to my 'plain story'. They went even farther. They agreed that God had given *me* the work of telling the Good News to all foreigners, just as he had given *Peter* the work of telling the Good News to the Jewish people. Both of us were doing God's work with God's help.

James and Peter and John—if anybody's word counts, theirs does—saw that it was God's work that I was doing. Barnabas and I were leaders of the friends of Jesus, they said, just as they were; and they shook us by the hand. Our work was clear: *we* were to look after the people of other lands; *they* were to look after the people of the Jewish nation.

They went on to ask us one thing: could we do something for the poor in the city who were suffering from famine? This was the beginning of the Christian Aid Fund.

The Christian Aid Fund.

Let me say something here about this fund. We were very keen to help, for such help might bring foreigners and Jews together. I went back to Ephesus to raise this fund to help the poor in Jerusalem.

My rule for the fund was this. Each Sunday, everybody was to put something by, and what he saved must match what he himself had earned. I should not then need to make a collection when I came myself. The money raised could be taken to Jerusalem, with a letter, by some of their leaders. I had not made up my mind then to take the gifts myself. If, when the time came, I thought I ought to go, these men could go along with me.

I told them all, when I was explaining the fund to them, that if we are really keen to give, God expects us to give only what we can afford, not to try to give more than we can afford. He doesn't want us to give so much to others that we go without what we really need ourselves. What God wants is that we share what we have together. If we've got more than we really need now and others are in need, we must help them; but some time it will be the other way round. God's will is, as I have said, that we shall share what he has given us—and share alike.

At Antioch

But our difficulties in getting the Good News clear were by no means over. This is the sort of thing that happened. Barnabas and I, some time later, were back in Antioch, and Peter joined us there. But I had to stand up to him and tell him that he was plainly in the wrong—on this same question.

When he first came there, he ate his meals with all of us; foreigner and Jew sat down together at the same table. Then some men came from Jerusalem (they said that James had sent them), and everything changed. He started to stay away from our common meals. He was frightened of these Jewish friends of Jesus who said that you couldn't become a friend of Jesus if you hadn't first become a proper Jew. Other friends of Jesus in Antioch started to do the same—even Barnabas was deceived.

This was cheating—and cheating about the very thing that makes the Good News really Good News. It was as plain as plain could be to me.

One day, when everybody was together, I tackled Peter.

'When you first came here,' I said, 'born and bred a Jew though you are, you "lived like a foreigner, not like a Jew", as these men put it. Why have you turned round, and now try to make foreigners "live like Jews"?'

I went on to put the Good News plainly. I myself am a Jew by race and not a foreigner. But I know that a man doesn't become a friend of Jesus by carrying out all the details of the Jewish religion. He becomes a friend of Jesus by just trusting Jesus himself. That is the heart of the matter.

I know what is the secret of my own life. I go on living my ordinary life, it is true, and yet, in a sense, I don't feel *I'm* living it—Jesus has taken charge of me. I live by trusting Jesus, God's Son, who loved me and gave his life for me.

I'm not going to say No to God's love. If living in God's Way is just a matter of rules and regulations, Jesus threw his life away.

TRAVELLING BY SEA: Paul often travelled in boats. This is a small coastal boat, and Paul would sometimes use such small boats as this. But on his longer journeys, he would travel in much bigger boats, built in the same style.

IN PRISON

My work in Asia, Macedonia and Greece was now finished; there was nothing more for me to do there. I could go now to Spain.

For many years I had dreamed of visiting Rome and the friends of Jesus there. I could call to see them on my way to Spain. I could spend a short holiday with them, and they could give me a good send-off.

But I had now made up my mind to go first to Jerusalem with the Christian Aid Fund. When I had been to visit the poor in Palestine and placed the money that had been collected safely in their hands, I would go on to Spain by way of Rome.

I wrote a letter to the friends of Jesus in Rome to tell them about these plans of mine. I wanted them to stand by me in my fight for the Good News, and to remember me in their prayers. I knew how dangerous my visit to Jerusalem would be; my life itself might be in danger. And I was afraid that the Jewish friends of Jesus there, who, as you know, didn't like me, might refuse to take the gifts I brought. But if all went well, I could go with a happy heart to Rome and enjoy my holiday there.

What happened was very different from what I planned, and I am now in prison in Rome. Yet all this misfortune has made the Good News more widely known; it hasn't stopped my telling people about it. Everybody here in Rome knows that I am in prison because I am a friend of Jesus; even the soldiers of the Palace Guard know it. And most of the friends of Jesus here have been really cheered by my being a prisoner. They bravely go out to tell the Good News to everybody, and show no fear at all.

Of course, the friends of Jesus here don't all agree with one another—or with me. Some tell the Good News because they love Jesus; some because they are jealous of me. But they all talk about Jesus. What can I say? Only one thing. If people talk about Jesus, either honestly or dishonestly, I'm quite happy. And I shall go on being happy—even if my imprisonment is to end in my death.

MY METHODS

Nobody can tell me what to do; I am free to live as I think I ought to live. But I've always chosen to be a slave to others—to persuade as many as I could to become friends of Jesus.

I've lived like a Jew among Jewish people. I've kept the Jewish law (though I had no need to do so) when I have been living among strict Jews. I've lived like a foreigner among foreigners (the Jews call them 'outlaws' but there's something more important than being 'Jews' or 'outlaws'—and that's being an 'in-law' of Jesus). I've tried to share the life even of people who had queer ideas about Jesus. I've done all this to get Jews (strict or not), foreigners, people who didn't share my Christian views, everybody, to become true friends of Jesus.

I have tried, you see, to live just like the people I've found myself with, and to share their way of living, as far as I could.

I've treated everybody like this, so that I might win some, in one way or another, for Jesus.

I've tried hard not to cause anybody to stumble. I didn't want them, if possible, to start criticising what I was doing. I wanted them to see that I was God's servant, not just pleasing myself. What a lot of trouble that has caused me! I've had to put up with all sorts of things—dangers and hard times and all sorts of difficulties; I've been flogged, put in prison, and beaten up; I've had to work like a slave, go without sleep and food.

And all through this, I've tried to live as Jesus lived. He was sincere in all he did; he knew what he stood for; he could put up with anything; he was very kind; he didn't just talk about loving people—he actually succeeded in loving them; he always told people the plain truth, for he knew God was with him and trusted in God's power. I've tried to live like that.

The only weapon I've had has been a straightforward life, but I've had to use it in a hundred different ways, and it hasn't been easy. People have sometimes honoured me, and sometimes insulted me; sometimes praised me, and sometimes blamed me. They thought I was lying—yet I always tried to tell the truth; they called me a nobody—yet everybody knew me; my life wasn't worth living—yet I have enjoyed every moment of it; I've had a rough time—yet they haven't finished me off; many things have made me sad—yet I've been a very happy man; I haven't had much money—yet I've made many people rich; I have lived like a beggar —yet the whole world's mine.

I've lived to make the Good News known. I've tried to warn everybody I met and to teach everybody I met. I wanted them to recognize nonsense when they met it, to be really grown-up—this is what it means to be a friend of Jesus. This is what I've worked for, with every ounce of strength God has given me.

My Daily Rule

My daily rule? I've never been too busy to pray—I've made a habit of it. And I didn't just say my prayers; I kept wide awake and always found something to say 'Thank you' for.

I've tried to be grown-up and sensible when I've been dealing with other people, especially those who are not 'our sort' of people. I've never wasted time. I've always tried to talk to people as friends, to make what I have to say interesting and worthwhile. Everybody has different questions to ask; I've always tried to learn how to deal with all their different questions.

My Friends

How many friends I have had! Their kindness to me has been like the scent of flowers!

Let me write some of their names down.

Timothy—he's been like a son to me; you know what a grand fellow he is;

Titus—who's worked by my side; he brought good news for me back from Corinth, you remember;

Priscilla and Aquila—who risked their lives for me, and the friends of Jesus who meet together in their home;

Stephanus and his family—the first people to become friends of Jesus in Greece, as Epaenetus was the first in Asia;

Relatives of mine—Andronicus and Junia who've been in prison with me; everybody knows them, for they have told the Good News to many people, and they were friends of Jesus before I was; and there's Herodion too;

Apelles—he's been a brave man;

Rufus—he's done fine work for Jesus (his father, you remember, carried the cross for Jesus); his mother who looked after me as if she were my mother too!

Gaius—I used to stay with him; he took care of me—and of all the friends of Jesus in his city too;

Erastus—the city-treasurer;

Stachys and Persis—both of whom I love very much indeed; what a hard worker Persis is!

Apollos—brother of mine in the service of Jesus; I began the work at Corinth, he carried it on, but it was God who made his work and mine grow;

TRAVELLING BY ROAD. Paul tramped along many roads—good Roman roads and rough country roads—on his travels. This is a modern road in Greece; you can see the wild country he had to cross.

Epaphroditus—brother of mine, too, in the service of Jesus; we worked together and fought our battles together. He was once taken very ill when he was away from his home in Philippi, and he was upset when he knew that his friends in Philippi had heard about his illness. As a matter of fact, he nearly died. He risked his life for me; he wouldn't leave me because the friends of Jesus in Philippi had sent him to look after me.

Philemon—leader of the friends of Jesus in Colossi; and Onesimus, once his slave and now a friend of Jesus and his friend too;

Aristarchus—who is a prisoner here in Rome with me;

Mark—cousin of Barnabas, and Jesus Justus; these are the only Jewish friends of Jesus who have helped me in telling the Good News; but what a help they've been;

Tertius—who wrote down some of my letters for me;

Luke—my doctor.

MEETING PEOPLE: in the Street. Paul, like Jesus, talked to people wherever he met them. He would stop to talk to them in the streets, where the crowds gathered round the workshops and in the bazaars. This is a corner of the bazaar in Damascus today.

A LAST WORD

I haven't yet got anywhere near being the kind of man I want to be;
and I haven't become as mature as Jesus was—by a long way.
But nothing's going to stop me now; I intend to be the kind of man
Jesus wanted me to be when he called me on the road to Damascus
City. I know I haven't got there yet; but I've set my heart on one
thing—to forget the past and live for the future. I'm like a long-
distance runner; I see the tape ahead and I'm going to get there—
and win the prize.

Who can take God's love away from us now—the love that Jesus
has made real? You know the sort of thing that can happen to any
of us in this world of ours—suffering, hardship, cruelty, hunger,
homelessness, danger, war. It's in just such a world that we who
are the friends of Jesus can now live more splendidly than the
greatest world conquerors—with the help of Jesus who loved us.

I'm quite sure that nothing—neither dying nor living, neither
what we're facing now nor what we may have to face tomorrow,
nothing in our own world or in outer space or in our own hearts—
can take God's love away from us.

Jesus is Lord in God's world.

Don't forget I'm in prison. The scars on my body are the
marks of the master I belong to—Jesus.

The graciousness of Jesus, our master, be with you all.

Paul

Rome

(Note: We have put a passage from one of Paul's letters later in the book (p. 219). It
gives us information, which Dr. Luke does not give us, about what was happening in
Corinth while Paul was in Ephesus.)

Dr. Luke's Story of Paul

In his letters Paul did not need to describe the many exciting events that happened in the cities he had visited. The friends he was writing to knew all about them. So 'Paul's own Story', which I made from his letters, had little to tell us about them. What stories he could have told we can see from his summary of his experiences in 'The Crowded Years' (p. 188).

Dr. Luke fills out the picture. How much we should have missed if he had not kept a notebook. So here I have set out Dr. Luke's stories, but followed Paul's own arrangement.

In this part of the book we are trying to find out two things: first, how Paul went about his work and what he tried to do ('In Anatolia' and 'On the Shores of the Aegean Sea'); secondly, what he had to say for himself when he was arrested and brought before Jewish and Roman judges ('On Trial in Palestine'). But we must remember that in these stories we are reading *Dr. Luke's account*; we must always check up what Dr. Luke tells us by reading Paul's own first-hand account of his convictions and his reasons in 'Paul's own Story' and in *Jesus, Leader and Lord*.

Before you begin to read this part, read again Dr. Luke's earlier stories about Paul which you will find in *From Galilee to Rome*. First of all read 'The Man who died for it: Stephen' (p. 150) and 'The Man who led it: Paul' (p. 160). Then read 'The great Plan' (p. 164) and 'How the Good News came to a Greek Island' (p. 168); these will tell you what happened just before our story begins. When you have finished reading *this* part, read 'How the Good News came to a "Barbarian" Island' (p. 173) and 'How the Good News came to the Capital of the Empire' (p. 178); these will tell you what happened to Paul after our story in this book is ended.

In Anatolia

Paul and Barnabas landed at the port of Anatolia (see the map on p. 140). It was probably here, in the low-lying, hot plain where Attalia and Perga stood, that Paul was taken ill.

The journey Paul and Barnabas were making was, in a real sense, a 'trial' journey. They were doing something which no friend of Jesus had tried to do before—telling the Good News to *foreigners*. They knew what to say to *Jews*; but how do you approach foreigners and what do you say to them? They had to find out, and it was here in Anatolia, that Paul made up his mind how this great work was to be done.

MEETING PEOPLE: outside Temples. Everywhere he went Paul found temples built for the worship of the many gods people believed in. He would find them in the cities and see them on the cliff-tops as his boat came into harbour. This is the Temple of the God of Medicine in Pergamum in Asia (modern Turkey). Tourists visit its ruins today.

Paul and his friends left the island of Cyprus behind them and crossed the open sea. They landed at the port of Attalia on the mainland, and went on to Perga City, eight miles inland.

John Mark left them and went back home, and Barnabas and Paul climbed the high mountain road to Antioch Town.

On the Saturday, the Holy Day of the Jews, they went along to the Jewish Meeting House and sat down. They listened to the reading of the Bible; and when this had finished, the leaders of the Meeting House spoke to them.

'Brothers,' they said, 'if you have anything to say to the people that would help them, come and say it.'

Paul stood up and raised his hand.

'My countrymen, and those among you who are not my countrymen but are here because you care for the true worship of God, listen to the Good News I have to tell you,' he said. 'Long ago our ancestors were slaves in Egypt. But God called them, led them out of slavery, and gave them a homeland—Palestine. They lived there as tribes under the leaders God gave them. Then, in the time of

Samuel, he gave them a king—Saul, a member of my own tribe—and, after King Saul, King David. The story I have to tell is about a descendant of King David, Jesus, the Great Deliverer God promised to send us. John the Hermit, just before he died, told us God's Chosen Leader would come after him. And so it happened. To us, in our own time, the Good News has been sent.'

Then he told them the story of Jesus, and how he died and how God raised him from the dead.

'And here we are,' he went on, 'to bring you the Good News—the Good News God promised to our ancestors. He has carried out his promise to us, their descendants, by raising Jesus to life again.

'Brothers, I want all of you here to know that through this man, Jesus, God offers you now his forgiveness. See that you don't say No to him now.'

As Paul and Barnabas started to leave the Meeting House, the people asked them to tell them the Good News again the next Saturday. Many of them, Jews and foreign worshippers, went along with them to the house where they were staying. And they talked to them there and told them to hold fast to what they now knew of God's love.

Next Saturday, it seemed as if the whole town had crowded into the Meeting House to hear the story of Jesus. The Jewish leaders were jealous when they saw how big the crowds were. They got up and said outright that Paul was quite wrong and that he was a liar.

That made Paul and Barnabas speak out more boldly.

'It was right to tell the story of Jesus first of all here in this Meeting House,' they said. 'But since you won't listen, there's only one thing for us to do—to go to the foreigners who live here. The Bible itself says, you remember—

> You shall be like the sun shining on everybody,
> setting the whole world free.'

The foreigners were glad to hear Paul talk like this.

'How good God's Way is!' they said.

Many became friends of Jesus, as God wanted them to be. And the story of Jesus was told far outside the town as well.

The Jewish leaders didn't like this, and they made trouble for Paul and Barnabas. They won over to their side some of the well-known women, who came to the Meeting House, and the town councillors, and got them to drive Paul and Barnabas out of the town. But those who had become the friends of Jesus were happy people and their hearts were filled with God's love.

Paul and Barnabas travelled on to Iconium Town, and went together into the Jewish Meeting House there. Again they told the people the Good News, and a great crowd of them—both Jews and foreigners—became friends of Jesus.

But some of the Jewish leaders didn't believe the Good News; and, as in Antioch Town, they made trouble for Paul and Barnabas. They tried to win the townspeople over to their side by their talk. But the town itself was divided into two parties; one thought the leaders of the Meeting House were right, and the other was for Paul and Barnabas. So the two of them went on boldly telling the Good News day after day. God was with them, showing his love in the good deeds they did.

Then a group of Jews and foreigners got hold of the town councillors, and planned to beat up Paul and Barnabas and kill them. But they were told about the plan, and escaped from the town.

They went to the towns of Lystra[1] and Derbe and into the villages in the countryside, telling the Good News to everybody who would listen.

Paul and Barnabas now turned for home.

They went back the way they had come—through the towns of Lystra and Iconium and Antioch. Here they met the friends of Jesus and told them what they would have to face.

'Living in God's Way isn't easy,' they said. 'We must be ready to face all sorts of dangers. Keep your hearts brave, and never forget the Good News.'

They chose leaders for each of the 'churches', as the friends of Jesus called their groups—older members who could look after them. This they did in simple services of prayer and fasting.

'Goodbye,' they said, 'we leave you in God's care.'

Paul and Barnabas then went down the steep mountain road to the sea. They passed through Perga Town, near the coast, and told the Good News there. Then they went down to the port of Attalia, boarded a ship and sailed for Antioch City where their journey had begun.

[1] The story of what happened at Lystra is told in *From Galilee to Rome* in the chapter 'How the Good News came to the Highlands of Anatolia' (p. 169).

Home at last, they called the friends of Jesus together and told them what had happened in the island of Cyprus and among the mountain towns of Anatolia—how God had helped them and how (as they said) 'God opened a door, and foreigners have become friends of Jesus and learned to trust in him.'

They stayed on there for quite a long time.

ON THE SHORES OF THE AEGEAN SEA

Paul's great work has now begun and he is quite clear what Jesus wants him to do. This is the first stage of that work; when this first part of his work is finished, he plans to go on to Spain, and visit Rome on his way.

Paul is now travelling through the most famous part of the ancient Mediterranean world—the home of Greek civilization. Everywhere he goes, the names of cities will remind him of the great days of old. He will come to Troy, now a large and important city but once the scene of a famous war sung by Greek poets (this is where the incident of the 'Trojan Horse' happened). He will come to Macedonia, the birthplace of Alexander the Great who conquered a world which stretched as far east as India. He will find himself in Athens, the most famous Greek city of all, and he will wander in the streets where Socrates, Plato and Aristotle once walked. He will come to Corinth where the Isthmian Games (like our Olympic Games) used to be held. He will live in Ephesus where the world's first scientists and philosophers had lived. We can imagine what his thoughts must have been. Now he is coming on a greater work, so he believed, than the work any of those soldiers and poets and scientists had been engaged in. He too, like Alexander, was taking part in the conquest of the world— but a different kind of conquest and in the name of a greater Captain than Alexander.

Looking for Headquarters

One day Paul spoke to Barnabas.

'Let's go back to the towns of Anatolia, where we told the story of Jesus, and see how the friends of Jesus there are getting on.'

Barnabas wanted to take John Mark, his nephew, along with them. But Paul wouldn't agree.

'You see,' he said, 'John Mark didn't go with us on that journey— he left us at Perga and went home.'

MEETING PEOPLE: in the Square. The city square was always crowded, and here Paul could easily talk to people. This is a square in modern Athens, very different from the Athens Paul knew. But the square is still crowded with people.

They couldn't agree about him. So they decided to go their own ways. Barnabas took John Mark with him and went across to the island of Cyprus. The friends of Jesus at Antioch City said goodbye to Paul and prayed that God in his love would take care of him.

Paul chose Silas as his companion and set off through Syria and Cilicia, his own homeland, and encouraged the friends of Jesus there.

He went on over the mountains, visiting old friends, and came to the towns of Derbe and Lystra.

There was a friend of Jesus called Timothy in Lystra Town. He was the son of a mixed marriage—his father, who was now dead, had been a Greek; his mother, who was also a friend of Jesus, was a Jewess.

The friends of Jesus in the nearby towns of Lystra and Iconium thought he was a very fine young man, and Paul wanted him to go along with him. But there was difficulty.

Timothy came, through his mother, as we have seen, from a Jewish family, but he had never become a proper Jew. There were many Jews living in the town, and they knew all about him. Paul didn't want them to think he didn't care at all about the Jewish Law —he was a Jew himself. So he got Timothy, half Jew as he was, made a proper Jew.

Then Paul and Silas and Timothy went on together and visited all the towns in Anatolia. Paul's visit made the churches there bold and strong, and their numbers grew day by day.

They went on over the mountains. Paul planned to go down the high road to Ephesus. But, when they were praying together about it, they felt that God did not want them to go there.

So they took the road to the north-west and came to the borders of Mysia. Here they thought of turning north and going to the towns on the shores of the Black Sea; but, again; when they prayed about it, they were quite sure that this was not where God wanted them to go.

On they went through Mysia and came down to the Roman colony of Troas.

(The Diary)

That night Paul had a dream. In his dream he saw a man from across the water, a Macedonian, standing on the opposite shore and calling to him.

'Come over into Macedonia and help us!' he was shouting.

Next day we made enquiries about getting across the water. We were sure now what God wanted us to do; we must go and tell the Good News in Macedonia.

We went aboard a ship in Troas harbour, and sailed straight across the open sea to the island of Samothrace. The following day we landed at New Town, where the road from Rome came down to the sea. We went inland to Philippi, a Roman colony and an important city in that part of the country.

A Roman Garrison Town

(The Diary)

We stayed some days in Philippi City.

On the Saturday, the Holy Day of the Jews, we walked down to the banks of the river, outside the city gate, where Jewish people used to meet for prayer. Some women were already there, and we sat down and talked to them.

A woman named Lydia, a cloth merchant from the city of Thyatira[1], was listening. She was not a Jewess, but she came to worship God in the Jewish Meeting House. As she listened to Paul, she felt God was very near. She and her family were baptized and became friends of Jesus.

'If you think I have become a true friend of Jesus,' she said to Paul, 'make my house your home.'

She was very eager for us to stay with her; so we made her home our headquarters.

That morning, as we were walking to the city gate, we passed a slave girl. She was a medium who could sound as if she were somebody else. She told people's fortunes and made a lot of money for her owners. She followed us; and for days after, whenever she met us, she shouted out in her strange voice.

'These men belong to the High God. They've got Good News to give you,' she said.

This upset Paul.

He turned to the girl and spoke to the 'Voice'.

'In the name of Jesus,' he said, 'come out of her, I tell you!'

[1] Thyatira was a city in Asia famous for its purple cloth.

And there and then, the girl stopped speaking in this strange way.

When her owners saw that they wouldn't now be able to make any money out of her, they took hold of Paul and Silas and dragged them to the market place where the law court was held.

'These Jews are upsetting the city,' they told the magistrates. 'They are telling us to do all sorts of things that are not Roman customs; they are trying to make us break the law.'

The mob started shouting, and the magistrates angrily ordered Paul and Silas to be beaten with rods. The police gave them a good flogging, locked them up in prison, and ordered the head warder to see that they didn't escape. Acting on this order, he locked them in the inner prison and fastened their feet in the stocks.

It was now about midnight.

Paul and Silas were praying and singing hymns together, and the other prisoners were listening to them, in their cells.

Suddenly there was a great earthquake. The whole prison shuddered to its foundations. All the doors sprang open and everybody's chains were broken off.

The head warder woke up, and saw the open prison doors. His first thought was 'The prisoners have gone!' and he drew his sword to commit suicide.

'Don't hurt yourself,' shouted Paul. 'We're all here.'

The warder called for torches and dashed into the cell. He was very frightened and fell down before Paul and Silas. Then he led them outside.

'Sirs,' he said, 'what must I do to know God as you do?'

'There's only one thing to do,' they told him. 'Put your trust in the Lord Jesus, and you and all your family will be all right.'

They told him and his family the story of Jesus. And there and then, in the middle of the night, he took them and washed their wounds, and, there in the prison, the warder and his family were baptized as friends of Jesus.

He led them into his own house and gave them a good meal. He and all his family were very happy, because they had come to know what God was really like and to trust him.

Daylight came, and the magistrates sent the police to the prison.

'Set the two men free,' were their orders. The head warder went to tell Paul.

'The magistrates have given orders for your release,' he said.

'You can leave the prison and go on your way. You won't have any more trouble.'

'We're Roman citizens,' said Paul. 'We've had no proper trial; we've been beaten with rods and thrown into prison. Now they want to throw us out by the back-door. Oh no! Let the magistrates themselves come and set us free properly.'

The police reported all this to the magistrates. When they heard that they were Roman citizens, they were very frightened indeed. They came along, asked their pardon, led them out of the prison and begged them to leave the city.

So Paul and Silas left the prison, and went to Lydia's home. There they met the friends of Jesus again and told them to be of good heart. Then off they went along the road to Thessalonica.

A Trading City

Paul and Silas walked along the great Roman road. They passed through two towns and came at last to Thessalonica, the capital city of Macedonia. There was a Jewish Meeting House there, and Paul, as usual, went along on Saturday morning to the service of worship.

'It is Jesus I want to talk to you about,' he said. 'He is God's Chosen Leader.'

For three Saturday mornings he explained the Bible to them. He told them what had happened to Jesus—how he died and how he was raised by God to life again—and showed them how the Bible made all this clear.

Two or three Jews were sure Paul was right and joined him and Silas; so did many of the Greeks and the wives of important city officials.

This made the leaders of the Meeting House jealous. So they got a mob of hooligans from the market together, and started rioting in the streets. They broke into the house of a man called Jason, looking for Paul and Silas to drag them out for the mob to beat up. They couldn't find them; so they got hold of Jason himself and some of the friends of Jesus who were there, and dragged them before the city magistrates.

'These are the fellows who have been making riots all over the world,' they shouted. 'Now they've turned up in this city—Jason's been hiding them in his house. The whole lot are rebels. "Down with the Emperor and the Empire" is their slogan, "we've another Emperor—Emperor Jesus".'

THESSALONICA TODAY. This is still today an important port, but it has changed very much since Paul's time. It stands on a fine bay and behind it are rich plains.

The crowd was excited by these charges, and the magistrates were frightened. But they put Jason and his friends on bail, and let them go home.

The friends of Jesus had to act quickly, and that night they got Paul and Silas out of the city in the darkness and off along the road to the town of Beroea.[1] Even here there was some rioting, and the friends of Jesus there hurried Paul off to the coast. Silas and Timothy stayed on in Beroea, but his guides sailed with him as far as the famous city of Athens. They then left him and went back home with a message.

'Come to Athens as soon as you can,' Paul wrote to Silas and Timothy.

Paul wandered about the famous city while he was waiting for them. Many learned men lived and taught there, and Paul met them and talked to them. They asked him to speak to them before the

[1] You will find the story of what happened at Beroea and at Athens in *From Galilee to Rome* in the chapters 'How the Good News came to a Jewish Meeting House' (p. 171) and 'How the Good News came to the Most Famous Greek City of all' (p. 171).

City Council. A few people—among them one of the city councillors
—became friends of Jesus.

Silas and Timothy still had not come, so Paul went on without
them southward to the port of Corinth.

A Great Seaport

Corinth was a great seaport and ships from all over the world
called there. Behind the city rose the mountain called 'High Corinth',
with its famous temple on its slopes.

A Jewish merchant, called Aquila, was living here. His boyhood
home was on the shores of the Black Sea. He had been living in Italy,
but, not long before, the Emperor had ordered all Jewish people
to leave Rome; Aquila with his wife, Priscilla, had come to live in
Corinth.

Paul went to see them. He found they were weavers, making
cloth from goat's hair—the trade he himself had learned as a boy.
So he stayed with them and worked in their workshop. On Satur-
days, the Holy Day of the Jews, he went along to the Jewish Meeting
House and talked about the Bible and the story of Jesus.

At last Silas and Timothy came down from Macedonia and found
Paul hard at work explaining to the Jews that God's Chosen Leader,
whom they read about in the Bible, was Jesus. But the members of
the Meeting House argued against him; indeed they went further
and even insulted him.

'All right,' said Paul, 'you've made your minds up, and that's
your business. I've done my best. In future, I'll deal with the people
who are not Jews.'

He didn't go to the Meeting House any more, but made his
headquarters in the house next door, which belonged to Titus
Justus, a foreigner who worshipped God. Many people became
friends of Jesus; among them were Crispus, the leader of the
Meeting House, and his family and many citizens of the city.

One night Paul had a dream, and in the dream he heard Jesus
speaking to him.

'Don't be afraid,' Jesus said to him. 'Go on telling the Good
News and don't give up. I am with you. Nobody shall do you any
harm, for I have many friends in this city.'

Paul stayed in Corinth for eighteen months, telling everybody
the Good News.

The Jews now went further. They got hold of Paul and took him before the Governor, Gallio.

'We have our Jewish Law,' they said, 'but this fellow is telling everybody it's all wrong.'

Paul was starting to put his case, when the Governor stopped him and turned to the Jewish leaders.

'This isn't the sort of question I'm here to deal with,' he said. 'If it had been a matter of some wrong done or some crime committed, I'd have listened to your complaint. But since it's a question of mere words and names and the meaning of your Jewish religion, use your own courts. I don't intend to start judging questions of this sort. The case is dismissed.'

He had them put out of the court. The crowd got hold of Sosthenes, the leader of the Meeting House, and beat him up. The Governor took no notice.

Paul stayed on in the city for quite a long time after this.

At last Paul said goodbye to the friends of Jesus in Corinth, and, with his friends Priscilla and Aquila, the weavers, set sail for Palestine. The boat put in at Ephesus on the other side of the Aegean Sea. Paul, as he often did, went into the Jewish Meeting House and talked about the Good News with the Jews who worshipped there. They asked him to stay on in Ephesus; but he said No.

The time came to say goodbye.

'I'll come back to you,' he said, 'if that is what God wants me to do.'

And he set sail for Palestine. Priscilla and Aquila stayed behind in Ephesus.

Paul landed at the port of Caesarea, which was the headquarters of the Roman army in Palestine, and went up and greeted the friends of Jesus there. Then he went on to Antioch, and stayed there for quite a time.

Paul—Right or Wrong?

This story begins in Antioch City.

Trouble began when some Jewish friends of Jesus came down from Jerusalem. They saw what was happening there; Jews and foreigners were living together as friends of Jesus—praying together and having their meals together.

'This is all wrong,' they said. 'You must become proper Jews before you can become friends of Jesus.'

MEETING PLACE: on the Quayside. Paul would find the quayside of the ports where he landed a very good place for meeting people. Crowds gathered to see the ships come in, and fishermen would be looking after the nets and boats. This fisherman lives on the island of Malta.

Paul and Barnabas denied this, and had a long argument with them. At last it was decided to send Paul and Barnabas and some of the other Christian leaders to talk it over with the leaders of the friends of Jesus in Jerusalem. The whole church gave them a good send-off.

They went southward along the coast road through Phoenicia; and then on through Samaria. Wherever they went they told how foreigners were becoming friends of Jesus; everybody was glad to hear about it.

The Christians in Jerusalem City welcomed them when they got there, and they told them the same story.

But some of the Jewish Christians there didn't like it.

'No,' they said. 'Foreigners must become Jews first, and they must keep the Jewish Law and all that Moses told us to do.'

A meeting of the leaders was called to get this matter clear.

Peter stood up.

'Brothers,' he said, 'you know that when, in the early days, we began to tell the Good News, God chose me to be the first to tell it to foreigners—Captain Cornelius and his family—and to call them too to become friends of Jesus. God can read men's hearts, and he gave Captain Cornelius his power just as he gave it to us. He didn't ask whether he and his family were Jews or foreigners; they trusted him, and he filled their hearts with love. Why do you want to tell God what to do and make our foreign friends keep laws that neither we nor our ancestors were ever able to keep? It is by trusting in the love of Jesus that we ourselves will become what God wants us to be —just as they will. There is only one way for all of us.'

Nobody in the room spoke. Then Paul and Barnabas told them about the great things God had done, through them, among foreigners.

When their story was ended, James spoke up.

'Brothers,' he said, 'listen to me. Peter has told us how God first received foreigners as friends of Jesus, as members of his Family. After all, this shouldn't surprise us—the Bible is quite clear about it. What I have to say is this: we ought not to make it difficult for foreigners to become friends of Jesus. We should send them a letter asking them to keep four of our Jewish laws about food. That would make it easier for friends of Jesus who feel they must still keep the whole of our Jewish Law to share meals with them; for there are Jewish Meeting Houses in all the cities of the world.'

ANATOLIA. These are the highlands (in modern Turkey) Paul and Barnabas visited, after Paul had been taken ill on the fever-infested coast. Here were the towns of Antioch, Iconium, Lystra and Derbe, 1,000 feet above sea-level.

The whole meeting agreed to choose some of their number to go along to Antioch with Paul and Barnabas. They chose Judas and Silas from among their leaders, and they gave them a letter to take with them to the foreign friends of Jesus in Antioch City and in Syria and Cilicia. Here is the letter:

'We send good wishes to all our foreign friends.

'We have heard that some friends of Jesus from this city have been upsetting you with their talk. We did not send them. We are now sending Judas and Silas with our beloved Barnabas and Paul— men who have risked their lives in the service of Jesus. They will tell you themselves all about our meeting here, and explain some rules we would like you to keep. Goodbye.'

Paul and Barnabas and their friends went back to Antioch City. The letter was read aloud in a meeting of the whole church; and everybody was very happy about it.

Judas and Silas stayed with them quite a long time; for they were men who could teach the Bible and they spent the time in helping the people to understand it. The friends of Jesus then let them go back home.

Seaport and Temple City

The Lecture Hall

Paul left Antioch and set off across the mountains of Anatolia for Ephesus City. On the way he looked up his Christian friends in the cities he passed through and gave them what help they needed.

In Ephesus, as in other cities, Paul went along to the Jewish Meeting House. For three months, he told them the Good News and talked with them about it and begged them to live in God's Way.

Then the trouble began. Some of the members of the Meeting House wouldn't listen to him; they didn't believe a word he said. They began to insult the friends of Jesus in front of the whole meeting. When this happened, Paul left them and took the friends of Jesus along with him.

He found a hall belonging to a man called Tyrannus. Here, each day, he used to meet and talk with people about the Good News. The only time he could use the hall was during the middle of the day when, because of the heat, most people rested—from eleven in the morning to three o'clock in the afternoon.

For two whole years this is how Paul carried on his work. The story of Jesus became known far beyond the boundaries of the city itself; and not only in the Jewish Meeting Houses but among the foreign population of the province of Asia as well.

The Talk of the Town

Paul didn't just talk about the Good News; he healed people 'in the name of Jesus', too. There were all sorts of stories told about him and the amazing things people believed he could do.

Many people believed that evil spirits made them ill; and travelling doctors, using magic words, claimed to be able to drive the evil spirits away and make people well.

Here's a story everybody in Ephesus was talking about.

There were seven Jewish travelling doctors, sons of a Jewish leader called Sceva. They heard about Paul, and began to use the words he used—'In the name of Jesus'—as their magic words.

'I am speaking to you,' they would say to a sick person, 'in the name of the Jesus whom Paul talks about.'

They went to a house, one day, so the story ran, to heal a sick man who believed an evil spirit was inside him. They used, as they had often done before, the words 'in the name of Jesus whom Paul talks about'.

But this time the spirit inside the man suddenly shouted out. 'I know who Jesus is,' it shouted, 'and I know who Paul is. But who are you?'

The sick man jumped on them, knocked them about and was so violent that they ran out of the house naked and badly beaten up.

This sort of story rather scared people, but at any rate they thought better of the name of Jesus.

Ephesus City was famous for magic, and it was now clear to people that God's Way had nothing to do with magic. Many of the friends of Jesus came and told Paul that they had been using magic spells. Some of the magicians even got their books of magic together and burned them for everybody to see. These books cost a lot of money; they reckoned that the value of the books burned was somewhere about £5,000.

So the Good News spread and the trade in magic dropped.

The Riot

At last Paul decided to go to Jerusalem, and to travel through Macedonia and Greece on his way. He believed that this was what God wanted him to do next.

'After I've been there,' he said, 'I must visit Rome too.'

So he sent his two helpers, Timothy and Erastus, on to Macedonia. But he himself stayed a little longer in Ephesus.

Just then trouble broke out about the Christians in the city.

There was a famous Temple in Ephesus City, the Temple of the Goddess Artemis. It was one of the seven wonders of the world and pilgrims came from all over the world to visit it. Many used to buy small images of the goddess and her temple to take home with them; and this kept the silversmiths and the shops busy.

Demetrius, one of the silversmiths, who was also a temple warden, called the craftsmen together.

'Men,' he said, 'you know where we get our money from. Now this fellow Paul has come along with his 'Good News'. Lots of people, not only here but throughout the province, aren't buying the images we make any more. You can see what's happening for yourselves. We're all in danger—and we shall get a bad name as well. But there's more at stake: all Asia and the world beyond worship the goddess Artemis here; soon, if this goes on, nobody will bother

EPHESUS. This city was Paul's headquarters. It is now in ruins. This is one of its main streets leading up to the Temple of Artemis; Paul would have often walked along this street. It has been partly restored, and many tourists come to visit it.

about her great Temple and she won't be a great goddess much longer.'

The speech turned them into a wild mob.

'Great is Artemis of the Ephesians,' they screamed and shouted.

Then the mob made one mad rush for the theatre, where public meetings were held, dragging two of Paul's friends with them.

Paul wanted to go in and face the mob. But his friends stopped him; and some of the county councillors, who were also friends of his, sent him a message, begging him not to risk it.

The meeting in the theatre was one great hullaballoo; most of the crowd hadn't a clue what it was all about—some were shouting one thing and some were shouting another.

A group of Jews pushed a man called Alexander, one of their leaders, to the front; some of the crowd thought he had something to do with the meeting and called to him. He beckoned to the mob with his hand and tried to explain that the Jews had nothing to do with the trouble. When the crowd realized he was a Jew, they burst out with one great shout—'Great is Artemis of the Ephesians!'

For two hours there was nothing but shouting. The town clerk at last got the crowd to be quiet.

'People of Ephesus,' he said, 'is there anybody anywhere in the world who doesn't know about our city, the Guardian of the Temple of the great Goddess Artemis, and of the holy stone which fell from the sky? Nobody's going to say this is nonsense. You must calm down; you mustn't start doing anything silly. You've brought these men here—but they've neither robbed the temple nor insulted our goddess. If the silversmiths, Demetrius and his friends, have got some trade dispute to complain about, there are law-courts and magistrates in this city; let them bring their charges against one another there. If you've got other matters to discuss, they can all be settled in the proper town meeting. We are in great danger of being charged by the Emperor with rioting here today, and we've got no excuse for going wild like this.'

With these words he closed the meeting.

When all the noise was over, Paul sent for the friends of Jesus. He told them not to be afraid but to go on telling everybody the Good News. Then he said goodbye and left the city, and went north to Macedonia. He gladdened the hearts of the Christians there as he talked to them about Jesus and the Good News. Then he went southwards to Greece, and stayed there for three months, for it was winter time.

A NOTE BY PAUL

Dr. Luke has not told us all that happened while Paul was in Ephesus. While he was there, trouble broke out among the Christians in Corinth. News was brought to him that quarrelling had broken out among them; they were divided into 'parties' and were arguing which was right. Paul went over to see them to try to put things straight, but they wouldn't listen to him. He then wrote to them a severe letter. At last everything was put right. He described what happened and how troubled he had been about it in a letter he wrote to them afterwards. Here is what he wrote; we have put it as if he were telling us about it.

When I first went to Corinth to tell them the Good News there, I didn't use big words or talk as if I knew everything. I had just come from Athens, and I'd made up my mind that there was only one thing to talk about—the plain story of Jesus and how he died.

I was hard up, but I wouldn't take a penny from them; the friends

CORINTH. This was the city on the isthmus linking northern and southern Greece; it had two ports, one on each side of the isthmus, and boats were dragged on rollers between them. Beyond the city rose a high mountain, near the top of which was a famous temple. Paul spent two years here. The ruins are those of a city temple.

of Jesus in Macedonia looked after me. To tell the truth, I was far from well; I was nervous and jumpy.

I know what some people in Corinth said about me—'His letters are full of big words; but when he himself turns up, you wouldn't look twice at him, and he hasn't got anything to say!' They were right. When I talked to them and told them the Good News, I didn't try to talk like a clever man; all I did was to let them see that I knew something of God's power and presence in my heart. It isn't cleverness that helps us to trust in God; it's realizing what God is doing for us that makes us trust him.

Some time later, when I was in Ephesus, news was brought to me from Corinth that they were all quarrelling with one another there. Things got so bad that I had to go over and see them. It was a very unpleasant visit, and I made up my mind that I wouldn't let that painful sort of thing happen again. It would only make matters worse.

So I wrote a letter to them. I actually wept over it, I was so unhappy about having to write it. I didn't want to upset them;

indeed I wanted them to know how much I cared for them—and I cared for them very much indeed. All this, as I have said, made me very unhappy. Yet I had to be straight with them.

I told them that if I did visit them again, I was afraid of what I would find. I shouldn't find *them*, I knew, the kind of people I wanted them to be; and they wouldn't find *me* the kind of man they wanted me to be. I was afraid that they would be still quarrelling with one another, and all I'd find would be jealous, angry, selfish people, telling all sorts of stories about one another, talking nastily to one another, proud of their own little groups, and all at sixes and sevens.

I warned all those who were causing trouble and everybody else as well—it's only what I had told them when I went over to see them—that if I came a third time I would just tell them, as plainly as I could, what I thought about them.

Titus took this letter to Corinth. I myself stayed on in Ephesus, and then went on to Troas. I had a very happy time there; doors opened everywhere. But Titus hadn't come back with an answer to my letter, and I was all on edge to know what my friends in Corinth would do. So, although there was plenty to do in Troas, I said goodbye and went on to Macedonia. But there I had to face all sorts of difficulties—trouble in the city and fears in my heart. But God cheered me up, as he always does when we get down-hearted— Titus came back from Corinth. It was good to see him, and I felt happy again. He told me how my friends in Corinth wanted to put things right; they were sorry for what had happened, and they were keen to help in every way they could. That made me happier still.

My letter *had* hurt them. I wasn't sorry that I had written it (as I was when I had just sent it off). It had only hurt them, I could see, for a short time—they soon saw what I was really troubled about. So I was happy again, not, of course, because they had been hurt, but because that straight letter had made them change their minds and see what God's Way was.

Before all this trouble had broken out, I had planned to leave Ephesus at Whitsuntide, and go through Macedonia to see the friends of Jesus there. After that I had planned to go south and stay with the friends of Jesus at Corinth, and perhaps spend the winter with them. They could then give me a good send-off on my next journey, wherever that might be.

I could now carry out these plans.

The friends of Jesus at Corinth, twelve months before, were the first to take up the Christian Aid Fund; they were very keen about it, and began collecting money at once. I'm afraid that they hadn't done much about it while they were quarrelling with one another. But now that they had got things straight again, they should finish what they had begun. They could see how much they could still collect.

'You've started them off again,' I said to Titus. 'What about going to help them to finish it off as well?'

Titus thought this was a fine idea, and off he went.

ON TRIAL IN PALESTINE

Paul's visit to Palestine turned out quite differently from what he had hoped. He came a free man; he left a prisoner. All his dreams of telling the Good News in Spain would now never come true.

After telling us about the riot in Jerusalem and Paul's arrest by the Commanding Officer of the Roman garrison, Dr. Luke wants us to read carefully what Paul had to say in his own defence. He did not get much chance of speaking properly to either the Jewish Council or to Governor Felix. The Jewish Council was too stormy and Governor Felix was not really interested. But two speeches in his own defence are important ones—the one he made to his own countrymen from the steps of the barracks (p. 229) and the one he made before King Agrippa (p. 236). When you have read them, read again what Paul himself has told us in 'Paul's own Story'—the chapters 'How I became a Friend of Jesus', 'Getting the Good News clear' and 'A last Word'. And remember that people can write much more freely and easily in a letter to friends than they can speak in a law-court.

As you read, ask yourself what are the most important points Paul is making; what does he think is the heart of Christianity?

Sailing to Palestine

(The Diary)

Troas

Paul at last set off from Corinth for Palestine. As he was about to board a pilgrim ship, he learned that some Jews had made a plot to murder him on the boat. He changed his plans and went the longer way round by road through Macedonia.

The representatives from the Christians of Beroea, Thessalonica,

TROY. This is the famous city of Troy; these are the ruins of the theatre. This city had long been buried in Paul's time, but it was in the new city nearby that he met Dr. Luke and dreamed of a Macedonian man calling him to go over to Macedonia and help them; and here Dr. Luke and Paul called on the last journey to Palestine.

Derbe and Ephesus were travelling with him. They were taking to Jerusalem the money they had raised for the Christian Aid Fund. At Philippi, they went on ahead to wait for us at Troas.[1]

We left Philippi by boat after Easter to meet them there. We were five days at sea, and we spent a week in Troas.

On the Sunday we met the Christians there to 'break bread'—to have supper together, as Jesus did with his friends on the night before he died.

Paul had decided to leave Troas the next day. He had a lot to talk to them about and he went on talking till midnight.

We were meeting upstairs on the third storey of the house, and there were many lamps burning in the room. A lad called Eutychus was sitting in an open window. Paul went on talking and talking;

[1] Dr. Luke joined Paul at Philippi and went with him to Palestine; so here he begins to use his diary again.

and the lad dozed off. He went so sound asleep that he fell out of the window into the street below and was picked up for dead. Paul went straight downstairs and bent over him and put his arms around him.

'Don't be frightened,' he said, 'there's life in him.'

He went back upstairs, 'broke bread' with the others and had something to eat, and went on talking until it was dawn. Then he went on his way.

They led the lad away—he was alive all right—and everybody was very glad it hadn't been worse.

Miletus

Paul decided to go by road, and we were to pick him up. So we went on ahead to the boat and set sail for the port of Assos. He met us there, and we took him on board and went on to the town of Mityline, on the east coast of the island of Lesbos.

There we stayed the night, and sailing at dawn, came that day opposite the island of Chios. We anchored for the night off the coast of the mainland, and sailed next day across the open sea to the island of Samos.

Paul had decided to sail past Ephesus; he didn't want to lose any time staying there. He wanted to be in Jerusalem by Whitsuntide, if he could, and he was in rather a hurry. So next day we sailed on to the port of Miletus, some forty miles to the south.

From Miletus Paul sent a messenger to the Christian leaders in Ephesus—twelve miles across open water and then twenty miles by road. He asked them to meet him in Miletus; and they came over.

MILETUS. Here the leaders of the Christian church at Ephesus came to say goodbye to Paul on his last journey to Palestine. It is forty miles south of Ephesus. These are the ruins of the theatre there; beyond it lay the bay which is now, as you can see, entirely silted up.

He talked to them about the work they had done together and how he had boldly told the Good News in market square and home to Jew and foreigner alike.

'And now,' he said, 'I am going to Jerusalem and I am sure that this is what God wants me to do. I don't know what will happen. All I know is that I may find myself in prison; in every prayer meeting we have held in the towns I have passed through, this has been made clear to me. I'm not bothered about myself—I don't matter; all I want is to do what Jesus told me to do, to tell everybody the Good News of God's love, and to go on telling that Good News to the end.

'I spent a long time with you, as you know; but this is my last goodbye—I am certain you will not see me again.'

He went on to remind them how he had lived among them—working with his own hands for his own keep and that of his helpers, and telling the Good News to all who would listen.

'After I am gone,' he said, 'you will have a hard time. But I leave you in God's hands. I have shown you, by the way I myself worked, that you must always help those who can't help themselves. Remember what the Lord Jesus himself said—"It's giving, not getting, that makes us happy."'

He knelt down and prayed with them all. Everybody was crying as they bade him goodbye; Paul's words about their not seeing him again had upset them very much.

They went down with him to his ship in the harbour. We said a last goodbye and went on board.

Tyre

We sailed across the open sea to the island of Cos, and came, the next day, to the island of Rhodes. From there we went across to the port of Patara on the mainland. Here we changed ships. We found a ship bound for Palestine and went aboard and set sail. We sighted the island of Cyprus to the north, made across the open sea and landed at the port of Tyre for the ship to unload its cargo.

We looked up the friends of Jesus in the town and stayed a week with them. In the prayer meeting, they told Paul that they believed God's will was that he should not go on to Jerusalem. But, when the ship was ready to sail, we left the house and went down to the harbour.

The friends of Jesus and all their families went with us through the streets and out through the city gate. We knelt down on the beach and prayed together, and then said goodbye. We boarded the ship and they went back home.

Caesarea

The day's sail from Tyre ended at the port of Ptolemais (its name was Acco in the old days). We made ourselves known to the friends of Jesus there and stayed the day with them. Next day we set sail again, and came at last to the port of Caesarea, where the Roman Governor had his headquarters.

We went up to the home of Philip, and stayed a few days with him. His four unmarried daughters were leaders in the church and taught the Bible to the others in the Sunday services.

While we were there, a Christian leader called Agabus came down from Jerusalem. In one of our meetings, he took Paul's belt and tied himself up with it, hands and feet.

'God has told me this,' he said. 'Just as I have tied myself up like this, so the Jewish leaders in Jerusalem City will bind the man who owns it, and they will hand him over to the Roman Government.'

This upset us and we begged Paul not to go up to the city; everybody in the meeting begged him not to go.

'You'll break my heart,' said Paul, 'if you go on crying like this. I'm ready for anything they can do to me in Jerusalem—I'll face prison and death itself, if that's what being loyal to Jesus means.'

Nothing could make him change his mind; it wasn't any use talking to him.

'God's will be done,' we said.

Riot and Arrest
(The Diary)

Meeting James

When our stay in Caesarea was over, we got ready to go up to Jerusalem City. Some of the friends of Jesus from Caesarea went with us, and took us along to stay with Mnason. (Mnason came from the island of Cyprus and had been a friend of Jesus from the earliest days.) On our arrival, the friends of Jesus in Jerusalem gave us a warm welcome.

We went next day to see James, the chief leader of the friends of

Jesus in Palestine, and the other leaders. Paul told them how glad he was to see them, and went on to tell them how he had taken the Good News to the foreign cities of the Aegean and what God had done there. He described all that had happened, city by city.

'How good God is!' they said. 'But we must be careful. You see, brother, there are many thousands of Jews among the friends of Jesus. They are all very keen still about keeping Jewish customs. They've heard a lot of untrue stories about you—how you tell the Jewish people who live abroad that they needn't bother about the Jewish religion and its laws.

'We know that these wild stories aren't true, but don't you think we ought to do something about it? They'll be certain to hear that you've turned up in the city.

'Do what we tell you—to set their minds at rest. There are four men here—Jewish friends of Jesus who feel that they themselves must still keep the Jewish law. They are going to the Temple to carry out their Jewish duty. Go along with them and pay their expenses. Everybody will then see that you yourself still care about Jewish customs, and that all the stories they have heard about you are nonsense. Foreign friends of Jesus, of course, needn't bother about our Jewish customs; we made that plain in the letter we sent to them, you remember.'

Paul agreed. He took charge of the four men, and next day went with them into the Temple. They were to spend a whole week there, carrying out their Jewish duties.

The Riot

Then it happened—just as the week was beginning.

A few days before, some Jews from Ephesus had happened to see Paul walking through the streets. They had recognized him— and the man who was with him, a foreigner from their own city. They now caught sight of him again. This time he was inside the Temple itself where no foreigner was allowed to go, and they jumped to the conclusion that he'd got his foreign friend with him.

They grabbed him and started shouting.

'Jews, help!' they shouted. 'Here's the traitor! Here's the man who's been attacking our customs all over the world! He's actually brought foreigners into the Temple itself—he's treating this holy place as if our law didn't matter at all!'

THE THEATRE AT EPHESUS. These are the ruins of the theatre where the rioting mob rushed to hold a town meeting to denounce Paul and the friends of Jesus.

Everybody began shouting and there was soon a great crowd. They got hold of Paul and dragged him outside the Temple, and the great Temple gates were closed. The crowd tried to beat him to death.

News was rushed to the Roman commander, Colonel Lysias, that there was rioting in the streets.[1] He called out the guard at the double, and ran down and charged into the crowd. At the sight of the colonel and the soldiers, the crowd stopped beating Paul up.

[1] The Roman barracks were in the Tower of Antonia nearby, and steps led down from them right into the Temple court.

Colonel Lysias went straight up to Paul and arrested him.

'Chain him up,' he told the soldiers, 'and double the chains.'
He turned to the crowd.

'Who is he? What's he been up to?' he asked.

People said all sorts of things, one man one thing, another
man something else. He couldn't make out what the riot was about;
so he ordered Paul to be marched into the barracks. Paul had to be
carried, for the mob was heaving and pushing all around and
shouting 'Finish him off!' The soldiers got him at last to the bottom
of the steps and were about to take him up the steps into the
barracks.

On the Steps of the Barracks

Paul stopped Colonel Lysias.

'May I say something to you?' he asked him in Greek.

'You speak Greek?' asked the colonel. 'Then you aren't the
Egyptian rebel who led four thousand "Dagger Men" into the
desert?'

'I am a Jew,' said Paul. 'I was born in Tarsus; I am a citizen
of a very important city. Let me speak to the crowd, please.'

The colonel had no objection.

Paul stood on the barrack steps and beckoned to the crowd with
his hand. There was silence. He spoke to them, not in Greek, but
in their native language, Aramaic; when they heard him speak in
Aramaic, you could have heard a pin drop.

He told them how he became a friend of Jesus—how he had been
taught by the great Jewish teacher, Gamaliel, in Jerusalem City;
and then how, on the Damascus Road, Jesus had called him to tell
the Good News to everybody everywhere.

'I then came back to this city,' he said, 'and I came into the
Temple here to pray. And while I was praying I saw Jesus.

' "Be quick," he said to me, "and leave the city at once; they
won't listen to what you've got to say here."

' "Lord," I said, "they know all about me. They know I went
from Meeting House to Meeting House and threw your friends into
prison and beat them up. Why, when Stephen was murdered, I was
the man in charge."

' "Go!" he said, "your business is to tell the Good News to foreigners all over the world." '

The crowd had listened quietly so far, but as soon as they heard the word 'foreigners' they started shouting again.

'Finish him off!' they roared. 'He isn't fit to be alive!'

They went on shouting, waving their clothes and throwing dust into the air.

'Into the barracks with him,' said Colonel Lysias.

'*I am a Roman Citizen*'

'Lash him with the whips,' said the colonel when they'd got Paul into the barracks. 'Find out what they are shouting about.'

The soldiers started to tie Paul up for the whipping.

'Is it right to whip a Roman citizen,' he asked the captain in charge, 'especially when he hasn't even been found guilty?'

The captain went straight off to the colonel.

'Do you know what you're doing?' he asked him. 'This man's a Roman citizen.'

The colonel came back to question Paul.

'Tell me,' he said. 'Are *you* a Roman citizen?'

'I am,' said Paul.

'It cost me a lot of money to become a Roman citizen,' said the colonel.

'I was born a citizen,' said Paul.

The soldiers didn't stop to see what happened next. The colonel, too, was very frightened—he had actually ordered his soldiers to handcuff a Roman citizen!

Before the Jewish Council

The colonel wanted to know what the riot was really about and what the crowds thought Paul had done. He set Paul free and gave orders for the Jewish Council to be called together. He took Paul down to meet them face to face.

Paul stared at the Council.

'Brothers,' he said, 'I have tried to do what God wanted me to do all my life.'

The High Priest told those who stood near Paul to hit him across the face.

'God will hit you!' burst out Paul. 'You're the white-washed wall the man of God spoke of long ago! Do you sit there as a

ILLYRICUM. This is the coast of the Adriatic Sea where the Roman province of Illyricum came down to the sea. Paul came as far west as this, he tells us. There were Greek colonies, some founded by merchants from Corinth, along this coast and its islands.

Jewish judge and tell them to hit me—and break the Law yourself?'

'Do you know what you're saying?' said the men nearby. 'You're cursing the High Priest who speaks in God's name.'

'I'm sorry,' said Paul. 'I didn't know that the High Priest would talk like that. I know, of course, what the Law says.'

Now Paul knew that the Jewish Council was divided into two parties who didn't agree with one another: there were the Pharisees who believed that those who die rise to life again and that there are such beings as angels and spirits; and there were the Sadducees who thought all this was nonsense.

'Brothers,' he called out, 'I am a Pharisee myself; I belong to their party. The real charge against me is that I hope, as they do, that men rise to life again when they die.'

That put the cat among the pigeons—the Council started arguing, and there was a lot of shouting.

Some of the Pharisees stood up and spoke up quite openly for Paul.

'We don't think this man is guilty of doing anything wrong,' they shouted. 'A spirit or an angel may have spoken to him.'

There was almost a riot in the Council Room. The colonel was afraid for Paul's safety; it looked as if he might be torn to pieces between the two parties. He told a squad of soldiers to force their way into the crowd and rescue Paul and take him back to the barracks.

That night Paul had a vision. Jesus stood over him.

'Don't be afraid,' he said. 'You have stood up for me in this city; you must stand up for me like this in Rome itself.'

Back to Caesarea

When daybreak came, more than forty Jews got together in a plot and vowed to go without food until they had killed Paul.

They went to the High Priest and members of the Jewish Council, and told them what they had planned.

'This is what we want you to do,' they said. 'Call the Council together and send word to Colonel Lysias to bring Paul down from the barracks. Tell him we want to give him a correct and careful trial. We will get him on his way here.'

Now Paul's nephew heard about this plot to ambush him. He went along to the barracks and told Paul about it. Paul sent for one of the officers.

'Take this young man to the colonel,' he said. 'He's got some news for him.'

The officer took him to the colonel.

'The prisoner, Paul, sent for me,' he said, 'and asked me to bring this young man along to you. He's got some news for you.'

The colonel took him on one side.

'What do you want to tell me?' he asked.

He told him about the plot.

'And now they are just waiting for you to say Yes,' he added.

'Not a word to anybody,' said the colonel. 'I don't want anybody to know you've seen me.'

And he sent him home.

Colonel Lysias sent for one of his captains.

'Call out two hundred soldiers and seventy cavalrymen,' he said. 'You'll need two hundred horses. Parade three hours after sunset tonight. You are to escort Paul and deliver him safe to Governor Felix. You must cover the sixty miles to Caesarea by tomorrow evening. And don't forget horses for the prisoner.'

He then wrote a letter to the Governor. It went like this:

'Claudius Lysias sends his good wishes to His Excellency Governor Felix.

'A Jewish crowd got hold of this man, and if I had not reached him and rescued him with a squad of soldiers, he would have been murdered. I find out he is a Roman citizen. I tried to discover what his crime was, and took him down to the Jewish Council. There was a lot of talk about their religion, but nothing on which I could sentence him to death or send him to prison. I have just discovered a plot to murder him. I am sending him to you at once, and I have told the Jewish leaders to put their case before you.'

The soldiers carried out their orders. By daybreak they had taken Paul halfway to Caesarea, as far as the town of Antipatris. The infantry went back to their barracks in Jerusalem, and the cavalry escorted him the rest of the way. They delivered the colonel's letter to the Governor and handed Paul over to him.

The Governor read the letter.

'What province do you come from?' he asked.

'Cilicia,' said Paul.

'I'll try your case when your accusers get here,' he said.

He gave orders for Paul to be kept under guard in Herod's Palace.

Before Governor Felix

Five days passed by.

Then the High Priest, Ananias, with some members of the Council, came down from Jerusalem City. They brought with them a lawyer, Tertullus, to put their case against Paul before the Governor.

The Governor called on Tertullus to speak.

'We enjoy great peace,' Tertullus began, 'and we owe it to you, Your Excellency. In every way and everywhere the life of our people has been made better; this, too, we owe to your care. We are glad about this and we are very thankful.

'I ask you to listen, with your usual kindness, to what we have to say. I will not speak long; I don't want to waste your time.

'This fellow here is a real trouble-maker—we've found that out all right. We've three charges to make against him. First, he's caused riots among Jewish people all over the world. Secondly, he's the ringleader of the Nazarenes—the followers of a man called Jesus. Thirdly, he went into the Temple with a foreigner and broke our Temple laws. That's why we arrested him.

'If you examine the prisoner himself, you can find out that all our charges are true.'

All the Jews there joined in the attack on Paul and said that this was what had happened.

The Governor nodded to Paul to speak.

'I know that for many years you have been a judge over our people,' Paul began. 'This makes me glad to make my defence before you. I haven't been in the country twelve days yet—you can check that fact yourself. I went up to Jerusalem to worship. There's nobody here who can prove I started an argument or a riot, in the Temple or in a Meeting House or in the streets of the city—they never found me doing anything of the sort. They can't prove any of their charges.'

He then explained that the friends of Jesus followed the teaching of the Jewish Bible and held the hope that when men die they rise again—a hope many Jews themselves hold.

'I've tried to live honestly before God and men,' he said.

'It's a long time since I was last here,' he went on. 'I came back this time to bring a gift of money to help the needy of my own people. This is what they found me doing. I was in the Temple carrying out my religious duty. No crowd was with me, and I was going quietly about my business. It was some Jews from Ephesus who started all the trouble. They ought to be here in this court now; they're the ones who should be making charges against me, if they think I did something wrong. Further, let these men here tell you what happened when I stood before the Jewish Council in Jerusalem. Did that court find me guilty of anything—except, perhaps, that I called out: "The one charge against me today is that I believe that men rise again to life when they die"?'

At this point the Governor said he would go on with the hearing of the case later. He knew all about 'The Way' (as the friends of Jesus were called).

'When Colonel Lysias himself comes down from Jerusalem City,' he said, 'I will give my verdict.'

He gave the captain of the guard his orders.

'Keep him under guard,' he said. 'But see he has some freedom. Don't stop his friends looking after him.'

Some days later the Governor was back in Caesarea, and his young Jewish wife was with him. He had Paul brought before him and listened to what he had to say about Jesus. Paul went on to tackle the Governor about justice and self-control and God's judgment, and this frightened him.

'You'd better go now,' he said. 'I'll find another time to talk to you, and I'll send for you then.'

He really wanted to get money out of Paul. That was why he often sent for him and talked with him.

Two years went by. Then the Emperor called Governor Felix back to Rome to give an account of himself and his government of the country.

The Governor wanted to keep the Jewish people friendly; so, when he went away, he left Paul in prison. Another Governor, Festus, was sent out to take his place.

Before Governor Festus

Festus took up his duties as Governor.

Three days later, he went up from Caesarea to Jerusalem City. The High Priest and the Jewish leaders at once brought their charges against Paul to his notice. They asked him, as a favour to them, to bring Paul back to the city; they intended to carry out their plot to murder him on the road.

'Paul stays in Caesarea,' the Governor answered. 'I am leaving the city quite soon, and you can go down with me. If the man has done anything wrong, you can make your charges against him there.'

He spent a week or more in the city, and then went back to Caesarea.

Next day he took his seat in the Court and ordered Paul to be brought before him. When Paul arrived, the Jewish leaders crowded round him. They made many serious charges against him, but they couldn't prove any of them.

'I have done nothing wrong,' said Paul, 'either against the Jewish religion or the Temple or the Emperor.'

The Governor wanted to please the Jewish leaders; so he turned to Paul.

'Do you want to go up to Jerusalem,' he asked, 'and be tried before me there?'

'I stand here in the court of the Emperor,' Paul answered, 'and that's where I ought to be. I've done nothing wrong against the Jewish people; you know that very well. I'm not trying to escape death—if I've done anything to deserve the death sentence. But if there's nothing in what these men say against me, nobody can hand me over to them. I claim my right to be tried by the Emperor himself in Rome.'

The Governor talked the matter over with his advisers.

'All right,' he said. 'You have appealed to the Emperor; to the Emperor you shall go.'

Before King Agrippa

Some days later, King Agrippa and his sister, Queen Bernice, came down to Caesarea to welcome Governor Festus and spend a holiday in the city. This gave the Governor the chance to ask him what he thought about Paul's case.

'Governor Felix left a man in prison here,' he said, and told him what had happened.

'They didn't charge him, you see, with crimes of any sort,· as I expected,' he said. 'It was all about their superstitions and about a dead man called Jesus who, Paul said, was alive. I didn't know where I was. What kind of questions do you ask in a case like this? I asked him if he wanted to go to Jerusalem and be tried there. He claimed his right to be tried before His Majesty the Emperor himself. So I ordered him to be kept under guard till I could send him to Rome.'

'I should like to hear the man myself,' said the King.

'Tomorrow,' said the Governor. 'You shall hear him tomorrow.'

Next day was a great day for the city. The King and the Queen wore their splendid robes; the army officers and important people crowded the Hall. Governor Festus gave the order for Paul to be brought in.

The Governor made a short speech.

'King Agrippa, Gentlemen,' he said. 'You see this man before you. In Jerusalem and in this city, the Jewish people have made many complaints about him. They actually demanded his death. But it was clear to me that he hadn't done anything to deserve the

ROME, THE CAPITAL OF THE EMPIRE. Here all Paul's journeys ended. He was brought here as a prisoner; here he was tried and executed. These are the ruins of the amphitheatre (the Colosseum) built in A.D. 80; the amphitheatre Paul knew was burnt down not long after his death. Here were held shows of fighting gladiators and wild beasts.

CAESAREA. These are ruins of the port of Caesarea, the headquarters of the Roman army in Palestine. Here Paul landed whenever he visited Palestine by sea; it was here Captain Julius took him on board ship, a prisoner ordered to stand trial in Rome.

death sentence. When he claimed the right to be tried in Rome, I decided to send him there. But I don't know what to put in my report to the Emperor. That's why I've brought him here before this assembly, and especially before you, your Majesty. When this examination is over, I shall know, I hope, what to put in my report. It seems silly to me to send a prisoner for trial without making clear what crime he's charged with.'

King Agrippa turned to Paul.

'You may tell us what you've got to say for yourself,' he said.

Paul raised his hand, and began to put his case to the court.

'The Jewish leaders have said a lot of things against me, King Agrippa,' he said, 'and I think I'm lucky to be putting my case today to you. You're no stranger, I know, to Jewish customs and to the questions we Jewish people disagree about among ourselves. I hope you will listen to me, even if I take some time about it.

'The Jewish leaders know all about me, though they won't tell you; they've known me for a long time. They know what I was like when I was young and living in Jerusalem; what an eager Pharisee I was—some of the best Jews are Pharisees. They know what lies behind this trial. The charge against me is about one thing, your Majesty—the hope our people have held for centuries. Why should anybody think God can't raise a man from death?

'Let me begin at the beginning.

'Deeply religious as I was, I did everything I could to stamp out the name of Jesus of Nazareth. In Jerusalem City I had many of the friends of Jesus thrown into prison; I did this under a warrant from the Jewish Council itself. At their trials, I voted with the rest for the death sentence. That is not all. Again and again I hunted them out in the Meeting Houses and tried to make them say "Cursed be Jesus". I hated them. I even hunted them out in cities far beyond the borders of Palestine.

'Then something changed my life.

'I was going one day along the Damascus Road with a warrant from the Jewish Council for the arrest of all Christians I found there.

'At midday, on that very road, your Majesty, I saw a light from the sky shining round about me and those who were with me— a light brighter than sunlight. We all fell flat on our faces. I heard a voice speaking to me—speaking in Aramaic, my native language.

'Saul, Saul,' the Voice said. 'Why do you treat me as an enemy? You're like a horse kicking against the sharp stick of its driver.'

'Who are you?' I asked.

'I am Jesus,' he said, 'and it's me you are treating as an enemy. Get up and stand on your feet; I've come to you to give you your orders. I make you my servant. You are to go and tell the whole world what you know about me now and what you will learn about me later. I will take care of you, whether your own people or foreigners attack you. It is to the whole world I send you, to all those who are not Jews. You must open their eyes, so that they may turn from their evil ways, receive God's forgiveness and become members of God's family.

'That is why, King Agrippa, I can never go back on what I saw that day; it was God's command.

'I told the Good News in Damascus first of all, then in Jerusalem, then throughout the whole country, to Jews and foreigners alike.

ROME, THE ARCH OF SETTIMIO SEVERO. This is one of several triumphal arches that were erected on the return of a victorious Roman general.

I told them all that they should change their ways and live in
God's Way. That's why the Jews got hold of me in the Temple
and tried to murder me.

'From the first day to this, I have had God's help. I tell the
Good News to everybody, to ordinary people and to rulers and
governors. I say nothing you won't find in the Bible. God's Chosen
Leader had to face death, and, by being the first to rise from the
dead, brought in a new day for all men everywhere—for the Jewish
people and for the people of every country in the world.

'I say that again here in this court today.'

Even while Paul was talking, the Governor Festus shouted at him.

'You've gone mad, Paul, quite mad. You've been reading too
many books. You're mad!'

'I am not mad, your Excellency,' said Paul. 'I am talking plain
common sense and telling the honest truth. His Majesty knows what
I'm talking about, and I'm talking to him from my heart. I am sure
that he hasn't been blind to what has been happening—it was no
hole-and-corner affair.'

He turned to the King.

'Your Majesty,' he said, 'do you believe what the Bible says?
I know you do.'

'In short,' said the King, 'you are trying to make me a Christian.'

'Short or long,' said Paul, 'I wish to God that everybody listening
to me now—not only you, Your Majesty—would become like me,
except, of course, for these handcuffs.'

King Agrippa, the Governor and Queen Bernice stood up and the
whole assembly rose.

The three of them went out, and talked together about Paul's
case.

They all agreed that he was doing nothing that deserved either
death or prison.

'If he hadn't appealed to the Emperor,' said King Agrippa to
the Governor, 'he could have left the court a free man.'

BOOK FIVE

JESUS—LEADER AND LORD

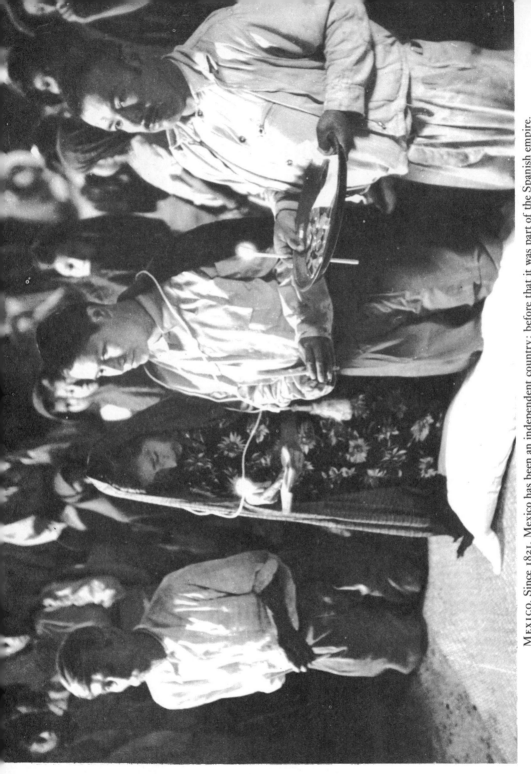

MEXICO. Since 1821, Mexico has been an independent country; before that it was part of the Spanish empire. Most of the people are Roman Catholic; there are 266,000 Protestants. (Population: 22 million)

Paul of Tarsus

Paul was a tireless traveller, and letters were the only way he could keep in touch with his many friends. Corinth and Ephesus were his headquarters for his work in the lands that bordered the Aegean Sea. They were his headquarters, not his home; for the ships and the roads often beckoned him. Perhaps it was from Corinth he once went westward through the Gulf of Corinth and up the coast of the Adriatic Sea—to Nicopolis ('Victory City', built in celebration of a sea battle) and beyond to Illyricum, modern Albania and Yugoslavia. A number of the towns on this coast had been Corinthian colonies, and he would hear about them in the streets and bazaars of the city. The valley behind Ephesus must have called him and he would hear stories of the coast and the islands from sailors in the harbour. He had friends everywhere; he could hardly help being a writer of letters.

Some forty years after his death, some of his letters were gathered together and published in two volumes. That would have surprised him. Perhaps this is how it happened.

At the beginning of the second century, the leader of the Christians in Ephesus was Onesimus. It seems very likely that this was the Onesimus who owed everything—his freedom and his love of Jesus—to Paul; you can read the letter Paul wrote about him to his owner, Philemon, on p. 326. Dr. Luke had recently published his book on the beginnings of Christianity, addressed to His Excellency Theophilus (*From Galilee to Rome*); and in this book, you will remember, he had told many stories about Paul. A copy of it came into the hands of Onesimus. As he read it, he remembered the letters of Paul that were still kept in the church chests at Ephesus and Colossae. These letters ought not to be hidden away, thought Onesimus; everybody ought to read them. Dr. Luke's book contained the names of other churches—Thessalonica, Philippi, Corinth, Rome—to which Paul had probably written letters. Onesimus was able to get copies of the letters they had received from Paul. When he had gathered the letters all together, he published them in two volumes; and, at the end, he put the little letter Paul had written to Philemon about Onesimus himself. People everywhere could now see for themselves how a great Christian leader Paul had been.

Paul's letters are not easy to read. I have taken passages from them, and arranged them under different headings. You can find out from his own words why he became a Christian and what he thought Christianity was about.

We begin with what he had to say about Jesus.

PAUL'S STORY OF JESUS

Paul did not need to write very much in his letters about what Jesus said and did in Palestine; everybody knew the story, and it was read and discussed every Sunday in the meeting for worship. None of the gospels had yet been written, but there were still many people alive in Paul's day who had known Jesus or been living in Palestine at the time.

Paul had, nevertheless, to remind his friends, from time to time, about what had happened to Jesus, and call their attention to its meaning. I have gathered together these passages about Jesus, so that you can read what Paul had to say about him.

Paul had a very clear picture of the kind of person Jesus was and of what he said and did. He himself had never met Jesus, but he had become a Christian only a few years after his death, and he had met his close friends (like Peter) and talked with them about him.

What Paul has to say about the story of Jesus should be compared with the fuller story in *The Beginning* and in *From Galilee to Rome* (Part One).

My own Experience

Let me begin by saying what Jesus means to me. God, who made this bright world, has filled my heart with light, the light which shines now I know what he is really like. This was the light which was shining from the face of Jesus.

I can only describe my experience as a friend of Jesus in this way: I go on living my ordinary human life; and yet, in a sense, I don't feel that *I'm* living it, but that Jesus has taken charge of me. I live by trusting in Jesus, God's Son, who loved me and gave his life for me.

Here are some important points about the story of Jesus.

What Jesus came to do

When the time was ready, God sent his Son to live among us.

He lived a life like ours, and grew up as a Jew in Palestine. But he came to help the whole world: to help his own people, the Jews, to be really 'God's People'; and to help all the peoples of the world to live as 'God's People' too.

We can put it in this way. He became the 'servant' of his own people for two reasons: he wanted them to see that all God had done for them throughout their long history from the earliest days of their Founding Fathers (Abraham, Jacob and Joseph) was no empty dream—God was a God they could trust; but he also wanted the whole world to know what God was truly like, a God of mercy, and to worship him with all their hearts.

In a word, he came to set us *all* free that we might live as free men.

What Sort of Man Jesus was

He was a descendant of King David. He had a number of brothers. One of them was James whom I got to know when I stayed a fortnight with Peter in Jerusalem City.

But the most important thing about him was that he made God real. That's what we mean when we call him God's Son. Yet he never did anything for his own pleasure. He is our example, and we must follow him.

These were the marks of his character.[1]

He cared for people—for everybody. He was a very happy man. People who couldn't get on with one another found it possible to be friends in his presence. He never gave up. He was very kind, a really good man, and he could always be relied on. He was gentle, yet master of himself. What people remembered about him was his 'graciousness'.

Jesus made his Purpose quite Clear just before he died

Yet he met a violent death at the hands of his own people, though he was executed by the Roman Government.

On the night when he was handed over to the Jewish leaders, he had supper with his friends. During supper he picked up the loaf of bread, said grace over it and broke it in pieces.

'This is my very self,' he said. 'I am giving myself up for you. Do this to remember me by.'

When supper was over, he raised the cup in the same way.

'This cup,' he said, 'means my death. I am dying to bring all men to God, as the Bible says, "from the least of them to the greatest". Whenever you drink it, remember me.'

And so he died and was buried.

---

[1] In this list of the marks of Christian character, Paul seems to be describing the character of Jesus himself (see also p. 272); hence the way I have translated it.

NORTH AFRICA. These people live in Kordofan (Sudan). Some of the tribesmen are great hunters, owning many horses. They were once slave raiders.

The Death of Jesus was not the End but the Beginning

On the third day he was raised to life. He was seen by Peter; then by 'The Twelve'. After that, he was seen by more than five hundred at once; most of them are still living, but some have since died. He was then seen by James, his brother; then by all his close friends.

Last of all, long after anybody could have hoped, he was seen also by me.

The heart of the Good News is that Jesus is not dead but alive. How, then, can some people say, 'There's no such thing as being raised from death'? If that is so, Jesus never conquered death; and if Jesus never conquered death, there is no Good News to tell, and we've been living in a fool's paradise. We've even been telling lies about God, when we said he raised Jesus from death; for he didn't— if 'there's no such thing as being raised from death'. And if 'there's no such thing as being raised from death', Jesus is just—dead. If Jesus is dead and has not been raised to life again, all we've lived for as friends of Jesus is just an empty dream, and we're just where we were, helpless to do anything about the evil in our hearts and in the world. And those who have died as friends of Jesus have now found out the bitter truth. If all we've got is a *story* about Jesus inspiring us just to live this life better, we of all men are to be pitied.

Of course, the whole idea of 'being raised from death' raises many questions for many people. For example—'How are dead people raised to life?' 'What sort of body do they have then?' But questions like these sound silly when we remember what kind of world God's world is and what God himself is like. Take the seed the farmer sows—it must die before it can grow. The seed he sows is only bare grain; it is nothing like the plant he'll see at harvest-time. This is the way God has created the world of nature; every kind of seed grows up into its own kind of plant—its new body. This is true of the world of animals, too, where there is a great variety of life, men, animals, birds, fish—all different from one another.

This shows us how to think about this matter of 'being raised from death'. There's the life men live on earth—that has its own splendour; and there's the life they live when they are 'raised from death' and live (as we say) 'in heaven'—and this world beyond our earthly world has its own different splendour.

The splendour of the sun and the splendour of the moon and the splendour of the stars differ from one another—even the stars differ in splendour.

So it is when men are 'raised from death'. Here the body is a 'physical' body; there it is raised a 'spiritual' body. Here everything grows old and decays; there it is raised in a form which neither grows old nor decays. Here the human body can suffer shame and shock; there it is raised in splendour. Here it is weak; there it is full of vigour.

This is the meaning of the words of the Bible—

'Death has been totally defeated.'

For the fact is Jesus *was* raised to life. God be thanked—we can now live victoriously because of what he has done.

It is all summed up in a hymn we sing.

> He bore the form of God;
> yet he did not think likeness to God
> just good fortune for himself alone.
>
> He gave up everything
> taking the form of a slave,
> living life like other men.
>
> As a man
> he faced the worst;
> obedience took him to his death.
>
> So God raised him to the heights,
> and gave him the name
> above every name—
>
> that at the name of Jesus
> the living and the dead
> should hail him as Lord,
>
> and everybody everywhere claim
> 'Jesus, God's Chosen Leader, is Lord!'
> to the glory of God the Father.

The Story of Jesus is Part of a much Bigger Story
(To the Christians in Rome)

The letter Paul wrote to the Christians in Rome (from which this chapter is taken) is different from his other letters. He was writing to Christians he had only heard about but not yet met. He wanted them to welcome him on his way to Spain and to help him in his work in the West. He knew that they must have heard all sorts of stories about him, many of them far from the truth. So he set down in this letter, carefully and honestly, what he believed and where he stood.

Jewish Christians had attacked him on three important questions—what Christianity is in fact about, what the importance of the Jewish religion in the history of mankind is, and how Christians should behave towards one another and towards other people. In this chapter we shall hear what he has to say about the first two questions—what Christianity is in fact about, and the importance of the Jewish religion.

To Paul, Jesus was the 'clue' to understanding what God is like and what he is doing, and to understanding the world in which we live and the story of humanity. Jesus helped him to begin to answer the serious questions men and women, all over the world and in all centuries, ask about this strange world in which we live—Why was it created? What is it all about? What has gone wrong? How can it be put right? What kind of world ought it to be? How can it become the kind of world it ought to be? Do individuals matter?

These are the questions he discusses in the first part of his letter to the Christians in Rome.

I have set out what Paul has to say under these headings:
    What the Good News means
    God shows himself to us in the Glory of his World
    God has no Favourites
    What the story of the Jews means
    Jesus
    All this makes a difference to the way we use God's Earth
    God's Love

In 'God's Love' we have repeated some words from 'Paul's own Story' in *From Galilee to Rome* for you to see that it is the conclusion of a serious argument.

In 'What the Story of the Jews means', I have put only a brief passage from Paul's letter. But I have added a very vivid description of Jewish history from another letter in the New Testament. This letter carries no name, but it may have been written by Paul's friend Apollos. Where Paul only refers to a few famous names, Apollos tells us something of the story which lies behind the names and helps us to see what kind of story it was.

What the Good News means

Let me begin by saying what I mean by the Good News. I am not ashamed of it, and this is why.

The Good News means, first of all, that God has given us the power to live in his Way.

The Good News makes it clear that all we need to do is to take God at his word; this is something that everybody, whoever he is, can do.

Last of all, the Good News is Good News for everybody everywhere; my own people were the first to hear it, but it is for the foreign people of every other country too.

In a word, the Good News tells us how God puts right what is wrong, and how he helps men everywhere to put wrong things right.

God trusts us, and we must trust God, from start to finish. That's what the Bible means when it says: 'The good man lives by trusting God.'

God shows Himself to Us in the Glory of his World

God has so made the world that men cannot defeat the truth— about God himself or about the world itself. If they try to defeat it, they only bring disaster on themselves and their selfish schemes.

He has made himself known to all men everywhere through the world which he has made; this is plain for all men to see.

What he is really like—his tireless energy and all that makes him 'God'—cannot, of course, be seen with our eyes as we can see the earth about us and the stars above us. But that doesn't mean that we can therefore say, 'We can't possibly know anything about "God".' For, from the beginning of human history, men have been able to think about what they see in the world about them and ask questions. As we can learn what a man is like from the things he has made, so we can learn what God is like from what God has made.

Men have known, therefore, something about what God is like; but they haven't acted on that knowledge and honoured him as they ought to have done. They haven't even been thankful for what he has done. So their thoughts, not only about God himself but about the world we live in, have all become twisted; their minds have become dark instead of becoming clear. They talk as if they were clever, but they are not being clever at all.

Look, for example, at what they have done—this business of idols.

GUATEMALA is in Central America. Taken by the Spaniards in the sixteenth century, it became an independent republic just over 100 years ago. Half its population is pure Indian. Most of its people are Roman Catholic.

'They have exchanged their glorious God
for the image of an ox that eats fodder',

as the Bible says. They have stopped thinking about God himself
(who never changes); they would rather have imitations instead—
sometimes in the shape of a man (who does change) and sometimes
in the shape of birds and animals and snakes.

What happened then? Men came to think that it wasn't worthwhile to find out what God was really like; so what they *did* think
about him was nonsense. Then their treatment of one another
became inhuman; they began to live more like animals than men.

Look at what goes on. Men are no longer just to one another;
they go on doing what they clearly know is wrong; they grab what
they want; they don't mind playing dirty tricks on one another.
The list of what they do is endless: jealousy, murder, gang quarrels,
plots, downright badness. They don't mind what they say about
one another—they don't hesitate to tell lies. They've got no use for
religion, of course. They are violent, proud of themselves, boasting
of their 'triumphs', inventing all sorts of crime, showing no respect
for their parents. They have no conscience, no love for anybody
but themselves, and no mercy.

God has no Favourites

Everybody will be judged by what he himself has done.

Those who have tried to live splendidly and honourably—
setting their hearts on what will always be worthwhile, and steadily
doing what they know to be right—will find out the secret of the
good life.

Those who try to grab what they can for themselves, play about
with the truth and don't mind how bad they are, will have to live in
the angry and furious world they have themselves made.

In all this, it doesn't matter who you are—Jew or foreigner.
God has no favourites.

But the story is not all dark; there's something else to say.
People all over the world, whatever race they belong to and though
they know nothing about the Bible, can begin to live in God's Way.
Their religion, strange though it may be, is real religion. Nobody has
told them what God is like—they have only their own hearts to
guide them; but they have used their minds and followed their
consciences. And when God, who has shown us in Jesus his Son

what his Way is like, judges them—some far from what Jesus stood for, some very near what Jesus stood for—the fact that their thoughts are all mixed-up will not be held against them.

The point is this. A good pagan is better than a bad Jew. Many people who do not seem to be religious are, in fact, doing what God asks us to do better than many whose outward lives seem to be religious. It isn't easy to tell if a man is religious; belonging to God's Family isn't just a matter of outward acts of worship. The truly religious man is the man who is such inwardly. True acts of worship spring from the heart; we don't do them because 'that's what religious people do', but because we ourselves, in our hearts, want to worship God. It's what we love with all our hearts that matters to God; it doesn't matter if we get no public praise.

What the Story of the Jews means
(The Old Testament)

But is there anything special about the Jews? What value for us has their religion? Very much indeed, however you look at it.

The most important thing about them is that God trusted them with the Good News. Through men like Moses, Amos, Isaiah and Jeremiah he told us his purpose for all mankind.

Here is a simple statement of what God has made clear to us through the Jewish people; through, that is, the great Men of God he sent them.

He made clear:
1. that he is our Father;
2. that he lives among us in all his glory;
3. how he wants us to live as his Family;
4. how he wants us to serve him;
5. what his purposes for all mankind are; these were made clear in the stories of Abraham, Jacob and Joseph, and, in our own day, in Jesus himself.

[Paul, in the passage you have just read, has briefly summarized his reasons for believing that the story of the Jewish people is important. But it was a thrilling as well as an important story. So I have put here a fuller description, from a letter of another friend of Jesus, which tells us more about what happened.]

'The heart of all religion is trust in God (this friend of Jesus wrote). It is this trust which makes our hope for the future a strong hope, and makes us sure about God himself whom we cannot see, and about the world which he made to be his world.

'This is what the Men of God, whose stories are in the Bible, saw very clearly; for God spoke through them. Look at what happened.

'Abraham trusted God. When God called him to go out to a land which would one day be the homeland of his descendants, he did what God told him to do. When he set off, he had no idea where he was going. He had only God's command. When he reached the land which was to be the future homeland of his descendants, it was still a foreign land to him. He didn't settle down in it; he went on living in his tents, as though he might still have to move on. So did his son Isaac and his grandson Jacob. His eyes were searching the horizon for a strong city designed and made by God himself.

'Moses trusted God. He refused to be a prince in the King's palace. He chose to share the hard life of his own people instead of enjoying the high life of Egypt. He knew that such high life would not last, and that God did not want him to have anything to do with it. In his eyes insults (such as God's Chosen Leader himself had to face) were greater riches than all the wealth of Egypt. He knew it would all be worthwhile. It wasn't the King's anger that made him leave Egypt; it was his trust in God. He could face anything; God was as real to him as if he could see him.

'Is there any need for me to go on to tell the stories of all the others? They would take too long. But what a roll call it would be— the heroes of the early days when we fought our way through the highlands; King David, the founder of our nation, and Samuel, who played so brave a part in that exciting story; and the great Men of God like Amos, Isaiah and Jeremiah. They all trusted God.

'See what they did. They defeated great empires; they made sure that justice triumphed; they proved that trust in God was not an empty dream. They took great dangers—wild animals, fire and war —in their stride. Their very weakness helped them to find out where their strength lay.

'They were tortured because they would not give in; for they knew that death itself could not defeat their hopes. Some were beaten up and lashed with whips, chained like animals and thrown into prison. Some were stoned to death and sawn in two and murdered. They knew what poverty was; the only clothes they had were the skins of sheep and goats. They were treated like dirt—men of whom the world ought to have been proud. They were outcasts, driven out on to the moors and the hills, with only caves and pits for a home.

'These men were not afraid to die; their secret was their trust in God. They did not see for themselves everything that God meant men to enjoy. They could only see it on the far horizon and greet it with a cheer. They were ready to live as foreigners and strangers in their own world.

'Such men show that what they were looking for was a new homeland, a new world. If they had been content with the world they had turned their backs on, they could have gone back at any time and lived in it. They didn't go back. The plain truth is that they longed for a better world—God's world. And God was not ashamed to be called their God—though their own world was ashamed of them as citizens. God's world is in the making, and they will have their place in it.

'Let us sum it all up. We remember all these men for one thing: they put their trust in God. They did not see the world they died for. God had a bigger plan than they dreamed of: he wants us all, everybody everywhere, to enjoy the world he is making. Nobody, not even such great men as we have been remembering, can truly enjoy God's world until we can all enjoy it together.'

[We can now go back to Paul's own words.]

Jesus

But now God has shown us clearly what he is like in a new way—how he stands for what is right, overthrows what is wrong and helps men to live in his Way.

This is not altogether a new Way, as we have seen—the Men of God of the Jewish people had begun to see how God puts wrongs right. But Jesus has made it quite plain. And if we are to live in God's Way, we must trust God; this means trusting in Jesus who has made God real to us.

This is true for everybody everywhere; for God, as we have seen, has no favourites. We have all done wrong; none of us has lived as splendidly as God intended him to live, though we were all created to live in his Way and be like him. But God treats us as if we had learned to live splendidly; his love is given to us freely. And it is Jesus who has won this freedom for us.

There is nothing in all this to make us proud of ourselves. Keeping all the rules wouldn't have stopped us being proud of ourselves. We have simply taken him at his word, and that leaves no room for boasting.

I am sure of this: everybody can really live as God wants him to live by simply trusting him, not by trying to keep all the rules. I mean everybody. Is God only the God of the Jewish people? Isn't he the God of all people everywhere? Of course he is, for there is only one God. So he puts Jewish people right—if they trust him; and he puts the people of other countries right—if they trust him.

When I talk like this, I don't make the Jewish religion worthless, as some people say I do; I am showing how important it is, for this is what it is all about.

Religion isn't a matter of rules and regulations—not even the Jewish religion, as you can see from the story of Abraham. God's Way was not a matter of rules and regulations for him. It would, of course, have been easy for him to boast if he had been the kind of man who could say: 'I'm all right; I've kept all God's rules.' But that would have counted only with his neighbours; it wouldn't have counted at all with God The Bible is quite clear. It says: 'It was Abraham's *trust* in God that made him a truly religious man.' Keeping rules and regulations is like working for wages. Wages aren't a *gift*; they are a *right*.

Friendship is different; friends don't help one another for what they get. If religion is just a matter of carrying out rules and regulations, there's no room for friendship with God—trust doesn't mean anything, and there's no point in making promises. The world is a hard world where, if you break a law, you pay for it—and that's that.

But this wasn't the way Abraham thought about God. He never once doubted that God was his *friend* and would keep his promises. This, for him, was the glory of God, and his trust in God grew stronger the longer he lived. He was quite sure that God would not let him down. That's why the Bible says: 'It was Abraham's trust in God that made him a truly religious man.'

But the Bible doesn't mean that this was only true for Abraham; it's true for everybody. And it's true for us who put our trust in God who raised Jesus to life again.

You see what it all comes to: our simple trust in God our Father puts us right, and we've nothing to worry about. This is what Jesus made possible. He made God's love real to us; and we are happy people, because we know that we can learn to be like God himself (we were created 'in his image') and live in his Way.

We can now be happy even when we have to face hard times. We know that hard times train us never to give in; never giving in is the secret of growing up; and being grown-up (as Jesus was grown-up), we look forward with high hope to the future. We aren't dreaming; for God himself lives in us, and our hearts are full to overflowing with his love.

So Jesus died at the right time. None of us was strong enough to deal with the mess we had got ourselves into; Jesus gave his life to get us out of it.

This is the wonder of it. It isn't often that a man will give his life even to save a decent fellow; sometimes, perhaps, a man will give his life for a good man. We were neither decent nor good; we were his enemies. Yet Jesus gave his life for us, and made us God's friends. This is proof of how much God loves us.

We may put it like this.

Jesus, by his death, made us God's friends—even though we were then God's enemies. Now we are God's friends, Jesus, living in our hearts, can all the more deliver us from what is evil and help us to live as God created us to live. And more: the very thought of God fills us with joy—we are his friends. This is what Jesus has done for us.

Those who, with God's help, try to live in God's Way are true members of God's Family.

You know what it was like before you became friends of Jesus. You didn't know what God was really like. You felt you were slaves, and you were always afraid. This will never·happen again. God's spirit does not make us slaves but members of his Family. When we pray, we speak to God just as Jesus did; we say 'Father!' God himself makes us quite sure in our hearts that we are his children. Children, as you know, inherit their father's wealth. If, then, we are God's children, we share his wealth as his heirs along with Jesus. But note: we must remember what Jesus went through before he became what he is; we must be ready to face what he faced, as well as share in his splendour.

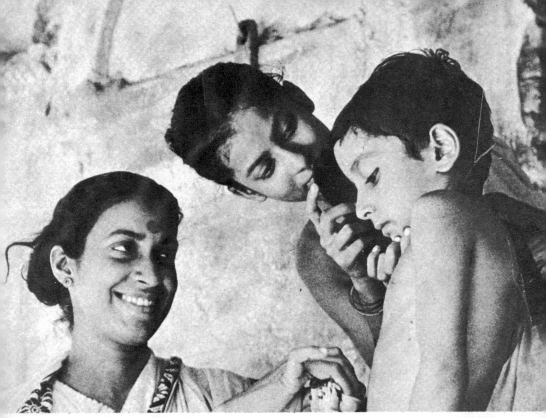

INDIA. About 560 million people live in the Republic of India. Their chief religion is Hinduism; other religions have their worshippers. There have been Christians here since the fifth century.

All this makes a Difference to the Way we use God's Earth

We look at everything differently now—the hard time we are going through and the very earth we live on. We see it all in the light of the glorious future which God will give us.

The earth itself is being spoilt by the way men live; it is, as it were, waiting for the time when the people who live on it will live, not as they do now, but as members of God's Family, with mercy and gentleness, sharing it together.

We know that the story of the whole world has been a story of much suffering. Animals know what suffering is; men and women know what it means, too. But it is not hopeless suffering; it is like the suffering of a mother when she has her baby—something is being born. Even we, who are the friends of Jesus and who have begun the new life, also know what suffering means all too well—but we look forward in hope to the time when we shall be fully members of God's Family, our whole personalities set free.

All this, of course, is only a hope now; we don't live as we ought to do. But this hope has made us new men. And we're going to hold on until the day comes when we can see it with our own eyes.

But we know now that the world is not the sort of world we once thought it was. It is a world where God works for all that is worthwhile, *alongside those who love him*. We are fellow-workers with God. This is what he was always calling us to be—with one purpose in mind, a purpose he planned and settled before history began. This purpose was that we might grow up to be the kind of person Jesus was; so that Jesus might be the elder brother of a great family of brothers and sisters.

God's Love

Looking back on all this, what shall we say?

If God is standing by us, what does it matter who opposes us? He did not spare his own Son; he gave him up for us all. With such a gift, will he not give us everything else as well?

Who can take God's love away from us now—the love which Jesus has made real to us?

You know the sort of thing that can happen to any of us in this world of ours—suffering, hardship, cruelty, hunger, homelessness, danger, war. In just such a world, we who are the friends of Jesus can live more splendidly than the greatest world-conquerors—with the help of Jesus who loved us.

I am quite sure that nothing—neither dying nor living, neither what we're facing now nor what we may have to face tomorrow, nothing in our own world or in outer space or in our own hearts, can take away from us God's love, made real by Jesus our Lord.

THE DIFFERENCE JESUS HAS MADE

To become a Christian makes a great difference to the way we feel and think and live. It made a great difference to those who became Christians in the early days. Here are two passages from Paul's letters where he discusses the difference becoming Christians had made in their lives.

The early Christians lived in a very different world from ours. As you read these passages, consider what difference becoming a Christian should make today.

CUBA is the largest and most populous of the West Indian islands. It is a republic. Its people are of white and negro origin.

'We've finished with the Old Ways of Living'
(To the Christians in Colossae)

We once lived as many people still do. But now all that's finished with; we must have nothing to do with sexual wrong-doing, indecency, lust, evil desires, the greediness that's always wanting more and more—using the world as if it were ours, not God's. But we must go further than this. We must do away with anger in our hearts as well as with angry words, with even wanting to hurt other people, and with all bad language. And, of course, we must never do anything but tell the truth to one another.

You see, we've finished with the old ways of living with all their nasty tricks. We're living in a new world—God's world—and every day God will make us better skilled at living in it.

You've heard people talking like this, haven't you?—'My country—right or wrong', 'Our religion's the right religion; other religions are just superstition', 'We're civilized; they're wogs', 'Some people are born slaves; they'll always be slaves'. We don't talk like that any more.

We stand—always and everywhere—for all that Jesus stood for.

Jesus has broken down all barriers. He is all that matters, and he is changing the whole life of mankind.

'We've found Something Bigger to live for'
(To the Christians in Corinth)

The love of Jesus drives us on—when we realize that he gave his life for all mankind, so that everybody should have something bigger to live for than just himself and what he can get for himself. Jesus gave his life for everybody.

We don't think of people now in the way people ordinarily think of one another. (I once thought of Jesus as my enemy and the enemy of my people. I don't think of him like that any more.) We try to think of people as God thinks of them.

When anybody becomes a friend of Jesus, the world's a new world for him; the old world has gone and a new world has been born.

WHAT JESUS MADE CLEAR

Jesus, for his friends, was 'the light of the world'. Knowing him was like stepping out of darkness into a world full of sunlight. They no longer stumbled, as men do when they are walking in the dark (see p. 375).

'I didn't understand myself,' Paul once wrote about the days before he became a Christian; and he did not understand a lot of other things too. For Paul, becoming a Christian was like hearing God say 'Let there be Light!' The world was still a place with strangeness and mystery in it, and there were many things still to learn. But it was not a dark place any more, where a man had to feel his way about; it was full of light. The day had dawned, and he could see where he was going.

I have chosen six important questions that Jesus made clear for Paul:

> What the world means;
> What freedom means;
> What God wants us to do;
> What it means to be a Christian;
> How to learn to live together;
> How to see life steadily and see it whole.

These are questions that *we* need to be clear about too. They are 'live' questions for us, as we face the making of a new world in which people of all races must have their place and part.

What the World means
(To the Christians in Corinth)

The world, we now know, is not a meaningless world. God has had a purpose from the beginning. He created the world so that men and women everywhere should learn to live gloriously as members of his Family.

This is God's 'secret' and his 'wisdom'.

Left: THE CITY DESTROYED—*Ossip Zadkine*, born 1890.
During the Second World War a great part of the old city of Rotterdam in Holland was destroyed by German bombing. This monument commemorates the dreadful loss of life and devastation, and was set up in 1953. The sculptor is Russian and of part Scottish descent, but now lives in France. He has produced many important pieces of sculpture including religious works of Christ on the Cross and the Pieta—Mary holding the crucified body of Christ.

This bronze figure is at least twice human size; and it stands amongst the new buildings of the city as a reminder of the suffering, not only of the people of Rotterdam, but of everyone in Europe at that time.

The governments of the world didn't realize what God was doing; if they had known anything about it, they wouldn't have executed Jesus as a criminal—Jesus who showed us, in the way he lived, what God was really like.

An old poem puts it clearly:

> 'Human eyes have never seen,
> human ears have never heard,
> human minds have never thought
> what God keeps ready
> for those who love him.'

All this God has made clear to us by giving us his Spirit—his presence in our hearts.

What Freedom means
(To the Christians in Anatolia)

You see what Jesus did: he set us free, to live as free men. Stand up, then, and live as free men, not as slaves.

But note this: don't let your freedom become an excuse for doing just what you feel like doing. With God's love in your hearts, be ready to do anything—and I mean *anything*—for one another. For all religion can be put in a single sentence: 'Love the next man as you love yourself.'

If you live like cat and dog, you'll just just destroy one another. Don't forget that.

Right : WINDOW IN THE BAPTIST CHURCH, ALABAMA—*John Petts*, born 1914.
Although the American negro was freed from slavery in 1865 he has never fully enjoyed equal rights with white Americans. In the Southern States, where the negroes were brought from Africa to work in the plantations, there is still strong opposition to equality between its black and white citizens and the whites have done everything in their power to segregate the races. In 1954 the Supreme Court ordered all state schools to desegregate immediately. This caused an uproar in the South and led to demonstrations and riots by the white population. There are now mixed schools but segregation still exists in many places.

In 1963 the late President Kennedy started a campaign to ensure that negroes are treated as American citizens. This has caused further strife in the South. On 17 September, 1963, a bomb exploded in the 'Sixteenth Street Baptist Church' in Birmingham, Alabama, when the negro congregation were assembled for worship. It partly demolished the building killing four Sunday school children and injuring twenty members of the congregation. This act of violence left an impression of horror around the world.

John Petts, an artist living in Wales, was moved to suggest that the Welsh people should contribute to the cost of a window to be presented to the church. A fund was started by a Cardiff newspaper and Mr. Petts was able to design this window which was presented to Alabama in the summer of 1965.

What God wants Us to do
(To the Christians in Corinth)

In Jesus, God is making everybody everywhere his friends; and he's not going to list the wrong and unkind things we have done and hold them against us.

He wants us to take this message of friendship to others; we are therefore the messengers of Jesus. It is as if God were speaking through us to everybody—'In the name of Jesus, be friends with God!'

What it means to be a Christian
(To the Christians in Anatolia)

Your trust in God your Father has made you members of his Family; Jesus has made this possible. For when you were baptized and became friends of Jesus, you began, with his help, to live in his way—as he lived in his Father's Way.

Living in God's Way means that you can't talk about one another as being 'white' or 'coloured', 'working-class' or 'upper-class', 'men' or 'women'—as though that were the only thing about them that matters. The most important thing is that as Christians you are one company of friends. And if you are friends of Jesus, you are members of God's Family as God meant you to be and promised to make you.

That is why, when the time was ripe, God sent his Son to live among us as one of us—to help us to live as his sons and daughters, grown-up members of his Family. Because this is what we now are, he has given us the spirit of his Son in our hearts. When we pray to him, we pray to him as Jesus did; we say, 'Father!'

You aren't God's slaves; God has made you, as I have said, his sons and daughters. And, as sons and daughters inherit their father's wealth, so all the wealth of God, your Father, is yours.

How to learn to live together
(To the Christians in Corinth)

I don't want you to have wrong ideas about the gifts which God has given us.

UNITED STATES. This is a picture of an American negro woman and her children. The negroes were brought over from Africa as slaves. They were set free in 1865, though only now are they beginning to enjoy full citizenship.

Different Gifts but one Spirit

First of all, God has given each of us different gifts, but he has given the one same Spirit—his presence in our hearts—to every one of us. There are different jobs to do, but we do them for the same Master. There are different kinds of work, but the same God helps all men in whatever they have to do.

To each of us God gives his spirit in our hearts in one particular way for the good of everybody. To one he gives the gift of talking wisely; to another the power to understand difficult problems and explain them; to another a special power to trust him fully; to another the skill of a doctor or nurse.

To one person God gives wonderful powers we do not really understand; to another the insight to understand his purposes and explain them clearly; to another the power to tell whether men are inspired by good or evil; to another strange mysterious experiences; to another the power to understand what these experiences mean.

But the one same Spirit—God's presence in our hearts—is at work in all these gifts, and God gives them to each of us, one by one, as he thinks best.

An Illustration—the Human Body

Take the example of the human body. The body is one body, but it has many parts. Though there are many different parts of the body, they all together form one body. Jesus, risen to life, is like that. It doesn't matter who we are—Jews or Greeks, slaves or freemen;[1] When we became friends of Jesus, we became one 'body' inspired by one Spirit, and we all share in that one Spirit.

[1] We could say now—'White or black, workman or boss'.

Look at the human body: one body, but many parts—not just one part.

Suppose all the parts of the body got jealous of one another. Suppose the foot said: 'I'm not the hand; so I'm not going to be part of the body'; it's still a foot, part of the body, isn't it? Suppose the ear said: 'I'm not an eye; so I'm not going to be part of the body'; it's still an ear, part of the body.

If the whole body were just one big eye, how could we hear? If the whole body were just one big ear, how could we smell anything? What God has done, you see, is to make the body out of many parts, arranging each part as he thought best. If all we had was one big ear or leg, there wouldn't be any 'body' at all. As it is, there are many parts, but that means that we can have something very different from the parts in themselves—a 'body' which does all sorts of things which none of the parts of the body, by themselves, could do at all.

That is why the eye can't say to the hand, 'I don't need *your* help'; the head can't say to the feet, 'I don't need *your* help'. That's nonsense. Why, we couldn't do without the parts of the body that seem to be the weakest. We know that; and we treat them, less attractive though they may seem, with very great care. We treat our private parts with great modesty; but we don't need to do that with our hair or face or figure. God has made the less attractive parts of the body more important than the attractive parts, so that there shall be no jealousy in the body. All the parts are made to fit in with one another as equally necessary. If something goes wrong with one part, all the parts are hurt; if one part wins honour, all the parts share its joy.

Christians are the Body of Jesus

All of you together are the 'body' of Jesus, and each one of you is part of his 'body'.

It works out like this. God has given everybody his own work to do, as a friend of Jesus.

First of all there are the Messengers, those who knew Jesus in Palestine and were there when he was raised to life. Then there are the 'Men of God', those who can explain the Bible and help us to understand what God is doing for us and the whole world. Then there are the teachers; then those to whom God has given unusual powers; then those who have the skills of healing; then those who have strange mysterious experiences. Is everybody a Messenger? or a 'Man of God'? or a teacher? Has everybody unusual powers? Can everybody heal people? Is everybody a leader? Does everybody have strange mysterious experiences? Can everybody explain what these strange mysterious experiences mean? Of course not.

What Love really means

In this matter of gifts, always put the emphasis on the most important gifts. Yet I will show you that there is something far more important than all these gifts; indeed they are worthless without it.

I may speak all the languages of earth and heaven, but, if I have no love in my heart, it's just like the old religions with the din and noise of gong and cymbal. I may be a 'Man of God' and be able to understand and explain all the wonders and secrets of God's Way; I may trust in God with all my heart, trust him as Jesus told us to trust him; but if I have no love in my heart, all this is worthless. I may give everything I've got to feed hungry people; I may be branded as a slave for what I believe; but if I have no love in my heart, I get nothing at all out of it.

This is what love is like.[1]

Love is never in a hurry, and is always kindness itself. It doesn't envy anybody at all, it never boasts about itself. It's never snobbish or rude or selfish. It doesn't keep on talking about the wrong things other people do; remembering the good things is happiness enough. It's tough—it can face anything. And it never loses trust in God, or in men and women; it never loses hope; and it never gives in.

Love holds good—everywhere, for everybody, for ever.

[1] Paul's description of love in the following paragraph is 'a portrait for which Christ himself has sat' (Dr. C. H. Dodd).

Make Love your Aim

This can't be said about even the most important of gifts.

There will come a time when there will be no need for 'Men of God' to explain God's Way. And all the strange mysterious experiences we mentioned will one day come to an end. There will come a time when learning will no longer be needed.

With all our learning, we don't know very much. All the 'Men of God' have told us about God's Way is only part of the truth about him. And all these will no longer matter when we know, as one day we shall, the perfect truth.

When I was a boy, I talked, thought and made my plans as a boy does. But when I became a man, I'd grown out of all my boyish ways. Our human life is like that. *Now* we are not seeing things as they really are; we are looking at them, as it were, in a clouded mirror, and they are not very clear. *Then* we shall see them directly, face to face. *Now* I know only a little bit of the truth. *Then* I shall know the whole truth, as God knows the whole truth about me.

All these things come and go. But there are some things that do not come and go. These three—trust, hope, love—last for ever. But love crowns them all.

See that you put love first.

How we see Life Steadily and see it Whole
(To the Christians in Corinth)

Get this clear. If any of you thinks he is 'clever' or 'wise', let him think again. Other people may pat him on the back, but he's just stupid in God's eyes. He must be ready to make a fool of himself in other people's eyes, if he wants to be really 'wise'.

Let me remind you of words you will find in the Bible:

God sees to it that the 'clever' man gets caught in his own tricks.

God knows that the schemes of a 'clever' man are stupid.

These are the facts:

The whole world is yours—all your 'star' leader has been able to do (whether he's Paul or Apollos or Peter is of no importance),[1]

---

[1] Paul is referring here to the quarrels which have been taking place in Corinth. See p. 287; and also *Paul the Explorer*, p. 219.

all the achievements of mankind, life and death, the present moment and the unknown future. All these, of course, are yours. But remember, they are only yours because you belong to Jesus and Jesus belongs to God.

BEGINNING TO LIVE IN GOD'S WAY

Paul saw clearly that Jesus did not want us to dream about God's Way; he wanted us to live in it. People must often have asked Paul: 'What must we do?' 'How do we begin to live in God's Way?' It is not easy for any of us, for we have to take the world as we find it and deal with people as they are. In his letters, Paul often gave them advice and guidance. Here is his well-known advice about Christian behaviour.

Paul believed that we have to train ourselves, if we are to learn to live in God's Way, as sportsmen have to train themselves. So I have added the passage where Paul talks about the runners and boxers at the Isthmian Games at Corinth.

How to go about it
(To the Christians in Rome)

Ourselves

We are members of God's Family, and I ask you to remember two things: keep God's kindness always in your minds, and give yourselves heart and soul to him—your energy, your heart and your mind. You belong to God, and it is service like this that makes God glad.

Don't try to do 'what everybody does'; let God keep your mind alive and ready to think new thoughts, and you'll be a very different person from what you were. In this way you will be able to find out what God wants you to be and to do—what is worth-while and right and grown-up.

I've learned something of God's love, and I say this to each of you: don't go about with high and mighty ideas of your own importance. Think sensibly about yourselves, in the light of what your trust in God has already taught you about God's love.

Ourselves as friends of Jesus

We who are the friends of Jesus are, as I have already said, like a human body with its different parts. We are many persons, but we are one 'body'. Each of us is like a different part of the body, and we are here to help one another, as the different parts of the body help one another.

BOTSWANA. The Bechuana people once lived in the north of Africa, but years ago they migrated to the south and made these highlands their home.

Each of us has different gifts; God has seen to that. We must use them. For example: some of us are able to understand God's Way more clearly than others; some of us deal with business better; some of us are teachers; some of us are speakers. Let us use our different gifts with God's help. And so with everything we do. If we give, let us be generous givers; if we are leaders, let us be energetic leaders; if we are helping others, let us be cheerful helpers.

Ourselves and Other People

Love must be sincere and straightforward. Have nothing to do with evil of any kind. Give your heart to everything that is good.

Be a real family, warm-hearted in your care for one another, thinking better of others than of yourselves.

When keenness is called for, let's have no laziness; on fire with the spirit of Jesus, give yourselves to his service.

SICILY, an island to the south of Italy, to which it belongs, has been the battlefield of Europe and Africa, and it has had many invaders. Life here has been very hard and difficult.

Look forward to God's new world with gladness. In hard times stand your ground; never forget to pray.

Take your part in helping other friends of Jesus when they are in want; make it your aim to keep the doors of your home open to those who need it.

Remember the words of Jesus: 'Bless those who treat you badly; bless them—don't curse them.'

Share other people's happiness and other people's sadness. Learn to respect everybody.

Don't be proud. Mix with ordinary people.

Don't talk as if you knew all the answers.

Don't injure anybody just because he has injured you; do the right thing that all men, in their hearts, know is right.

As far as you can, be friends with everybody. Never try to get your own back, my friends; leave that in God's hands. You know what the Bible says: ' "I will see justice done," says God; "punishment is in my hands." '

Remember what the Bible also says:

> If your enemy is hungry,
>   give him food;
> if he is thirsty,
>   give him drink.
> If you do this,
>   you will make him ashamed of himself.

Don't be beaten by evil; beat evil by doing good.

Ourselves and our Duty

Don't be in debt to anybody—except in the matter of caring for one another. He who loves the man next door, whoever he may be, has got to the heart of all religion.

The Ten Commandments—and all other commandments—can be put in a single sentence: 'Love the next man as you love yourself.'

This is what 'love' means, and love cannot do wrong to anybody; that is why it is the heart of religion.

The Need for Training
(The Christians in Corinth)

You know what happens in a race: all the runners compete; but only one wins the prize. Run to win—that's what you must do. Every runner at the Olympic Games has to train hard. He runs for a wreath that withers; we run for a prize that never withers.

I try to remember all this.

I run, and I know where I'm running. Or, if you like, I box; and when I box, I don't punch the air!

And I'm tough with my body; I let it know who's master. After spending my life training others, I'm not going to be left at the post myself.

TACKLING THE JOB

There were many problems the friends of Jesus had to tackle and do something about. Sometimes they wrote to Paul to ask him to help them. I have gathered together here what Paul had to say about seven problems.

Some are special problems they had to face.

Slavery was common in those days. What do you do if you are a slave or slave-owner when you become a friend of Jesus? If you are a slave when you become a Christian, ought you to try to get free?

The meat sold in the butchers' shops in those days had first been offered in worship to idols in the temple; ought Christians to be vegetarians and have nothing to do with it?

Other problems were ones that we know something about.

What attitude ought we to take to people in authority, many of whom are not Christian and do not try to live in God's Way?

What about sex? (We know what many people do.)

What ought we to do when, as often happens, Christians disagree with one another about important matters? (For example, the Jews kept Saturday as a Holy Day; were Christians to go on keeping Saturday a Holy Day, as many Jewish Christians did? Or were they to do what many of them were doing, keep Sunday as a Holy Day, the day when Jesus was raised to life again? Or did they not need to have a special Holy Day at all, but just live every day in God's Way?)

What ought we to do when Christians divide themselves up into groups or parties, or start quarrelling?

When you have read what Paul had to say, discuss some of *our* problems today, as Paul discussed the problems of his day.

Perhaps you don't agree with what Paul thought Christians ought to do. Why?

Slavery
(A Letter to a Christian Slave-owner in Colossae)

My dear Philemon, friend and fellow-worker,

When I am saying my prayers and I come to your name, I always thank God for you. People often tell me how much you love and trust Jesus, and how much you love and trust all the friends of Jesus too.

This love and trust is something we all share together; and sharing it together has shown us how much Jesus means to us, how good now it is to be alive. Your love has meant a lot to me and made me very happy. And what's more, you've cheered the hearts of all the friends of Jesus, too, my brother.

Now, I've got something I want you to do. I wouldn't be afraid, as a friend of Jesus, just to tell you what your duty is, and leave it at that. But I'd rather appeal to the love we both have for Jesus and one another. I'm an old man now, you know, and, what's more, I'm a prisoner as well for the sake of Jesus; and I am appealing to you for my boy.

It's Onesimus I'm talking about—I became like a father to him here in prison.[1] I'm sending him home to you—and sending my heart with him. I should have liked to keep him here with me; he could have been a great help, and taken your place by my side, prisoner as I am for the Good News. But I wouldn't do anything unless you said Yes. I know, of course, that you'd do the right thing; but I want it to be your choice, not mine.

He was perhaps taken away from you for a short time so that you could have him back again to stay with you always—no longer a slave but something far better than a slave, a real brother. He is a brother to me now; and he will be much more a brother to you, both as a man and as a friend of Jesus.

If you think of me as your partner, welcome him as you would welcome me.

If he's done you a wrong or is in debt to you, put it down to my account.

I, PAUL, WRITE THIS WITH MY OWN HAND—I WILL PAY YOU BACK.

I don't need to remind you that you owe your very self to me. Now I come to think of it, I'd like to make something out of this— the sort of thing that Jesus would make out of it. Cheer me up, as the real Christian you are.

I know you'll do what I ask. I wouldn't have written to you otherwise. In fact, I know you'll do more than I ask.

And while you are about it, get a room ready for me. I know you've been praying for me; I hope God will answer your prayers and give me back to you.

---

[1] Here Paul made a pun of the name of Onesimus which I have not translated.

Remember me to Apphia our sister; and to Archippus our fellow-soldier; and to all the friends of Jesus who meet in your home.

Epaphras is a prisoner here with me; he sends you his best wishes. So do the others who are working here with me—Mark, Aristarchus, Demas and Dr. Luke.

How real Jesus has made God's love and peace! May the graciousness of Jesus be with you all.

Paul (a prisoner here in the cause of Jesus) and Timothy.

People in Authority
(To the Christians in Rome)

Everybody must obey those who rule over us. God gives some men the right to rule, and the present government is put there by God, even though the Emperor and his officials are not friends of Jesus.

So a rebel against the government is a rebel against God, and such men get what they deserve. A good man doesn't need to be afraid of the magistrates; a bad man should be. If you don't want to be frightened of the magistrates, do what is right and win their praise. For the magistrate is God's servant, working for your good. If you do wrong, you have every reason to be afraid. Government officers don't wear the sword for nothing; the government is God's servant to see that justice is done, and that the man who does wrong doesn't escape.

You must, therefore, be good citizens—not just to escape punishment, but because that's the way you ought to live. That is why you should pay your taxes. Government officers are God's officers, and they've got to carry on the government properly.

Do your duties, then, as a citizen. Pay your rates and taxes; show respect and honour to those who have the right to them.

'My Job'
(To the Christians in Corinth)

God has given us whatever gifts we have; let us go on living as we were when he called us to be friends of Jesus. That's the rule I follow in all the churches everywhere.

Were you a Jewish citizen when you became a Christian? Don't try to hide the fact. If you weren't a Jewish citizen when you became a Christian, don't try to live like a Jewish citizen.

Being a Jewish citizen or not being a Jewish citizen is a matter of no importance at all. What matters is living in God's Way.

Let each man stay what he was when he became a Christian. Were you a slave when you became a Christian? Never mind. If you get a chance of becoming a freeman, take it. But remember that if you were a slave when you became a friend of Jesus, you are now a freeman of Jesus; if you were a freeman when you became a friend of Jesus, remember that you are now his slave.

Your freedom was bought at a great price—Jesus gave his life for you. Don't become the slaves of·men again.

Here, then is the rule: whatever you were when you were called to become a Christian, stay like that. God is with you.

Sex

(To the Christians in Corinth)

'I'm free to do what I want,' you say.

Yes, that's true. But not everything is good for us.

'But I *am* free to enjoy everything,' you repeat.

I agree; but there's nothing that's going to make me its slave.

'Food for the stomach; the stomach for food'—you quote that, do you? Neither of them will last for ever.

I'd rather say this: 'The body for Jesus; Jesus for the body.' For whatever our bodies were meant for, they weren't meant for any kind of sexual wrong-doing. They were meant for bigger things than that; that is why God raised Jesus to life, and why he will raise us to life—real life.

You are parts of the 'body' of Jesus, as I have said, and that means that your physical bodies belong to him, too. Can I, then, take my body, which is part of the 'body' of Jesus, and hand it over to a prostitute? Never.

So, keep clear of sexual wrong-doing. All the other wrong things a man does are, in a sense, outside his body; a man who indulges in sexual wrong-doing wrongs his own body itself.

You know, don't you, that your body is the home of God's own Spirit? You don't belong to yourselves; you were bought at a great price—Jesus gave his life for you. Then use your bodies for God's praise.

Other People's Points of View: The Question of Butchers' Meat
(To the Christians in Corinth)

Let us look at this matter of buying meat in the market—meat, as we know, that has already been used in the idol-worship of the temples. That's the problem. What do we do about it?

Now, let's be clear. We all know that 'an idol is just an idol and doesn't mean anything at all', and that 'there's only one God'. And even if we agree (for the sake of argument) that there are many beings called 'gods' in the sky and on earth—we know that the towns and villages are crowded with 'gods' and 'lords'—yet for us there is only one God, our Father, who made the world in which we live and whose Way is our way. And we know that there is one Lord Jesus, who has shown us what the world we live in is really like and who has helped us to come really alive.

But this is the point. There are many friends of Jesus who have not learned to think like this yet; they are only beginning to understand all that Jesus means. Some of them were once regular worshippers in the temples, and have only just become friends of Jesus; they can't eat butchers' meat, which they know has been used in the temples, without feeling that it is wrong to do so; idols still feel real to them. When they eat it, they feel guilty, for they cannot make up their minds yet what is wrong and what is right.

Now food doesn't make any difference to what God thinks of us. If we refuse to eat the meat, we are no worse off; if we eat it, we are no better off. But make sure that this right of yours to eat what you like doesn't make it difficult for these friends of Jesus, friends who honestly can't make up their minds on these questions.

For example, if somebody like this, who can't make up his mind about what's wrong and what's right, sees a good man like you, with all your understanding of God's Way, sitting down to a meal in a temple where idols are worshipped, what will happen? Might he not say, 'Oh, it's all right for him; so it must be all right for me'? So he goes on into the temple and has a meal there. And all the time, in his heart he feels guilty; he feels he ought not to do it, and he's all mixed up in his mind.

With all your 'knowledge', you haven't helped him, have you? You've done him great harm, a brother for whom Jesus gave his life. You've made him do something he believed to be wrong—and that's **wronging your brother and wronging Jesus.**

For myself, if I thought that a question of food made it difficult for a brother to be a true friend of Jesus, I wouldn't touch butchers' meat again. I don't want to do anything to make another friend of Jesus do something he feels, in his heart, is wrong.

So, as a general rule, eat the meat sold in the meat-market,

JAPAN. Japan used to be a feudal state, isolated from the world. Within the last hundred years, she has transformed herself into a modern state, and is one of the great industrial countries.

and don't start asking yourself 'Is it right?', 'Is it wrong?'. For quite clearly, as the Bible says,

The whole world belongs to God
and everything in it.

Again, if somebody who isn't a friend of Jesus asks you out to dinner and you want to go, go and have dinner with him. Eat whatever he's got ready for you, and don't start asking yourself 'Is it right to eat this?', 'Is it wrong to eat that?'. We've settled that question.

But if somebody at the dinner table looks across at you and says, 'This meat was used in the worship in the temple, you know', that raises another question altogether—the question of what *he's* thinking and what *he* believes is right and wrong (it isn't, as we have seen, a question for you at all). For his sake, don't eat it. For the point now is this: we've got to make it quite clear what we, who are the friends of Jesus, think of idol worship; and this isn't something that doesn't matter.

'What!' you say, 'has my freedom to be spoiled because of somebody else's queer ideas of what's right and what's wrong? Look, I enjoy everything I eat, and I always thank God for everything that he's given us. Why should anybody say I'm not a good friend of Jesus?'

Really, it can be put quite simply. Do everything—eating, drinking, whatever it is, everything—to the honour of God. But don't ever make things difficult either for a Jewish citizen (with all *his* convictions), or for a Greek (with all *his* convictions) or for members of the Christian community (with all *their* different feelings). That's what I've tried to do—to look at things from other people's points of view, not to bother about myself but to find out what I could do to help other people. I want everybody to be a true friend of Jesus.

Follow my example, as I try to follow the example of Jesus.

Other People's Points of View: The Question of Sunday
(To the Christians in Rome)

One man thinks that Sunday is more important than all the other days; another thinks that every day is just as important as any other. In matters of this kind, everybody must make up his own mind carefully. If a Christian keeps one day in a special way, he keeps it in honour of Jesus.

This is exactly the same question as that of buying butchers' meat in the meat-market. Some friends of Jesus eat it, and they do so in honour of Jesus and give thanks for his goodness; some won't eat it, and they also act in honour of Jesus and give God thanks for his goodness.

This, you see, is the heart of the matter: none of us lives or dies just for himself; we live and die in honour of Jesus. For **both in life and death we are the friends of Jesus. Jesus died and was raised to life to be the Lord of all humanity, the living and the dead.**

Why do you, sir, find fault with your brother? Or you sir, why do you look down on your brother?

God is the judge of us all.

Do you remember what the Bible says?—

'As I live' God has said,
'every knee shall bow before me,
every tongue shall praise God.'

Each of us, you see, will have to give an account of himself to God.

Other People's Points of View: Some Suggestions
(To the Christians in Rome)

Let's stop finding fault with one another. Let us make up our minds that we won't get in the way of anybody who's trying to live in God's Way.

Take this question of food.

You know what Jewish people—and many Jewish friends of Jesus—believe. They believe that God has forbidden us to eat certain kinds of food. Now, if there's one thing which Jesus has made quite clear to me and which I'm absolutely sure about, it is this: this is a mistake—no food of any kind is wrong to eat. But that isn't the end of the matter.

Here are some things to think about.

1. If anybody really believes that certain foods are wrong to eat, they are wrong to eat—for him.

2. If the feelings of another friend of Jesus are hurt because you eat anything you fancy, you are not really making love your aim.

3. Don't let mere food cause anybody to give up trying to live in God's Way. Jesus gave his life for him—as well as for you.

4. Don't let your Christian ideals get a bad name.

GHANA is one of the new African states. Europeans came here in the fifteenth century to carry on the slave trade. Now she is making herself into a modern nation.

5. God's Way has nothing to do with food—what you eat and what you drink. But it has everything to do with (a) putting wrong things right, (b) learning to live together as friends, and (c) enjoying being alive because you know, in your hearts, that God is Father. Anybody who 'follows Jesus' by living like this is the sort of person God wants him to be—and his fellow men respect him too.

6. Whatever we do must have two clear aims: it must help people to live together as friends, and it must help to build up God's Family.

7. Don't let questions like that of food hinder God's work.

8. Everything God has made is good; but it's a bad thing if arguing about food shakes somebody's trust in God. We ought to do nothing—eat, drink or what you will—that shakes anybody's trust in God.

9. Keep your convictions about things like food to yourself—and God. You're a happy man if you've nothing to regret about the way you've upheld the truth.

10. If you've got any doubts about certain foods, don't eat them. If you do, you're doing wrong; you aren't, in this matter, trusting God. You're acting out of bravado, or because you don't care, or for some such reason; that's wrong. We must always let our trust in God direct our lives.

11. If we are strong, our business is to help people who are weak. We have no right just to 'please ourselves'. It's the fellow next to us we should 'please'—to help him to be himself and to grow up. Remember—Jesus never 'pleased himself'.

Groups
(To the Christians in Corinth)

You are members of God's Family, and I beg you to learn to agree with one another. We mustn't break up into quarrelling groups, arguing about who's right and who's wrong. You know what Jesus wanted. You must be real friends, sharing one another's thoughts and sharing one another's convictions.

News has been brought to me that you are quarrelling with one another; some of Chloe's business agents told me. To put it plainly, you are divided into quarrelling parties with your party-cries: 'I belong to Paul's party', 'I'm for Apollos', 'Peter's the man for me', 'I've no use for parties; I just follow Jesus'.

This is all wrong. Can the friends of Jesus be divided into parties with cries like this? It's like dividing Jesus himself. Get things straight. Have I died for you on a cross? Were you baptized 'In the Name of Paul'?

If you are going to be jealous of one another and quarrel with one another like this, you are living as though you'd never known Jesus and you're behaving like any Tom, Dick or Harry in the city. When you shout your party cries—'I belong to Paul's party', 'I'm for Apollos'—aren't you just like anybody else in the world?

What's Apollos, anyhow? Who's this Paul? I'll tell you— just servants through whom you became friends of Jesus. That's all. We were only doing what Jesus told each of us to do. We're like gardeners: I put the plants in and Apollos watered them; but it's God who made them grow. The gardeners don't matter, whether their job is to set the plants or to water them; only God, who makes things grow, matters. The man who sets the plants and the man who waters them work together as a team, and they get paid according to the job they do. We are fellow-workers, and we work together for God, not for ourselves. You are simply God's field where we work.

Or, if you like, you are God's building. I am like a skilled master-builder. I laid the foundations. God gave me the strength to do this; I couldn't have done it by myself. Then somebody else put the building up.

I have talked like this about myself and Apollos to help you to see the real point of being a friend of Jesus—living in God's Way. You won't do it by boasting about this leader and attacking that. Who gave you the right to go about boasting of your own importance like this? Hasn't everything you've got been *given* to you? And if this is the truth about us—that everything we have is given to us by God—why all this showing off as if you were the 'big noise'?

Quarrels

(To the Christians in Corinth)

Do you mean to tell me that you go off to the ordinary law-court when something goes wrong between you and another friend of Jesus? Doesn't it occur to you that this sort of thing ought to be settled between yourselves? We who are the friends of Jesus know what God's Way is and that this is the standard by which everybody everywhere is to be judged: isn't that clear to you? What's the point of claiming to know what God's Way for the whole world is, if we can't settle little matters of this sort? Don't you know that God's Way is the Way for both heaven and earth, let alone for the everyday matters of our daily life?

And if you have to settle everyday matters like this, why choose as judges people who don't take our point of view? You ought to be ashamed of yourselves. Haven't you got anybody sensible enough to settle questions like this between one friend of Jesus and another? Must one friend of Jesus go to law against another friend of Jesus, and get people who don't accept our Christian standards to settle who's right and who's wrong?

To go to law at all with one another shows you've failed to live in God's Way.

Isn't it better to put up with wrong? Or let yourself be robbed?

THREE THINGS TO REMEMBER

These three passages give us a summary of Paul's thought about the Christian life. It can be lived now—if we are prepared to 'have a go' and keep our eyes on Jesus. And it is worth it.

Remember—Everybody is needed
(To the Christians in Ephesus)

You are no longer outsiders and foreigners in God's world; you are fellow-citizens with all the friends of Jesus everywhere and members of God's Family.

Let me make what I mean clear with an illustration.

Think of building a house. The builders lay the foundations, use the stones to build the walls and hold them together with a key-stone.

God's Family is like a house. Inspired preachers among us (like Agabus)[1] and the first close friends of Jesus (like Peter and Andrew) are the foundations; Jesus is the keystone; you are the stones.

Jesus holds God's Family together and helps it to grow; but he needs you, as the keystone needs the stones that make the walls.

Spend your Time on what is Worthwhile
(To the Christians in Philippi)

One last word. Give your minds to what is true and noble, right and clean, lovely and graceful. Wherever you find excellence—things really worth getting excited about—concentrate on them.

[1] See *Paul the Explorer*, p. 226.

Remember who you are

(To the Christians in Colossae)

Remember who you are: God has chosen you, you belong to him and he loves you. His way must be your way.

Care for people. Be kind and gentle and never think about yourself. Stand up to everything. Put up with people's wounding ways; when you have real cause to complain, don't—forgive them.[1]

Here is your clue: God's forgiveness of you is the measure of the forgiveness you must show to others.

It is love like the love of Jesus that makes all these things possible, holding everything in its grip and never stopping half way. Master every situation with the quietness of heart which Jesus gives us. This is how you were meant to live; not each by himself, but together in company with all the friends of Jesus. Thank God that it is so.

Remember Jesus, and keep the Good News, with all its wealth of meaning, day by day in your mind. Here is real wisdom, in the light of which you can help one another, deepening one another's understanding and warning one another, if need be.

How full of songs your hearts will be, songs of joy and praise and love, songs to God himself! In this spirit you can take everything in your stride, matching word and deed, as the friends of the Lord Jesus. Make him the centre of your life; and with his help let your hearts be filled with thankfulness to God—your Father.

---

[1] Paul here gives a list of the marks of the Christian character. But, as in another letter (see p. 272), he is painting a portrait of Jesus.

WEST AFRICA. The new African states are building modern cities and developing modern industries. But they cannot do everything at once, and life in many villages goes on in the old ways.

John of Ephesus

'I have not written about the many other "signs" which Jesus did in the presence of his friends. If I had, I should have filled the world with books! I have written as I have to help you to see that Jesus is God's Chosen Leader, God's Son—to stake your life on this fact and to live splendidly as his friend.'

THE PURPOSE OF JOHN'S BOOK

At the end of the first century, some forty or more years after the death of Paul, a new account of the story of Jesus was written in the city of Ephesus, Paul's headquarters during the last years he spent in the area of the Aegean Sea. We know very little about its author; his name was John.

People were asking new questions about Jesus and the meaning of his story. It was seventy years after the first Easter Day. Most Christians then living were not Jews, and Palestine and its stormy history meant little to them. They had grown up in Greek cities and they thought in Greek ways. Was the Good News, they were asking, really Good News for the Greek and Roman world? Could the story of Jesus—a story of something that happened long ago in a far-off province on the edge of the Roman Empire—really mean anything to educated people in cities like Ephesus and Corinth? Jesus had not even been a citizen of the Empire—he was a mere provincial; how could what he was and said be important in the changed world of a new century?

Many people today ask questions like those. 'Can the story of Jesus mean anything in the twentieth century?' they ask. 'It happened so long ago and so far away. Times have changed.'

John was the first great Christian thinker to show, in the language of a new age, that the *story of Jesus matters always and everywhere to everybody*.

Mark and Matthew and Luke had told the story of Jesus much as it had been told from the beginning, using words and language that anybody who had grown up in Palestine and thought in Jewish ways could understand. Dr. Luke sometimes changed a Palestinian word or phrase into its Greek form; when he described a house, for example, he pictured a Greek house, not a Palestinian house. This was not enough. Something bolder had to be done.

In the city of Ephesus, Christians met, as Christians all over the world did, on Sunday, the First Day of the week, for prayer and teaching and 'the breaking of bread' (see p. 247). At this service of worship, they heard the story of Jesus read aloud, the story that had been read aloud ever since Paul's day and that went back to the memories of the friends who had known Jesus in Palestine. The Christians in Italy and Greece used similar stories of Jesus in their services of worship; their version of the stories of Jesus lies behind the accounts of Mark and Dr. Luke in *The Beginning*, *The Message*, and Part One of *From Galilee to Rome*.

When these old stories had been read in the services of worship in Ephesus, John had often been asked: 'But what do these stories mean *now*?' 'What do they mean to *us*?' He had often talked about them, and shown his Greek friends how full of meaning for everybody these old stories were. He was getting old, and his friends asked him to put down in writing what he had told them in his many talks.

So he sat down to write a new kind of book about Jesus. He would not just tell the story again as Mark and Matthew and Luke had done. He would tell it in a new way so that everybody would be able to see its world-wide meaning. He would take some of the old stories and draw out their meaning in language that his Greek friends used in their conversations with one another. His theme would be, not 'What Jesus did and said', but 'What Jesus means to us now'. He would use the old stories, but he would use them in a new way.

THE PLAN OF HIS BOOK

You will remember how Mark planned his book about Jesus. He told a straightforward story. He began with the Baptism of Jesus by Jordan River; he went on to tell of his work in Galilee, his exile in the north and his journey south; then he ended his story with the last days in Jerusalem. Matthew and Luke followed his plan, and put in other stories and sayings where they thought they best fitted in. John had a new plan.

He divided his book into three parts: the Introduction; 'The Book of Signs'; and 'The Book of the Passion'.[1]

He begins, in the Introduction, with a poem, and then the story of the Call of the first friends of Jesus. He wants us to see what Christianity is about, and he helps us to do this by setting the story of Jesus against the background of world history, and showing us what Jesus meant to four men.

In the central part of his book, 'The Book of Signs', he uses nine stories of Jesus, familiar to his readers because they come from the stories they heard read aloud in the Sunday services. Some of them you will have already read, in Mark's and Dr. Luke's versions, in *The Beginning*, *The*

[1] The word 'Passion' means 'suffering' and refers especially to the death of Jesus.

Message and *From Galilee to Rome*; some are new to us. But he used them in a new way, as a poet does, to make clear what Jesus means to everybody everywhere.

Then, in the last part of his book, 'The Book of the Passion', he tells the story of the last days of Jesus. But he tells us the story in his own way— first the 'Table Talk' of Jesus, then the plain story of his death, then some stories of his resurrection.

JOHN'S METHOD OF WRITING

We can see that John had a special way of writing about Jesus when we notice that he called the stories of Jesus he used, not 'stories', but 'signs'. To him they were more than stories of something that happened long ago; if we read them carefully and think about them, they tell us more than just what Jesus did in Palestine—they are 'signs' of what he means to us and all men *now*.

How does John help us to see this?

He begins by telling the story very much as it was told in the early version of the stories of Jesus used in the worship of the Christians at Ephesus—as Mark and Dr. Luke would have told it. He wants us to remember that he is dealing with a story of something that once happened (only in one 'Sign', 'The Sixth Sign', does he put what he has to say in a story of his own making, much as Jesus put what *he* had to say in the form of stories). So, to begin with, he puts the story down very much in the words as they lay before him, though he adds a phrase here and there to bring out their meaning. If the Christians at Ephesus wished to find out just what happened, there was always Mark's *The Beginning*.

Then, when he has told the story, he adds longer 'Dialogues' (or 'Conversations'). These are his own work. He is writing as a poet does, using his imagination and his own words to bring out the meaning of the old story, though he weaves into his 'Dialogues', from time to time, actual sayings of Jesus that everybody knew. This is how he talked to his Christian friends at Ephesus when they asked him, 'What do these stories mean *now*?' He is drawing on his long Christian experience and telling them what Jesus has meant to him. 'This,' he is saying, 'is not just what Jesus did for particular people but what he always does in a different way for all of us who love him, whoever we are and wherever we are living.'

This way of writing a book about a great man had been used before. Plato, the friend of the great Greek thinker Socrates, explained what Socrates had stood for by writing Dialogues. In these Dialogues he imagines Socrates talking to all sorts of people; the words of the Dialogues are Plato's; but the picture of Socrates is a true picture, helping us to understand what Socrates stood for. In John's Dialogue, the words are mostly John's; but the picture of Jesus is a true picture.

John introduces us to friends of Jesus we have not met in Mark's and Dr. Luke's stories. Nathanael came from Cana in Galilee. Others are Jerusalem friends, and one of them belonged to an important city family. He is referred to as 'the friend Jesus loved dearly' and the 'other friend'. It was the 'other friend', John tells us, who took Peter past the doorkeeper into the High Court in Jerusalem. It was too dangerous to name him.

READING JOHN'S BOOK

We read Mark and Dr. Luke's books (*The Beginning, From Galilee to Rome*) chiefly as history books. They believe that Jesus is the Son of God (as John also does) and they do not hide what they believe about him. But they are telling 'the plain story' of what happened. We must read John's book as we read a drama (like the plays of Shakespeare). John believes that it is important to be sure what actually happened, but he is telling us *what the story means*, as we have said. That is why, like a poet or a dramatist, he has arranged his story in his own way. He begins, as we have seen, with a poem. He sets out 'The Book of Signs' like a play with seven acts, and he explains the meaning of each act in his Dialogues.

As we read John's book, we must look carefully at the details of his story and ask ourselves: 'Why did he choose *that* detail?' 'What is he helping us to understand about Jesus?' He uses words, as poets do, to suggest more than they actually seem to say.

'Light', 'Day', 'Night', 'Darkness' mean for him, not merely actual day and night, but also the light and darkness of our minds. Jesus is 'Light' and he has come so that men do not 'stumble in the darkness'. It was 'Night' when Nicodemus came to Jesus—night in his mind as well as night in the street outside. The friends of Jesus crossed Galilee Lake *in the darkness* and alone—after the Desert Meal they, too, were puzzled about Jesus and did not understand him. John uses other words in the same way—'running water' ('living water'), bread ('the Bread of Life'), the vine ('the true vine' means God's Family), shepherd (Jesus is the Good Shepherd), wine (the true worship of God). So, as we read, we must note first the *ordinary meaning*, and then ask, 'With what *special meaning* does John also use the word?' John deals with their special meaning in the Dialogues.

Note the characters of his stories. John seems to have chosen them to make clear that Jesus came to help everybody: men and women, old and young, religious leaders and ordinary people, friends and strangers, Jews and Greeks. Jesus meets them in many places—the house and the Temple, the village and the city, in the street and by a well and on a country road.

It may help us to realize how John uses the details of his stories, if we

CHINA. For over two thousand years China has been a civilized country. In 1911 her people overthrew the monarchy and made themselves a republic. In 1948–9 she became a Communist country.

remember how Shakespeare uses the details of *his* plays. For example, Shakespeare begins his terrible tragedy of *Macbeth* with a scene which helps us to *feel* the darkness of his story—'A desert Heath. Thunder and lightning'—and we *feel* immediately something of the darkness and storm of the story he is going to tell us. This is what John does. He tries to help us to feel the darkness in which Nicodemus was groping for the truth by beginning his story with the words, 'Nicodemus . . . once came to Jesus *when it was dark*'; he makes us feel the darkness in the heart of Judas when he tells how he left the supper in the upper room—'He went straight out *into the night.*'

So John's stories prepare us for what he has to tell us about Jesus in the Dialogues.

There are two words John loves to use—the name Jesus used to describe God's character, 'Father', and the word 'world'. In these two words we can see what John believed was the most important thing about Jesus, made clear by what he said and the way he lived and died and rose again to life: he came to help everybody everywhere to know God as Father and to live in his Way.

A LETTER

About the time John wrote his book, a circular letter, written in Ephesus, was sent to the churches in the surrounding province of Asia. It may have been written by John himself or by a close friend and pupil of his. The letter tells us simply and clearly what Christianity really means, and summarizes the great theme of John's own book. These passages from the letter are worth reading before you begin to read the book itself.

The theme of our message is the Good News—the Word that makes real life possible.

It has always been true, but now we have direct evidence of its truth, the evidence of our own eyes and ears and hands—we have actually seen him face to face:

> The Word became human
> and lived a human life like ours.[1]

We have the evidence of our own eyes—we speak as witnesses—and we tell you the secret of real life, life lived in the presence of God our Father and now shown to us for us to see clearly what it is like.

What we want you to be quite sure about is that we are not guessing—we are telling you what we've seen and heard.

The message of this letter is that we all should be partners together, members of God's Family, friends of Jesus his Son.

[1] See the poem 'The Word of God', p. 299.

The secret of unclouded joy—that's what our letter's about.

'The daylight's here: the night's gone for ever.' This is what Jesus had to tell us—Good News about God.

See how great is God our Father's care of us—he calls us his sons and daughters! That, in fact, is what we really are. Here and now we are members of his Family. God has not told us what we shall one day be; but we are sure of this—when he does make it clear to us, we shall share his likeness, for we shall see him as he really is.

My dear friends, let us really care for one another; such care and love is God's gift to us. Everybody who loves and cares is his son or daughter, and knows God. Those who have no love in their hearts for anybody haven't the slightest idea what God is like, for the very heart of God is love.

This is how God's love has been made clear to us: he sent his only Son to live among us to help us to live splendidly. I'm not thinking, you see, of the way we love God, but of the way he loves us. He loved us enough to send his Son to help us to get rid of all that is wrong in our hearts and lives. That's how we know what love means.

If God loves us like this, my friends, we must love one another like this too. Nobody, of course, has ever *seen* God himself; yet, if love of one another marks everything we do, God lives in our hearts, and he makes our love real love like his.

God is love itself. So, if we live in love—and we can see what this means by remembering how Jesus lived—we live in God's presence and he lives in our hearts. With love like this in our hearts—love for God and love for one another—there's nothing that can ever make us afraid, for such love drives all fear away. You see, God loved us first, and we learned how to love from him.

We can test our love for God. If somebody says 'I love God' and yet cares nothing about the man he meets at work or in the street or about another friend of Jesus, he is just a liar. If he can't love somebody he's seen, that shows he doesn't love God whom he hasn't seen. Indeed, Jesus told us plainly: if we love God, we must love the man we meet at work or in the street as well.

The Introduction

John begins his account of the meaning of Jesus with a poem. We must read it, as we read all great poetry, many times.

It begins with an echo of the opening words of the Book of Genesis, the first book of the Bible, where the creation of the world is described. In the coming of Jesus, John suggests, God is completing the creation of the world, so that it shall be the world he intended it to be, a world where men and women live together as members of his Family.

The word 'Word' has many meanings; John wants us to keep them all in mind. It means first of all just what it says—an ordinary word (how powerful *words* can be!); it also means 'reason', 'the thought behind the word'; and finally, for John, it is the best name for Jesus, for he is God's 'word', God explaining himself to us.

I have put the words from the Book of Genesis at the head of the poem for you to read; and then divided the poem into its three parts. The headings of the parts are mine, to guide you in following John's argument.

Then John gives us some stories about the call of the friends of Jesus. Perhaps he put Andrew first because he was well-known in Ephesus, But these stories are given to us to show us that Christian experience—the experience of his friends—points to the truth of the poem. This is what Jesus means to those who love and follow him.

The poem and the stories should be read quietly. There is more in them than we shall find in one reading.

The Word of God

What Jesus really means

> At the very beginning of all things
>   God made the universe we know.
> The earth lay empty and dead,
>   darkness blacked out the deep seas,
>   great winds lashed the water.
> God spoke—
>   'Let there be Light!'
>   and the world was filled with Light.
>   (The first words of the Bible)

The Word

> At the beginning of all things—
>   the Word.
> God and the Word,
>   God himself.
> At the beginning of all things,
>   the Word and God.
>
> All things became what they are
>   through the Word;
>   without the Word
> nothing ever became anything.
>
> It was the Word
>   that made everything alive;
> and it was this 'being alive'
>   that has been the Light by which men have found their way.
> The Light is still shining in the Darkness;
>   the Darkness has never put it out.

'It'?—or 'He'?

> The real Light
>   shining on every man alive
>   was dawning.
> It was dawning on the world of men,
>   it was what made the world a real world,
>   but nobody recognized it.
>
> The whole world was its true home,
>   yet men, crown of creation, turned their backs on it.
> But to those who walked by this Light,
>   to those who trusted it,
> it gave the right to become
>   members of God's Family.
>
> These became what they were—
>   not because 'they were born like that',
>   not because 'it's human nature to live like that',
>   not because men 'chose to live like that'—
> but because God himself gave them **their new life**.

Not 'It' but 'He'

> The Word became human
>> and lived a human life like ours.
> We saw his splendour,
>> love's splendour, real splendour.

> From the richness of his life,
>> all of us have received endless kindness:
> God showed us what his service meant through Moses;
>> he made his love real to us through Jesus.

> Nobody has ever seen God himself;
>> the beloved Son,
> who knows his Father's secret thoughts,
>> has made him plain.

The First Friends

John the Hermit and two of his friends were standing one day talking together by Jordan River. Jesus walked by, and John saw him.

'Look,' he said, 'God's Chosen Leader!'[1]

The two friends heard what he said and went after Jesus. Jesus turned round and saw them coming.

'What are you looking for?' he asked.

'Sir,' they said, 'where are you staying?'

'Come and see,' said Jesus.

So they went along with him and saw where he was staying and spent the day with him. It was about four o'clock in the afternoon.

One of John's friends was Andrew. His first thought was to find his brother Simon.

'We've found God's Chosen Leader,' he told him, and took him back to Jesus. Jesus looked him over.

'So you are Simon?' he said. 'I'll give you a new name—Peter.'[2]

The next day, Jesus made up his mind to go north to Galilee.

He met Philip.[3]

---

[1] John said 'Lamb of God', an Old Testament name meaning 'God's Chosen Leader'.

[2] 'Peter' means 'Rock'.

[3] Philip came from the same town as Andrew and Peter—Bethsaida on the northern shore of Galilee Lake.

'Come along with me,' he said.

Philip found Nathanael.

'You know the Leader the Bible talks about,' he said, 'the Leader God is going to send us. We've found him. He's Joseph's son, Jesus, and he comes from Nazareth village.'

'You can't expect anything from a place like Nazareth!' said Nathanael.

'You'd better come and see for yourself,' said Philip.

Jesus saw Nathanael coming to meet him.

'He's a true member of God's Family,' he said. 'There's nothing false about him.'

'How do you know what sort of man I am?' asked Nathanael.

'Before Philip spoke to you,' said Jesus, 'I saw you in the shade of the fig tree.'

'Master, you are God's Son,' said Nathanael. 'You are the King of Israel.'

'You trust me just because of what I said about the fig tree,' said Jesus. 'This is nothing to what you will see. You remember Jacob's dream? He saw a ladder set up on earth and reaching up to heaven and God's angels linking heaven and earth. It was a dream for Jacob—believe me, it will be fact for the Son of Man.'

THE BOOK OF SIGNS

We come now to the central part of the book, the Book of Signs and its Conclusion. I have marked the Narratives and the Dialogues so that you can see which are which.

Read the Narrative first. If the same story occurs in *The Beginning* or in *From Galilee to Rome*, compare it with the version there. You can discuss, if you like, exactly what happened. But the important thing is to see how John has used the story and to find out why he has chosen just this one at this point. The title I have given the story will guide you. Then read the Dialogue which follows and think about it carefully. Here John is trying to help us to see some truth about the whole meaning of Jesus, what he does for us if we trust and love and follow him.

Each 'Sign' takes one great truth about Jesus, and all the 'Signs' together form a single argument. It runs something like this. Christianity is nothing less than a 'new creation'; *Jesus makes everything new* and, whatever we have been like, if we follow him we can start again (the First Sign). *He offers us the power to 'live splendidly'*; he is not merely a good example (the Second Sign). But we must play our part; *our new*

RUSSIA. The greatest revolution of this century took place in Russia in 1917. It was a backward agricultural country; now it has become one of the two most powerful industrial states of the modern world.

life must be sustained, as we have to eat food if we are to be strong and healthy (the Third Sign). We are not forced to accept the offer Jesus makes us to live in a new way; *we can say Yes or No to him*, we can accept him or reject him (the Fourth Sign). And so *we judge ourselves* (Jesus does not judge us) by the choice we make (the Fifth Sign). Nevertheless, *God's purpose will succeed*, for what God cares for is that we should really be ourselves as he created us to be. Life will conquer Death; *Christianity is a victorious faith* (the Sixth Sign). Then we come to the heart of the matter. Jesus seemed weak when he died on the cross; but this was really his hour of victory. Mysterious though it may seem, *Life conquers in and through Death;* seeming weakness is strength. This is what Paul meant by 'the foolishness of God' (the Seventh Sign). So we come to the end of the

Book of Signs with a simple Conclusion that leads us on to the story of the death and resurrection of Jesus.

Here is an outline of the Book of Signs. I have added beneath each title a saying of Jesus and a quotation from Paul, each dealing with the same theme. You will see that both Paul and John are helping us to realize what Jesus stood for.

First Sign   *A New Beginning*

Jesus: Anyone who does not welcome God's Way like a little boy or girl won't get into it.

Paul: When anybody becomes a friend of Jesus the world's a new world for him; the old world has gone and a new world has been born.

Narratives   New Wine
                New Temple
Dialogues   A Conversation at Night
                A Conversation by a Well

Second Sign   *New Life*

Jesus: You remember what the Bible says?—
            Blind people see again,
               lame people walk about;
            lepers are made well,
               deaf people are hearing;
            dead people are alive again,
               hopeless people are told the Good News.

Paul: The Good News means first of all that God has given us the power to live in his Way.

Narratives   A Boy is healed
                A Cripple is healed
Dialogue   New Life

Third Sign   *'Our Daily Bread'*

Jesus: Give us today our bread for tomorrow.

Paul: I go on living my ordinary life; and yet, in a sense, I don't feel that *I'm* living it, but that Jesus has taken charge of me; I live by trusting in Jesus, God's Son, who loved me and gave his life for me.

Narrative   The Desert Meal
Three Dialogues   Living Bread
Conclusion   Nearly all the friends of Jesus desert him.

Fourth Sign   *Yes or No?*

Jesus: Why don't you make up your own mind about what is right
         and wrong?
Paul: Everybody must make up his own mind carefully.
Narrative   Jesus goes up to the Feast.
Seven Dialogues Who is Jesus?

Fifth Sign   *We judge Ourselves by the Choice we make*

Jesus: The measure you give
              will be the measure you get.
Paul: What you sow you reap.
Narrative   A blind Man sees.
Dialogues   Many points of View
                     The Shepherd and his Sheep
Conclusion   'Trust what I do'

Sixth Sign   *Triumphant Life*

Jesus: For as the lightning lights up the whole sky
         God himself will light up the whole world.
Paul: We can now live more splendidly than the greatest world con-
         querors—with the help of Jesus who loved us.
Narrative and
   Dialogue   The Death of Lazarus.
Conclusion   The Jewish Council plots the Death of Jesus.

Seventh Sign   *Seeming Weakness is Strength*

Jesus: If you forget all about yourself because you are keen on helping
         me, even if you lose your life, you'll be all right. You will really be
         yourself.
Paul: 'My love, given freely to you, is all you need,' God once told me.
         'It's when you have no strength left that you will know how
         strong I am.' I've proved that. It is when I'm weak I am strong.
Narratives   The Anointing at Bethany
                     Jesus rides into the City
Dialogue   Foreigners meet Jesus

The Conclusion   The Light of the World

This arrangement of the Book of Signs (as indeed the arrangement of the whole of John's book) follows the suggestions of Dr. C. H. Dodd in the two very important books he has written about the gospel John wrote ('The Fourth Gospel'). We owe a great debt to Dr. Dodd for the way in which he has made John's argument plain.[1]

The First Sign—A New Beginning

Two Narratives : New Wine

On the third day there was a wedding in Cana in Galilee. Jesus and his friends had been invited, and his mother was there, too.

They ran short of wine.

'There is no wine left,' his mother said to Jesus.

'You mustn't bring me into this yet, mother,' he said. 'My time has not come.'

'You do just what he tells you,' said his mother to the servants.

Six stone water pots stood nearby (each held twenty or thirty gallons). They were kept to hold water for religious purposes.[2]

'Fill the water pots with water,' said Jesus to the servants, and they filled them to the top.

'Draw some of the water out,' said Jesus, 'and take it to the master of ceremonies.'

This is what the servants did.

The master of ceremonies tasted the water, now become wine. He hadn't any idea where it had come from; the servants who had got the water, of course, knew.

He called the bridegroom over.

'Look here,' he said, 'most people serve the best wine first. Poor wine's kept till everybody's a bit drunk. You've kept the best wine till now.'

New Temple[3]

Just before the Great Feast Jesus went up to Jerusalem City. He went inside the Temple, and found the Foreigners' Court

---

[1] The two books are *The Interpretation of the Fourth Gospel* and *Historical Tradition in the Fourth Gospel*.

[2] See *The Beginning*, p. 20.

[3] See *The Beginning*, p. 32; *From Galilee to Rome*, p. 125.

being used as a cattle market. There were oxen and sheep and doves everywhere, and money-changers busy at their tables.

He made, as it were, a cattle whip of some cords and drove sheep, cattle and the whole crowd out of the Temple. He tipped the coins of the money-changers on to the ground and pushed their tables over.

'Take these things out of here,' he said to the dove-sellers. 'Don't make my Father's house into a market.'

'Where's your warrant for treating us like this?' the crowd demanded.

'You can destroy this Temple,' he said, 'but in three days I'll make it into a real Temple again.'

'Indeed,' they said, 'it took nearly fifty years to build and you're going to rebuild it just like that!'

Jesus, of course, was not talking about wood and stones; he was talking about his 'body'—the company of his friends and the work he would do through them.

(His friends remembered this saying after his resurrection. They knew, then, that the Bible was right, and that Jesus had spoken nothing but the plain truth.)

Two Dialogues : A Conversation at Night

Nicodemus, a Jewish leader, once came to Jesus when it was dark.

'Sir,' he said, 'we Jewish leaders have no doubt that you are one of God's teachers. Nobody could do what you do without God's power.

*   *   *

'Believe me,' said Jesus, 'you must begin all over again if you are to see what God is doing in the world of men.'

'How can an old man begin all over again?' asked Nicodemus. 'He can't start life again as a baby, can he?'

'No,' said Jesus, 'but let me put it this way. If a man is to live in God's Way, two things matter: he must change his ways—this is the point John the Hermit made—and be baptized as a sign that he has done so; and he must receive God's power in his own heart.

'Man's power is only man's power, when all is said and done; only God's power is strong enough to help a man to live in God's Way.

'Don't be so surprised when I tell you, "You must begin all over again". Strange things happen in our world. Take the wind, for

FRANCE. During the last war, France was occupied by the Nazi armies and suffered great losses. She has played a great part in the story of Europe, and all the world owes much to her thinkers, writers and artists.

example. It blows where it wants to. You can hear its noise, but you haven't any idea where it's coming from or where it's going to. Doesn't that help you to understand what God's power is like in the lives of men?'

'How can this sort of thing happen?' asked Nicodemus.

'You're a very learned man,' said Jesus, 'and you're a teacher of men yourself; can't you really understand how God works? Believe me, I am talking about what I know at first hand and reporting what I have seen; but you will not believe that these are plain reports. If what I said about the wind means nothing to you, how can what I say about God make any sense?'

*   *   *

This is the measure of God's love for everybody everywhere: *he gave his beloved Son*. He does not want men to destroy themselves; he wants them to live—and to live splendidly. The secret of splendid living is to stake your life on his beloved Son. God did not send his Son to judge the world; he sent him to save it.

Men stand or fall by the attitude they take to Jesus; the great question is—Will they risk their lives, if need be, for what he lived and died and rose again for? This is how men judge themselves; the day has dawned—and they liked the darkness better. What they were doing would not stand examination. The man who has something to hide detests the light; he keeps out of it if he can—he does not want to be 'shown up' for what he is. The man who has nothing to hide welcomes the light; he does not mind everybody seeing how he lives—with God's help and for his sake.

A Conversation by a Well

Jesus once had to cross Samaria, and he came, about midday, to Jacob's Well, outside the Samaritan town of Sychar. His friends went off into the town to buy some food. The long walk had tired Jesus and he sat down, just as he was, near the well.

A Samaritan woman came along to draw water.

'Could you please give me a drink?' he asked.

'Indeed!' she said. 'You're a Jew—and you're asking a Samaritan woman like me to give you a drink?'[1]

'If you only understood the Jewish religion,'[2] said Jesus, 'and who it is who is asking you for a drink, you would have asked him for a drink and he would have given you, not well water, but living water.'

'But sir,' she said, 'you've got no bucket, and it's a very deep well. Where are you going to get "living water" from? Jacob, the founder of our nation, made this well for us; he and his family and his cattle used it. Are you a greater man than he was?'

'This water will not really quench a man's thirst,' said Jesus. 'Before long, he will be thirsty again. The water I give is not like that. If a man drinks it, he will never be thirsty any more. It will

---

[1] Jews, in those days, wouldn't even drink from the same cup as a Samaritan.

[2] Jesus said 'Gift of God'. For Jews God's greatest gift was the Law (the first five books of the Old Testament) which sets out what religion meant to them. The Samaritans also had their own version of the Law.

be as though he had a living spring of water in his heart, the secret of living in God's Way.'

'Sir,' she said, 'give me this water. I shan't be thirsty, then, and I won't have to come all the way to this well to get water.'

* * *

'Go and fetch your husband,' said Jesus, 'and come back here.'

'I haven't a husband,' said the woman.

'That's an honest answer,' said Jesus. 'You've been married five times, but you aren't married to the man you're living with now. You've answered quite straightforwardly.'

'You're a Man of God, I can see, sir,' she said. 'But, you know, we don't think you Jews worship God properly. Our ancestors worshipped God on this mountain here; you say God can only be properly worshipped in Jerusalem City.'

'The time is near, believe me,' said Jesus, 'when the worshipping of God as Father will not be on this mountain or in Jerusalem City alone. I said the time is near, but indeed the time has already come when God's true worshippers, who know him as Father, will worship him everywhere with their whole hearts and their whole lives. That is the kind of worship God our Father asks for. God is not Someone you can meet on a mountain. God is Spirit—you can meet him anywhere; what we must give him is the service of our lives and hearts.'

'Well, it's all rather difficult,' said the woman, 'but we know that when God's Chosen Leader comes, he will make it all plain.'

'I am God's Chosen Leader—I who am now talking with you,' said Jesus.

* * *

At that moment his friends came back from the town. They were amazed to find him talking with a woman. They were too amazed even to ask him if he wanted anything to eat, let alone why he was talking with her.

The woman left her pitcher by the well and went off back to town.

'Come on!' she said to people she met. 'Come and see a man who could read my life like a book!'

And out of the town they came, along the road to where Jesus was.

In the meantime, his friends asked Jesus to have something to eat.

'I've food to eat you know nothing about,' said Jesus.

UNITED STATES. These two boys, both American though of different races, are friends. Friendship is the way in which differences of race and colour can be dealt with.

'Has someone brought him some food?' his friends asked one another.

'My food is a different kind of food,' said Jesus. 'It is doing God's will and finishing the work he sent me to do. That's the food I live on.'

*   *   *

'You know the proverb "It takes time to grow a harvest," ' Jesus went on. 'Believe me, if you'll only use your eyes and look at the fields, you'll see they are golden harvest fields already. The reaper is at work and the corn is being harvested. Sower and reaper are celebrating together.

'You remember that other proverb—"One man for sower and another for reaper." That is true too. The harvest I sent you to reap was sown by somebody else. Other people worked long and hard in the fields; you inherit their hard work.'

*   *   *

Crowds of the townspeople came to trust Jesus just because of what the woman told them. (You remember what she said, 'He read my life like a book!')

When they met Jesus, they asked him to stay with them, and Jesus spent two days in the town. Many more came to trust him when they heard what he himself had to say.

'You know,' they said to the woman, 'we don't trust him now just because of what *you* told us. We've listened to him ourselves and we are sure that he is indeed the Saviour of the world.'

The Second Sign—New Life

Two Narratives: A Boy is healed[1]

There lived in Capernaum a royal official whose son was ill. He heard that Jesus had left the south and come north into Galilee. Off he went to meet him. He asked Jesus to come down to heal his son, who was very near death.

'Trust based on miracles,' said Jesus, 'is not enough.'

'Sir,' he said, 'come down or my son will be dead.'

'Go home,' said Jesus. 'Your son will live.'

The man took Jesus at his word and went off home.

On the way home, his servants met him.

'Your son's going to live!' they said.

He asked them the exact time he began to get better.

'It was one o'clock yesterday afternoon,' they said. 'It was then his fever left him.'

The father realized that it was at one o'clock Jesus spoke the words 'Your son will live'. He and all the members of his household became friends of Jesus.

A Cripple is healed [2]

By the Sheep Pool in Jerusalem City, there was a building with five arcades.[3] In these arcades lay a crowd of sick people—blind, crippled and paralysed.

One of the men lying there had been ill for thirty-eight years.

Jesus caught sight of him and realized how long he had been ill.

'Do you want to get better?' asked Jesus.

[1] See *From Galilee to Rome*, p. 120.
[2] See *The Beginning*, p. 18.
[3] Its Aramaic name is 'New House'.

'I've got no friends, sir,' he said. 'When the water bubbles up, there's nobody to put me into the pool. Somebody always gets down before me when I'm trying to reach it.'

'Get up,' said Jesus, 'pick your bed up and walk.'

The man was cured then and there. He picked up his bed and started to walk.

Dialogue : New Life

The day happened to be Saturday, the Holy Day of the Jews.

'It's the Holy Day,' said some Jewish leaders to the man who had been cured. 'You shouldn't be carrying your bed.'

'The man who cured me told me to pick up my bed and walk,' he said.

'Who told you to do this?' they asked.

The man had no idea, for Jesus had disappeared into the crowd.

Some time later, Jesus found the man in the Temple.

'Look,' said Jesus. 'You're a healthy man now. Don't do anything that's evil. Something worse than illness may happen to you.'

The man went off and told the Jewish leaders that it was Jesus who had cured him.

It was because he did things like this on the Holy Day, that the Jewish leaders became his enemies.

He made his attitude quite clear.

'My Father is always at work,' he said. 'He's at work now. So am I.'

*   *   *

'Believe me, he who listens to what I have to say, and trusts God who sent me, has learned the secret of real living. He is God's free man. He's no longer "half dead", as we say—he's full of life.

'Believe me, the time is soon coming—in fact, it is here now—when people who are living "half dead" lives will hear the voice of the Son of God, and all who listen will learn the secret of being really alive. The Father is the source of all real life; he makes the Son the source of real life too.

'I do not try to please myself; I try to do the will of God who sent me.'

The Third Sign—'Our Daily Bread'

Narrative : The Desert Meal[1]

One day, just before the Great Feast, Jesus went over Galilee Lake. People had watched him cure the sick, and a great crowd of them followed him.

He climbed the hillside, and he and his friends sat down.

He looked up and saw the crowd coming towards him.

'Where are you going to buy bread to feed a crowd like this?' he asked Philip.

'If you spent £20 on bread,' said Philip, 'you wouldn't have enough—they'd only get a bite each.'

'There's a boy here with four barley loaves—and two fish!' said Andrew. 'Do you think that's enough for a crowd like this?'

It was a grassy spot, and the five thousand men who had gathered there sat down on the grass.

Jesus took the boy's loaves, said Grace over them, and gave them out to the men sitting there. He did the same with the fish, too—as much as they wanted. And they all had enough.

'Pick up the bits of food left over,' said Jesus to his friends. 'We don't want to waste anything.'

They picked up enough bits of food to fill twelve wicker baskets—all left uneaten by the crowd from the five barley loaves.

The crowd had been watching, and they were soon talking among themselves.

'This is surely the Man of God we were expecting to come and save us,' they were saying to one another.

Jesus saw what was going to happen—they were planning to force him to be their king.

He slipped away, alone, to the hills.

After sunset, his friends went down to the beach, got into the boat and put across the Lake to Capernaum. It grew dark, and Jesus had not joined them. A rough sea was running before a gale. They had gone three or four miles over the water when they caught sight of Jesus walking by the sea and coming towards the boat. They were terrified.

'It's me,' said Jesus. 'Don't be frightened.'

They were about to take him on board, but at that moment the boat grounded on the beach ahead.

[1] See *The Beginning*, p. 21.

Three Dialogues : Living Bread

The crowd met Jesus on the western shore.

'Master,' they said, 'when did you get here?'

'Believe me,' said Jesus, 'you didn't hunt me out because you understood the meaning of what I have been doing; it's because you had a good meal. Bread like that goes stale quickly; you must not make that the chief aim of your lives. Work for the food that keeps a man really alive. This is the food the Son of Man will give you. God has given him his own power.'

'What ought we to do,' they asked, 'if we are to live in God's Way?'

'Living in God's Way means just this—trust in the one he has sent.'

*   *   *

'I am the living bread,' said Jesus.

'Nobody who becomes my friend ever goes hungry.

'Nobody who trusts me ever goes thirsty.

'I will never send away any man who wants to be my friend. I have come from God, not to please myself, but to do his will—he sent me. His will is that I should keep safe everybody he has given into my charge, to share the glory of God's Great Day.[1] It is his will, too, that everybody who trusts in me shall know what life really means. I am the living bread—the living bread which comes from God himself. He who makes this bread his food will learn the secret of the life that nothing can destroy. The bread I give is my life, and I give it for the life of the world.'

*   *   *

'This sort of talk is more than we can stand;' said some of the friends of Jesus as they were listening to him. 'Why listen to him?'

Jesus realized that his friends were displeased with him.

'Does this upset you?' he asked. 'Suppose you saw the Son of Man going home to God! The Spirit is the source of real life; human nature by itself gets nowhere. My words—all I have said to you—are full of God's power and they are the secret of real life.'

---

[1] See *The Beginning*, p. 5; *The Message*, p. 91.

UNITED STATES. This is Fifth Avenue, New York. Our modern industrial world is a world of cities, and in the last 150 years cities everywhere have grown and spread. But, we have not yet learned how best to build them and how to live happily in them.

Conclusion: The Friends of Jesus desert him

After this, many of the friends of Jesus gave him up and would have no more to do with him.

'Are you going off too?' Jesus asked 'The Twelve'.

'Sir,' said Peter, 'who else is there to go to? There's one thing we're really sure about—you are the one who has shown us what life really is. *We* have come to trust you, and we know you are God's Chosen Leader.'[1]

The Fourth Sign—Yes or No?

Narrative: Jesus goes up to the Feast

Jesus could move freely in Galilee in the north; but in the south—in Judea—his life was in danger.

This incident happened shortly before the Feast of Tents in the middle of October[2]—celebrated, remember, in Jerusalem City in the south.

His brothers spoke to him.

'You shouldn't stay up here in the north,' they said. 'You should move down to Judea. Your friends in the south ought to see what you are doing, how important it is. Nobody keeps to himself what he wants everybody to know. If what you are doing really means what you say it does, come out into the open.'

In fact, even his own brothers thought he was crazy.

'The right time for me has not yet come,' said Jesus, 'but you can do what you want at any time. You're in no danger; I am—because I've said publicly to government and people that their way of life is the very opposite of God's Way. You do what you like; I'm not going to be hurried by anybody.'[3]

With these words, he stayed on in the north, and his brothers went up to the Feast.

A few days later, Jesus himself went up, not as a pilgrim, but just quietly by himself. The crowds were expecting him to be there.

'Where's he got to?' they were asking.

---

[1] See *The Beginning*, p. 24.

[2] The Feast of Tents was the feast Jesus attended during 'The Last Days' (See *The Beginning*, p. 31).

[3] The brothers of Jesus were making fun of him. Jesus seems (*a*) to have refused to let his actions be determined by hostile public comment; (*b*) to have made up his mind to go up to Jerusalem, not as a pilgrim, but incognito.

There was a lot of whispering going on about him.

'He's all right,' said some.

'No, he's not,' said others, 'he's a dangerous agitator.'

People whispered this sort of thing to one another; they were scared of the Jewish leaders.

Seven Dialogues : Who is Jesus?

The Feast was half over when Jesus went up to the Temple and spoke openly to the people. Everybody was amazed.

'Where's this man picked up his education?' they were asking. 'He's no scholar.'

'My teaching is not my own,' said Jesus. 'It is the teaching of God who sent me. Anybody who really wants to live in God's Way will realize whose teaching it is—whether it's God's truth or whether I'm just airing my own ideas. A man who is airing his own ideas is just boasting; but anybody who is really trying to understand God in all his glory is honest and straightforward.'

Jesus was the talk of the town.

'Isn't this the man the government want to get rid of?' some people were asking. 'And here he is talking publicly to the crowds and they don't say a thing to him! Can they have decided that he's God's Chosen Leader after all? Yet we know this man's parents; but nobody will know anything at all about the origin of God's Chosen Leader when he comes.'

'You think you know me,' said Jesus, 'and you think you know where I come from. Yet I haven't come of my own free will; I was sent by the only authority who really counts. You may think you know him, but you don't. I know him because I've come from him and he sent me.'

There was some attempt made to arrest Jesus, but it didn't get as far as actually taking him in charge—his 'right moment' had not yet come.

Many of the crowds who heard him came to put their trust in him.

'God's Chosen Leader couldn't do more than this man to make God's Way plain,' they said.

All this whispering came to the ears of the Jewish leaders and they sent the police to arrest him.

*   *   *

It was the last 'Great Day' of the Feast. The ceremony of the Feast included the drawing of water and the lighting of the golden candlesticks; all this was now over.

Jesus stood up and called the crowd.

'If anybody is thirsty, let him come to me,' he said. 'Whoever trusts me, let him drink.'

(In all this Jesus was speaking about our Christian experience— God's power in our hearts which those who trust in him are given. But this experience was not yet possible; it was only possible after his death and resurrection.)

These words of Jesus impressed people in different ways.

'This, indeed, is the Man of God we were told would come,' said some.

'This is God's Chosen Leader,' said others.

'God's Chosen Leader can't be a Galilean,' said others. 'The Bible says quite clearly that God's Chosen Leader will be a descendant of King David and come from Bethlehem, King David's village, in the south.'

All these different views were held. There was some attempt made to arrest him, but again, it didn't go as far as actually taking him in charge.

*   *   *

The police went back to the Jewish leaders.

'Why haven't you brought him here under arrest?' they demanded.

'Nobody ever talked as this man talks,' said the police officers.

'Have you been taken in by him, too?' they exclaimed. 'Have any of *us* joined him? These common people are no good; they haven't a clue about the real meaning of religion, and God's got no use for them.'

Then Nicodemus stood up. Leader though he was, he had been to talk to Jesus, you remember.

'Isn't it illegal,' he said, 'to pass sentence on a man before you've heard his own evidence and found out what he's been doing?'

'Are you a Galilean patriot, too?' they retorted. 'You look up your Bible—there's nothing there about a Man of God coming from Galilee.'

*   *   *

Jesus spoke again to the people.

'I am the light of the world,' he said. 'Whoever follows me shall not wander in the darkness; he shall have light to live by.'

'We've only your own word for it,' said the Jewish leaders, 'and your own unsupported word isn't good evidence.'

'Even if you do have only my own word for it,' said Jesus, 'my own word is in itself good evidence. It springs from my deep convictions about my origin and about my destiny; and you know nothing about these. You judge men by their appearances; I don't. But if I do venture to make judgments as you do, my judgment is reliable, because it really isn't my judgment alone; it is God's judgment—God who sent me—as well as my own.'[1]

Jesus was speaking in the Treasury at the time. Nobody arrested him; his 'right moment' had not yet come.

*   *   *

These are some words of Jesus.

'When you have lifted up the Son of Man,' he said, 'then you will realize that I am the man I claim to be. I do nothing just because *I* think it's right; I speak what God the Father has made clear to me. God who sent me stands by me. He has not left me to myself; for I have given my whole life to his service.'

Many people believed him, when they heard him talk like this.

*   *   *

Jesus spoke to those who believed him.

'If you live loyally, in the light of all I have made clear to you,' he said, 'you will be true friends of mine. You will come to under-

---

[1] Jesus is here appealing to his own inner convictions, and to the true interpretation of the Old Testament which he believed the Jewish Leaders misunderstood.

stand the real truth about God's Way, and this truth will give you your freedom.'

'Our freedom?' they exclaimed. 'We're loyal Jews; we've never been anybody's slaves. What do you mean by saying that we will be *given* our freedom?'

'Believe me,' said Jesus. 'Everybody who does what is wrong is a slave. Slaves, you know, are not permanent members of a home; the son is a permanent member of the home he belongs to. If the Son gives you your freedom, you are really free.'

The Fifth Sign—We judge Ourselves by the Choice we make

Narrative : A Blind Man sees[1]

One Saturday, the Holy Day of the Jews, Jesus was walking with his friends through the streets of Jerusalem City. He had been in the Temple and was just coming away.

He noticed a blind man who had been born blind.

'Sir,' asked his friends, 'blindness like this is God's punishment, isn't it? Somebody must have done something wrong. Was it the man himself or his father and mother?'

'Nobody,' said Jesus, 'neither the man himself nor his father and mother, but that the power of God shall be seen in his cure.'

He spat on the ground and made some mud paste and put it on the man's eyes.

'Go and wash yourself in Siloam Pool,' he said.

The man went away and washed himself; and came back clear-eyed.

Dialogues : Many Points of View

The Neighbourhood

Neighbours and passers-by knew the blind man as a street beggar.

'This is the street beggar, isn't it?' they began to say.

'Yes, it is.'

'No, it isn't, it only looks like him.'

'I *am* the beggar—I am,' the man himself kept saying.

'Then how did you get your eyes put right?' people asked.

'A man called Jesus made some mud paste and put it on my eyes,'

[1] See *The Beginning*, p. 16.

he said. 'Then he told me to go and wash in Siloam Pool. I did—
and now my eyes are all right.'

'Well, where *is* the man?' they asked.

'I've no idea,' he said.

The Jewish Leaders

The crowd took the beggar to the Jewish leaders.

'He used to be blind,' they said.

So he was questioned all over again.

'How did you get your eyes put right?' the leaders asked him.

'The man put mud paste on my eyes and I washed myself and now
I can see,' he said.

'The man's no good,' said some of the leaders. 'Why, he takes
no notice of the Holy Day.'

'How can a bad man do things like this?' asked others.

They were all at sixes and sevens.

'What have you got to say about him yourself?' they asked the
beggar. 'You say he put your eyes right.'

'He's a Man of God,' he said.

His Father and Mother

The leaders just wouldn't believe that the man had been born blind
and been given his sight—until they called his father and mother.

'Is this your son?' they asked. 'You say he was born blind?
Well, how can he now see like this?'

'He's our son all right,' they answered. 'We know that. And we
know he was born blind. But don't ask us how he can see now and

---

Right: IN GETHSEMANE—*Ivan Meštrović*, 1882–1962.

Born of a Serbian peasant family, Meštrović started as a small child to carve in wood
and stone whilst looking after the village flocks of goats and sheep. He was apprenticed
to a stone-cutter at the age of 15 and later studied in Vienna and Paris.

Meštrović was intensely patriotic and helped, through his work, the nationalists who
were working to free all the southern Slavs from Austro-Hungarian rule. After World
War I, Serbia became part of the new state of Yugoslavia and Meštrović was able to
devote himself to less political themes and many of his religious sculptures date from this
period.

Meštrović was imprisoned for a time when Yugoslavia was overrun by the Germans
during the Second World War. He could not support the Communist Government
which was set up in 1945 and so accepted an invitation to live and work in America.

This wood carving is one of many depicting the life of Christ which decorate the
nave of a church at Kašlet, Yugoslavia.

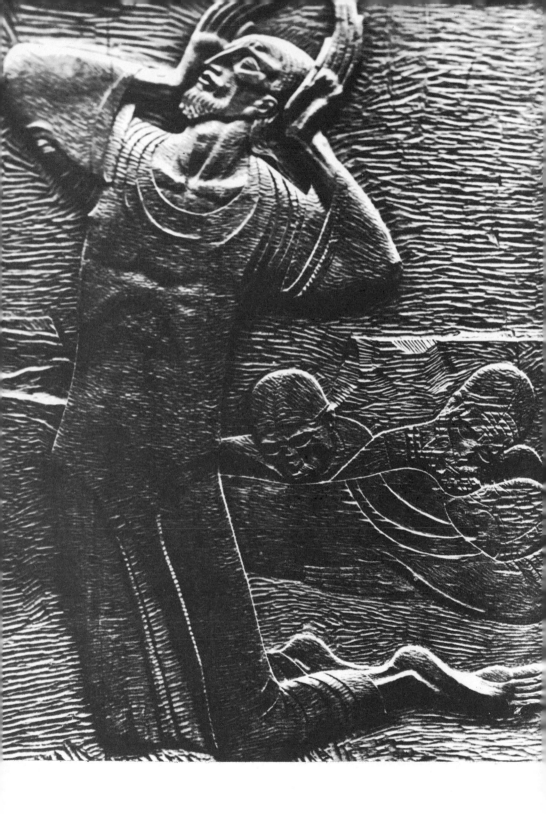

who put his eyes right—we don't know a thing about it. He's old enough; ask him—he can speak for himself.'

They were frightened of what might happen to them; for the Jewish leaders had threatened to make anybody who followed Jesus an outcast. That is why they answered as they did.

The Man himself

So, for the second time, the Jewish leaders called the man himself before them.

'Tell the truth and shame the Devil,' they said. 'This man you said put your eyes right is a bad lot.'

'I don't know whether he's bad or not,' said the beggar. 'But there's one thing I do know. I was once blind and now I'm not—I can see.'

'What did he do to you?' they asked. 'How did he put your eyes right?'

'I've told you already,' he said. 'You don't listen when people talk to you, do you? Do you want to hear it all again? It looks as if you want to become friends of his.'

'None of this impudence,' they said, 'it's you who are a friend of his. We stick to Moses; we know where we are with him—God really spoke to *him*. This man's a nobody.'

'Good gracious!' said the beggar. 'It's amazing! You don't know anything about him and you say he's a nobody; yet he put my eyes right. God doesn't listen to bad men—we know that all right. He only listens to people who take him seriously and live in his Way. I was blind when I was born and now I can see—has anybody heard of *that* happening before? If this man was a bad man, he couldn't have done a thing!'

'You were not only born blind,' they said. 'You were born bad. Are you trying to tell us our job? Get out.'

And that was that.

Jesus

Jesus heard that they had stopped the beggar from going to the Meeting House. He met him again.

'Do you trust in the "Son of Man"?' he asked him.

'Who is he, sir?' he asked. 'I'd like to trust him.'

'You've seen him,' said Jesus. 'He's talking to you now.'

'I trust, sir,' he said, and knelt down on the ground at his feet.

Epilogue

These are the words of Jesus.

'The kind of judgment I was born to give is this:
>Blind people see,
>the people who see become blind.'

Some of the Jewish leaders were there when he once talked like this.

'Are we blind, then?' they asked.

'If you were really blind,' said Jesus, 'you wouldn't be bad men. What makes you bad is the way you say: "We can see perfectly well, thank you." '

Dialogue : Shepherd and Flock

Jesus told these two stories.[1]

'Believe me,' said Jesus, 'the thief or bandit does not enter through the gate of the courtyard, where the sheep are kept, but climbs in over the wall. The shepherd, whose sheep they are, uses the gate, and the gatekeeper opens the gate for him.

'Again, sheep know the sound of the shepherd's voice. He calls them by their names and leads them out to the hills. He walks ahead of them and they follow; they know the sound of his voice. They won't follow a stranger; they scatter at the sound of *his* voice—they don't recognize it.'

The people who heard these two stories did not understand what he was saying.

'Believe me,' Jesus went on, 'I am the gate for the sheep. All those who have claimed to be God's Chosen Leader before me[2] were nothing more than thieves and bandits.[3] The sheep took no notice of them. I am the gate; anybody using this gate will be safe—he will come in and go out and find the pasturing grounds.

'The thief only thinks of stealing, killing, smashing things up. I came to help people to live—and to live splendidly. I am a true shepherd—a shepherd who will give his life for his sheep. The man who is paid to look after the sheep—no proper shepherd owning his own sheep—runs off at the very sight of a wolf and leaves the

---

[1] See *The Message*, p. 61.

[2] See *From Galilee to Rome*, p. 146.

[3] The word for 'bandits' also means 'rebels', and was used to describe members of the Resistance Movement.

sheep to their fate, and the wolf worries them and chases them in every direction. What happens to the sheep means nothing to him.

'I am a true shepherd. I and those who are mine really know one another (as the Father knows me and I know the Father) and I give my life for the sheep. I have other sheep, too; they do not belong to this sheepfold, but I must gather them in. They will recognize my voice. There will then be one flock, one shepherd.

'The Father loves me because I give my life that I may receive it back again. Nobody takes my life from me; I give it freely. I have the right to give it and the right to receive it back again. These are my Father's orders.'

The people who listened could not agree about these words of Jesus.

'He's got a demon inside him—he's just mad,' many said. 'Listening to him's a waste of time.'

'This isn't the way a madman talks,' said others. 'Can a demon make blind people see?'

Conclusion : 'Trust what I do'

It was the Feast of Lights in Jerusalem City, and it was winter. Jesus was walking in Solomon's Cloister in the Temple. People gathered round him.

'How long will you keep us guessing?' they asked. 'If you are God's Chosen Leader, tell us in plain language.'

'I have told you,' said Jesus, 'and you do not believe. The evidence is simply in the life I live, for all I do is done in the service of my Father.'

The people picked up stones to stone him to death.

'I have done many good things to make plain to you that it is with God my Father's help I do everything. Which of these is the reason for your wanting to stone me?'

'We are not stoning you for doing good,' they replied, 'but for blasphemy—you, a mere man, make yourself out to be God.'

'You are forgetting what the Bible says,' said Jesus. 'Do you remember the words—

I say "You are gods,
sons of the Most High, all of you." ?

'The writer, to whom God spoke, calls them "gods"—and you cannot put the Bible on one side. I said "I am the Son of God"—

CZECHOSLOVAKIA. A class of Jewish boys with their teachers in central Europe, a part of the world that has seen great changes, revolution and war, in this century.

and God dedicated me and sent me to the world. Why do you say I am guilty of blasphemy? If I am not living in God my Father's Way, do not trust me. But if I live in his Way, trust what I do even if you do not trust me. It will be clear to you then that the Father lives in me and I live in him—and you will understand.'

They tried to arrest him, but he escaped.

The Sixth Sign—Triumphant Life

Narrative and Dialogue : The Death of Lazarus

Lazarus, the brother of Mary and Martha,[1] was ill. They lived in the southern village of Bethany, two miles from Jerusalem City.

The sisters sent to Jesus.

'The friend you love is ill,' they said.

'This is not a fatal illness,' said Jesus when he received the

[1] See *From Galilee to Rome*, p. 119.

message. 'It has happened so that God's own presence among men may be clearly seen; and that it may be clearly seen, too, that the Son of God makes God's own presence real for men and women.'

Jesus was very fond of Martha and her sister and Lazarus. So when he heard about the illness of Lazarus, he stayed on, where he was, for two days more.

'Let us go back into Judea,' said Jesus to his friends at the end of the two days.

'But Master,' they said, 'not long ago the people there were wanting to stone you to death. You're not going back?'

'There are twelve working hours in the day, aren't there?' said Jesus. 'Nobody need stumble in the daylight—he has the whole light of the sun to see by. Walking by night's a different matter—a man easily stumbles when the light's gone.'

'Our friend Lazarus has fallen asleep,' Jesus went on. 'I am going to wake him up.'

'If he's sleeping, sir,' said his friends, 'he'll get better.'

Jesus had really been talking about his death; his friends thought he had been talking about ordinary sleep.

'Lazarus is dead,' said Jesus bluntly. 'In a sense, I'm glad—for your sakes. It will help you to trust in me. Let us go to him.'

'Let us go too,' said Thomas, 'and let us die with him.'

*   *   *

When Jesus got there, he found that Lazarus had already been buried four days.

Many of the city people had come to console Martha and Mary in their bereavement. When Martha heard that Jesus was on his way, she went out to meet him. Mary stayed at home.

'If only you'd been here, sir,' said Martha, 'my brother wouldn't have died. But even now he's dead, God will give you whatever you ask him, I know.'

'Your brother will rise again,' said Jesus.

'I know he'll rise again when all men rise again at the last day,' she said.

'I am the resurrection,' said Jesus 'and I am the source of life. Whoever trusts me shall come to life again, even though he dies; nobody who is alive and trusts in me shall ever die. Do you believe this?'

'Yes I do, sir,' she replied. 'I firmly believe that you are God's Chosen Leader, the Son of God, the Coming One.'[1]

With these words, she went to call her sister Mary.

'The Master's here and wants you,' she told her in a low voice so that the others shouldn't hear.

As soon as she heard that, Mary got up quickly and went to Jesus. He was still where Martha had left him, outside the village.

The people in the house who had come to console Mary saw her get up quickly and go out. They followed her, thinking that she was going to the tomb to mourn there.

Mary reached the spot where Jesus was standing, and, as soon as she saw him, she fell down at his feet.

'If you'd only been here, sir,' she said, 'my brother wouldn't have died.'

Jesus saw her crying—and all the people with her crying; he was deeply moved and troubled.

'Where have you buried him?' he asked.

'Come and see, sir,' they said.

Jesus wept.

'He must have been very fond of him,' the visitors said.

'He can make blind people see,' said some. 'Couldn't he have done something to stop this man from dying?'

Jesus was again deeply moved as he reached the tomb. It was a cave with a large stone closing its opening.

'Move the stone out of the way,' said Jesus.

'The smell must be very bad by now,' said Martha. 'He's been dead four days.'

'Didn't I tell you,' said Jesus, 'that you would see what God can do—if you trust in him?'

The stone was moved.

Jesus looked up.

'I thank you, Father, for listening to me. I know that you always listen to me. I say this for the sake of those who are standing round me. I want them to be sure that you have sent me.'

Then he called loudly, 'Lazarus, come out!' and the dead man came out. His hands and feet were bound with bandages, and his face was wrapped in a cloth.

'Undo him,' said Jesus, 'and let him go.'

---

[1] 'The Coming One' was a title for the Deliverer the Jewish people believed God would send to save them from their enemies.

Conclusion : The Jewish Council plots the Death of Jesus

Many of the people who had come to visit Mary and had seen what Jesus did came to trust in him. But some of them went back to the Jewish leaders and told them all about it.

The Jewish leaders called a meeting of the Council.

'What's our line of action?' they asked. 'This man is performing many signs. If we don't do anything to stop him, everybody will be joining him. Then we shall have the Romans stepping in and that will be the end of our temple and our nation.'

Caiaphas, who was High Priest that year, addressed the Council. 'You're talking a lot of nonsense,' he said. 'Use your heads. Isn't one man's death better than the death of the whole nation?'

From that very moment they began to plan the death of Jesus.

The Seventh Sign—Seeming Weakness is Strength

Two Narratives : The Anointing in Bethany[1]

Six days before the Great Feast, Jesus came to Bethany, the village of Lazarus. They made a supper for him. Martha was in charge of the meal, and Lazarus was one of the supper party. Mary brought a pound of real Indian ointment, poured it over the feet of Jesus and wiped them with her hair. The house was filled with the smell of the ointment.

'Why wasn't this ointment sold for thirty pounds?' said Judas Iscariot. 'The money could have been given to the poor.'

It wasn't the poor he cared about. He was a thief, and stole the money in the common money-box he looked after.

'Leave her alone,' said Jesus. 'Let her keep it for my burial day.

---

[1] See *The Beginning*, p. 38.

Right : LAZARUS—*Sir Jacob Epstein*, 1880–1959.

Epstein was born in New York of Russian-Polish–Jewish parents. He settled in this country in 1905 and his work soon became known. It was often unpopular because the public mistook his more imaginative work for primitive lack of ability. However, he eventually became famous for his portraits in bronze and for his work on public buildings. One of his statues, 'War Memorial', can be seen at the T.U.C. Headquarters in London.

He produced many religious sculptures as well. For example, 'St. Michael and the Devil' at the new Cathedral, Coventry; the 'Risen Christ' in Llandaff Cathedral; and the 'Madonna and Child' which stands over the entrance to the Convent of the Holy Child in Cavendish Square, London.

The statue of Lazarus was finished in 1948 and stands in the chapel of New College, Oxford.

Reproduced by courtesy of the Warden and Fellows, New College, Oxford.

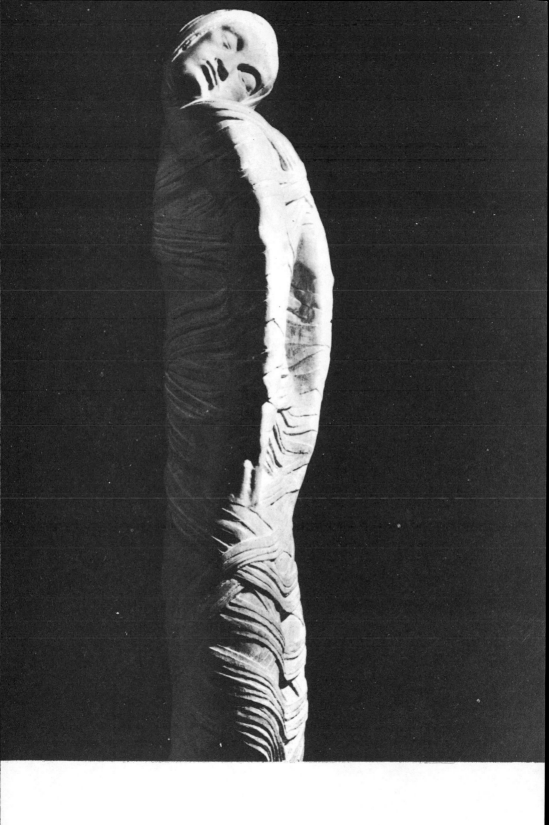

There are always poor people among you; I shall not be with you for ever.'

Jesus rides into the City[1]

The great crowd that had come up for the Feast heard next day that Jesus was on his way to the City. They took palm branches and went out to meet him. These are the words they shouted:
> 'Hurrah!
> Happy is he who comes in the Lord's name!
> God bless the King of Israel!'

Jesus mounted a donkey he found.

'The situation's hopeless,' said the Jewish leaders. 'Everybody's on his side!'

Two Dialogues : Foreigners meet Jesus

There were some Greeks among the pilgrims at the Feast.

They approached Philip (from Bethsaida in Galilee).

'We'd like to meet Jesus,' they told him.

Philip told Andrew, and the two of them told Jesus.

'This is the great moment for the Son of Man, the crown of his work,' said Jesus. 'Believe me, a grain of wheat just remains a grain of wheat—unless it falls into the earth and dies. But if it dies, it produces many seeds. He who just cares for himself, ceases to be himself; he who does not put himself first becomes truly himself and learns the secret of the life that is really worth living. If anybody wants to do me service, he must follow me. Where I am, my servant will be. My Father honours anybody who does me service.'

*   *   *

'Now I am torn in two,' said Jesus. 'What am I to say? "Father save me from the suffering that lies ahead"? But it was for this I came. "Father, bring your great work to its fulfilment."'

A voice came from heaven—

'My great work has been carried on—and will be carried on.'

The crowd nearby heard it and said that it thundered.

'An angel spoke to him,' said others.

[1] See *The Beginning*, p. 31.

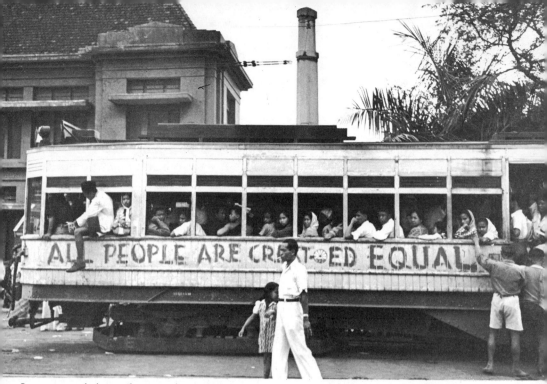

INDONESIA is in south-east Asia, one of the poorest and most underdeveloped parts of the world. If the people who live here are to live full and happy lives, they will need the help of those who live in rich countries.

'It was for your sake the voice spoke,' said Jesus, 'not for mine. This is the testing time of the world. The evil powers that rule the world will be defeated. I will draw everybody to myself—when I am lifted up from the earth.'

(These words of his make clear the meaning of his death.)

'We understand, from the teaching of our religion,' said the crowd, 'that God's Chosen Leader never dies. How can you say that the Son of Man must be "lifted up"? Who is the Son of Man?'

'It's only for a short time that you have the light shining on you,' said Jesus. 'Go on your way while you have the light to walk by—you do not want the darkness to overtake you. He who walks in darkness has no idea of his direction. While the light is shining, trust it. In this way you will become people who can live in the full light of God's world.'

After saying this, Jesus went away into hiding.

Conclusion of the Book of Signs—The Light of the World

'Whoever trusts me is not just trusting me but trusting in God who sent me,' said Jesus with great urgency.

'Whoever sees what I stand for, sees what God, who sent me, stands for. I have come into the world as light, so that he who trusts in me shall not stay in darkness.

'I do not judge the man who listens to what I have to say and takes no notice of it. I did not come to be a judge of men; I came to save them. The man who has no use for me and takes no notice of what I say has a judge: the very words I have spoken will be his judge on God's Great Day. What I have said is not my own idea; God my Father, who sent me, has told me what to say and what to speak. I say what God my Father has told me to say.'

THE BOOK OF THE PASSION

John has now finished the main part of his book where he has shown us what Christianity really means. The stories of what Jesus did and said in Palestine have a timeless meaning. He turns now to the story of the death and resurrection of Jesus.

Note, first of all, how he changes his method. In the earlier part of his book his method was to tell the story or narrative first and then to add the dialogues to explain its meaning for everybody everywhere. Here, he puts the dialogues first, and then, in simple language and without comment, he lets the story of how Jesus died speak for itself.

For John, the death of Jesus is the historical 'plain story' that most of all has timeless meaning. Although he has shown us, in the later 'Signs', how Death can be the means of Life and weakness the source of strength, he has not yet dealt with the death of Jesus and all it means to us and the whole world. So, now, he gives us more dialogue then he has given us for any of the other stories. The 'Table Talk' and 'The Prayer of Jesus' are really an explanation of what the best man in the world lived and died for.

He begins with a short story of what happened on the last night when Jesus and his friends had supper together. It is a story we have not yet heard, about how Jesus, taking the place of a slave, washed the feet of his friends. It was a slave's duty to wash the dusty feet of visitors when they came to a house. On this evening there was no slave to wash his friends' feet; Jesus had only hired or borrowed the room. He did the job himself. This is the sort of person he was.

Then comes the 'Table Talk'. Here the whole meaning of the death of Jesus is explained, in the light of this simple short story—and how his death is not the End but the Beginning.

Then, without comment, he tells us what happened in the garden and in Jerusalem and at Skull Hill.

He brings his story to its conclusion with an account of Easter morning, what happened later in the day and then, some time later, by Galilee Lake. (This last story he added after he had finished his book, as an appendix to it.)

Jesus—Servant

The Great Feast of the Jewish people was near. Jesus was having supper with his friends.

He got up from the table and took off his long robe. He picked up a towel and tied it round him like a belt. He poured water into a basin, and began to wash his friends' feet.

When he had washed their feet, he picked up his long robe, put it on and sat down again at the table.

'I have shown you what you must do,' he said. 'You must do what I have just done for you. Believe me—

A slave is not greater than his master,
a messenger than the man who sent him.

'I hope you understand all this. You will be happy men if you live as I have shown you.'

Table Talk

Jesus was talking with his friends at the supper table. He stopped talking and became very troubled.

'One of you is going to hand me over to the government,' he said.

His friends stared at one another; they had no idea whom he was talking about.

One of his friends, one he loved very dearly, was sitting by his side on his right.

Peter nodded to him.

'Find out who he's talking about,' he whispered.

The friend leaned back close to Jesus.

'Sir,' he asked, 'who is it?'

'When I've dipped a piece of bread in the sauce,' said Jesus, 'I'll give it to the man I'm talking about.'

He dipped a piece of bread in the sauce, picked it up and gave it to Judas, the son of Simon Iscariot.

'Be quick about what you're doing,' said Jesus.

Nobody grasped what all this was about. Judas was treasurer.

Some thought Jesus had told him to buy in food for the Feast; some that he was to go and help some poor people.

Judas took the piece of bread from Jesus. Then he went straight out into the night.

*   *   *

'I shall not be with you much longer,' said Jesus to his friends after Judas had gone out of the room. 'Love one another—this is my "new commandment". Love one another in the same way as I have loved you. This will be the mark by which everybody will recognize that you are my friends—the way in which you love one another.'

'Sir,' said Peter, 'where are you going?'

'You cannot go with me now where I am going,' said Jesus. 'You will go with me later on.'

'Sir,' said Peter, 'why can't I go with you now? I'll die in your defence.'

'You'll die in my defence?' said Jesus. 'Believe me, before the cock crows, you will say three times that you are no friend of mine.'

*   *   *

'Stop worrying,' said Jesus. 'Keep trusting God and keep trusting me. There are many different places in my Father's home for people to live. I would have told you long ago, if this was not true. I am going away now to make sure that there is a place for you. Then I shall be back again to welcome you into my own home, where we shall always be together.

'You know my direction and my road,' he added.

'We don't know where you're going, sir,' said Thomas. 'How can we know the road?'

'You know me—what I am and how I live,' said Jesus. 'I am the Road. The End of the Road is to know God as Father; to help people to know God as Father has been my work and mine alone. If you had known me as I really am, you would have known God as Father. From now on you know him as Father—you have seen him for yourselves.'

'Sir,' said Philip, 'help us to know God as Father; that's all we need.'

'We have been friends together for a long time,' said Jesus. 'Don't you know me yet, Philip? He who has seen what I really am has seen the Father. Why do you keep on saying "Help us to see God as Father"? Don't you believe that I live in the Father and that the Father lives in me? I don't just invent the words I speak; God the Father is living in me and at work in me. You must trust me at this point if you don't understand; my words—"I live in the Father and the Father lives in me"—are the plain truth. If you find this difficult to believe, look at my whole life and trust me for what I do. Believe me, the man who trusts me will be able to live as I live; indeed he will be able to do much more than I can do here—because I am going to the Father. Remember, I will do whatever you ask—if you ask *in my name*.

'If you love me, you will obey my orders, and I will ask the Father to give you another Helper to stand by you always—the Spirit who helps us to understand the whole truth about God—what he is like and what he is doing.

'I will not leave you without a teacher; I am coming back to you. In a very short time, I shall pass from the sight of men; but you who love me will see me. Because I live, you too will live. When I have risen to life again, you who love me will be quite sure that my words and deeds are my Father's words and deeds; and what will make you quite sure of this is the strength of our friendship—you in me and I in you.

'He who hears my orders and obeys them is the man who really loves me; and he who really loves me will know in the depth of his being that God my Father loves him. I will love him, and through my love for him I will show him who I really am.'

'Sir,' said Judas (not the Judas who handed Jesus over to the Jewish leaders), 'what has happened that you are not going to show the whole world who you really are—that you are only going to show us, your friends, who you really are?'

'The man who loves me,' said Jesus, 'will take what I say seriously. My Father will love him, and we will come to him and make our home in his heart. The man who has no love for me doesn't bother about anything I say. What you hear me say, I do not say on my own authority; it is what God, my Father, who sent me, says.

'I have talked to you like this while I am still with you. But the Helper, the Spirit God the Father will send in my name, will explain everything to you, and call back into your minds all that *I* have said to you but which you did not understand at the time.

'When we leave one another we say "Peace be with you".[1] But my goodbye is no casual goodbye. Peace is my parting gift to you— my own peace which nobody else can give you. Don't panic, and don't be cowards.'

*   *   *

'I am the real vine[2] and my Father is the farmer who looks after it. He cuts off every unfruitful branch, and he prunes every fruitful branch to make it more fruitful still. A branch dies if it gets broken off the vine—no fruit can grow on it. It is thrown on one side, and becomes a dry stick; the sticks are picked up and used for the winter firing. So it is with our friendship; if your friendship with me is not a real friendship, you will become like that dead branch. I am the vine, you are the branches. If your friendship with me is a real friendship—you in me and I in you—it will bear a great harvest; but there will be no harvest at all, if our friendship is broken—you need me.

'I have loved you as my Father has loved me. Hold fast to my love of you. The way to hold fast to my love is to obey my orders; . I have obeyed my Father's orders and held fast to his love.

'In talking to you as I have done,' said Jesus, 'I have had one aim in view: I wanted you to know the happiness I know. I don't want anything to spoil your happiness. This is the secret of it—my secret, your secret: love one another as I have loved you. For a man to die for his friends—that is the greatest love we know. You are real friends of mine—if you do what I have told you.

'I don't want you to be my "slaves", just doing the things you are told to do, without knowing at all why you are doing them. I want you to be my "friends": that's why I shared with you all I have learned from my Father.

'You did not choose me, you remember; I chose you. And I chose you for one purpose: I want you to go on growing, producing a rich and lasting harvest.

'This, then, is my order: love one another.'

*   *   *

'I have spoken to you like this so that you will not let me down. The Jewish leaders will forbid you to worship in the Jewish Meeting House. Indeed, before long, anybody who kills you will think he is

---

[1] See *From Galilee to Rome*, p. 119.
[2] In the Old Testament the vine represented 'The People of God'.

being loyal to God and obeying his commands. The reason is clear—
they do not know God as Father and they do not know who I
really am. I have spoken to you as I have to warn you; when this
sort of thing happens, you will remember I warned you. I have not
talked to you like this before, because we were together. But now I
am going to him who sent me. None of you asks me where I am
going; my words have just made you miserable.

'Yet it is for your good that I should leave you—this is the truth.
If I do not leave you, the Helper will not come to you; if I go,
I will send him to you.'

*   *   *

'There are many things that I still have to tell you, but you
could not now take what I have to say; but when the Spirit, who
understands the whole truth about God, comes, he will lead you,
step by step, into the whole truth about him.'

*   *   *

'In a short time, you will see me no longer; again, in a short
time, you will see me,' said Jesus.

His friends talked this over among themselves.

'What's he trying to tell us?' said some of them. 'We don't
understand what he is talking about.'

Jesus knew that they had many questions they wanted to ask him.

'Is it what I said about your not seeing me and then your seeing
me again that you are arguing about? Believe me, this will indeed
happen—you will find yourselves a group of mourners and the world
outside will be delighted. Your grief will be very real, but it will be
changed into joy. Think of the birth of a child. The mother has to
endure much pain while the child is being born. But her pain is
swept away by joy—she even forgets all about it—when the child
has been born: a human being has come into the world. Your
experience is like hers: short sorrow, and then great joy—when I
see you again. Nobody will rob you of this joy. You will be asking
me no questions then.'

*   *   *

'See, the time is coming—it has already come—when you will
go back home, scattered like sheep, and you will leave me alone by
myself. Yet I am not alone; the Father stays by my side.

'I have told you all this that you may have "Peace", as I said. You will have to face hard times when you go out into the world. Don't be afraid—I have conquered the world.'

The Prayer of Jesus

'Father, the time has come.

'Glorify your Son so that your Son may glorify you.

'I have glorified you among men. I have finished what you gave me to do.

'I have made you known—Father—to the men you gave me. They left their ordinary life to come with me (they were your choice, you gave them to me) and they have been loyal to the Good News about you. They are now quite sure that all you gave me really is *your* gift to me. I told them what you told me; they listened and are quite sure I came from you, and they have staked their lives on the fact that you sent me.

'I am praying for them.

'My earthly life is over, but they have to face the world as it is and I am coming to you. Holy Father, keep those whom you have given to me loyal to you, so that they may be one as we are one. Now I am coming to you. I speak like this now here in the world so that they may know, in all its fullness, the joy I know.

'I have given the truth about you into their keeping. The outside world treats them with hatred—they do not share its way of life as I do not share its way of life. My prayer is not for you to take them out of the world, but to guard them from its evil power. Set them apart as messengers of your truth. The Good News about you and your purpose is truth. As you sent me into the world, I also have sent them into the world; and I set myself apart for their sake, that they also may be set apart as messengers of the Good News.

'My prayer is not only for them. My prayer is also for all those who, through their message about me, stake their lives on its truth.

'I pray that they may all be one, as you, Father, and I are one— you in me and I in you. May they live in us, so that men and women everywhere may be convinced that you have sent me.

'Righteous Father, men and women in the world outside have not learned to know you. I have known you, and these, my friends, have learned that you sent me. I have made your nature as Father clear to them, and I will go on making it clear; so that the love with which you have loved me may fill their hearts, and I may be in them.'

The Last Days[1]

In the Garden

Jesus left the house with his friends and crossed the Kidron Brook to the other side of the valley. They came to a garden and went inside. They knew it well, for Jesus and his friends had often met there.

Judas knew this, and he led a detachment of Roman soldiers and a company of Jewish police straight to the spot. They were fully armed and carried lanterns and torches.

Jesus stepped out to meet them.

'Who do you want?' he asked.

'Jesus from Nazareth,' they answered.

'I'm the man you want, then,' said Jesus.

At these words, they stepped back and fell on the ground.

'Who do you want?' asked Jesus again.

'Jesus from Nazareth,' they repeated.

'I've told you—I'm the man you want,' he said. 'If it's me you're after, let these men go.'

Peter drew his sword and struck at a slave of the High Priest and cut off his right ear.

'Put your sword up,' said Jesus. 'Do you want to stop me facing what God the Father has set before me?'

The soldiers then arrested Jesus and handcuffed him.

Before Annas

The soldiers took Jesus before Annas, the most powerful man in Jerusalem City. He was not the High Priest of the Jewish people. Caiaphas was the High Priest that year; Annas was his father-in-law.

Now Jesus had a friend whose name we do not know. He was not one of 'The Twelve', but belonged to one of the most important families in Jerusalem; the High Priest knew him well. He was the 'other friend'.

Peter and the 'other friend' followed Jesus along the road. When they got to the courtyard, the 'other friend' went straight in with Jesus; Peter was left standing outside at the door. The 'other

[1] See *The Beginning*, p. 40; *From Galilee to Rome*, p. 127.

friend' came back and had a word with the girl on duty at the door and then took him inside.

'You're one of this fellow's friends, too, aren't you?' the girl asked Peter.

'Not I,' said Peter.

It was a cold night, and the slaves and court officers had lit a charcoal fire. They were standing round it, trying to keep warm. Peter joined the crowd round the fire; he wanted to get warm too.

The High Priest asked Jesus about his friends and what he stood for.

'What I have had to say,' said Jesus. 'I have said openly for everybody to hear. I have talked in the Meeting Houses, and I have talked in the Temple to Jewish people from all over the world. I have not been plotting in back rooms. Why ask me questions now? Ask the ordinary people in the villages and in this city. They heard me. They know what it was I talked about.'

One of the court officials standing near him gave him a slap on the face.

'Is that the way to talk to the High Priest?' he said.

'If I did something wrong,' said Jesus to the officer, 'prove it. If I didn't, why hit me?'

Annas had Jesus handcuffed again and sent to Caiaphas.

Peter was still standing near the fire, getting warm.

'You are one of this fellow's friends too, aren't you?' said some of the men by the fire.

'Not on your life,' said Peter.

Now it happened that one of the court officers standing there was a relative of the man Peter had slashed with his sword.

'I saw you in the garden with him, didn't I?' he asked.

'No, you didn't,' said Peter.

At that moment, somewhere in the distance a cock crowed.

Before the Roman Governor

It was now Friday, the day before the Great Feast.

Just before dawn Jesus was marched into the headquarters of Pilate, the Roman Governor.

The Jewish leaders stayed outside the building (it was 'unclean'[1] to them because it belonged to foreigners, and, if they had gone

---

[1] See *The Beginning*, p. 20.

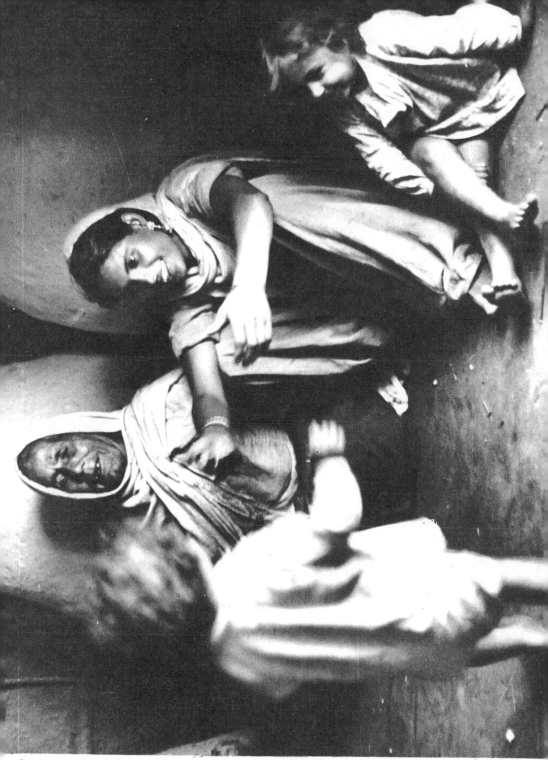

REFUGEES. The wars and revolutions of this century have made many people refugees. These are refugees from the Punjab. The United Nations has helped them to reclaim land in India, free it from malaria and turn it into flourishing farms.

inside, they would not have been allowed, by Jewish law, to take part in the Great Feast). So Pilate came outside.

'What's the charge against this man?' he asked.

'He's a criminal,' they said. 'Would we have brought him here if he wasn't?'

'Well, take him off and deal with him yourselves,' said Pilate. 'You've got your own laws and law-courts.'

'But we can't pass the death sentence,' they replied.

Pilate went back into the building and had Jesus brought before him.

'So you're the Jewish King, are you?' he said.

'Are those your own words?' asked Jesus. 'Or are you just repeating what other people have told you?'

'Do I look like a Jew!' said Pilate. 'You've been brought here by your own leaders. What have you been up to?'

'I'm no nationalist,' said Jesus. 'My men would have been out on the streets fighting, if I were—they wouldn't have let me be arrested so easily. My "kingdom" has nothing to do with that sort of thing.'

'So you *are* a "king", then,' said Pilate.

'The word is yours,' said Jesus. 'I was born to defend the truth. Anybody who cares for the truth knows what I am talking about.'

'What is truth?' said Pilate.

And with that he went outside again.

'As far as this court is concerned,' he told the crowd, 'there is nothing this man can be charged with. I've been in the habit of setting one prisoner free for you at the Feast. What about letting "the Jewish King" go free this year?'

The crowd broke into a roar.

'Not this man, but Barabbas!'

(Barabbas was one of the toughs of the Resistance Movement.)

So Pilate had Jesus flogged, and the soldiers—as was often their custom with prisoners—made sport of him. They made a crown out of some thorn twigs and crowned him with it, and dressed him in a soldier's purple cloak. Then they kept coming up to him, saluting him with 'Long live Your Majesty!' and slapping him on the face.

Pilate went out to the crowd again.

'Here he is,' he said. 'I'm going to bring him out to you to make it clear that there is nothing this court can charge him with.'

Jesus was brought outside, still wearing the mock crown and the purple cloak.

'There's the man!' said Pilate.

When the Jewish leaders and their officers caught sight of him, they started shouting.

'The cross! Let's have him on the gallows!'

'Take him and put him on a cross yourselves,' said Pilate. 'He's done nothing this court can deal with!'

'But we've a law of blasphemy,' they answered, 'and by that law he ought to be executed—he claims to be equal with God himself!'

That last sentence frightened Pilate. He went back again into the building.

'Where were you born?' he asked Jesus.

Jesus didn't speak.

'I'm the Governor, you know—why don't you say something?' said Pilate. 'Don't you know I can set you free or have you executed?'

'You would have no power over me at all,' said Jesus, 'if God had not given it to you. The man who handed me over to you is more guilty than you.'

From that moment Pilate made up his mind to set him free.

But the shouting of the crowd went on.

'If you let this man go, you're no friend of the Emperor! Anybody who calls himself a king is an enemy of the Emperor!'

Pilate heard what they were shouting.

He brought Jesus outside again, and took his seat as Governor and Judge at the place called 'The Pavement'. It was now just midday.

'Here's your "King"!' he said.

'Take him away! Hang him on a cross!' the crowd shouted.

'So it's your "King" I'm to hang on a cross?' he asked.

'The Emperor is the only King we've got!' they shouted back.

Pilate handed him over for execution.

At Skull Hill

The soldiers marched Jesus off, and, with his own cross on his shoulders, he went out of the building to Skull Hill, a place quite near the city. And there they hung him on the cross. Three men were hung on crosses that day—Jesus in the middle, the other two on either side of him.

Pilate had a notice written out in three languages, Jewish, Roman and Greek: JESUS OF NAZARETH, THE JEWISH KING. He had it fastened on the cross. Crowds of citizens read it.

'Don't put THE JEWISH KING,' the Jewish leaders protested to Pilate. 'Put—HE SAID HE WAS THE JEWISH KING.'

'It stays as I wrote it,' said Pilate.

*   *   *

When the four soldiers had carried out their orders, they picked up the clothes of Jesus and made four bundles, one for each of them. Then they picked up his tunic. This was one piece of cloth, woven from top to bottom, not made up of several pieces.

'We mustn't tear it up,' they said. 'Let's toss for it.'

That is what they did.

*   *   *

All this time, his mother, his aunt Mary, the wife of Clopas, and Mary from Magdala were standing near the cross itself. Jesus caught sight of his mother—and the friend he loved dearly standing by her side.

'Mother,' he said, 'take my friend as your son.'

'Take my mother as your mother,' he said to his friend.

And from that time, his friend took her into his own home.

*   *   *

'I am thirsty,' said Jesus.

A full jar of sour wine had been put nearby for the guard. The soldiers soaked a sponge in it, stuck it on a javelin and put it up to his mouth. Jesus drank it.

'My work is done,' he said.

His head dropped, and he died.

*   *   *

The Jewish leaders did not want the bodies on the crosses to stay there over the Saturday, the Holy Day of the Jews, especially since this was a very important Saturday, the first day of the Great Feast. They asked Pilate to have the men's legs broken to make them die quickly, and then to have the bodies taken away.

This is what the soldiers began to do. They broke the legs of the two men hanging on either side of Jesus, one after the other.

They went up to Jesus, but they found that he was already dead. They didn't break his legs, but one of the soldiers jabbed a lance into his side, and water and blood flowed out. (This is what happened; it is the evidence of an eye-witness who can be trusted.)

*　　*　　*

After all this, two men went to Pilate—Joseph from the village of Arimathea (he was a member of the Jewish Council; he had kept his friendship with Jesus a secret, for he was afraid of what the Council might do) and Nicodemus (who, as we have told, first met Jesus at night).

Joseph asked Pilate to let him take the body of Jesus down from the cross, and Pilate agreed. So his friends came and took his body away, and wrapped it in linen sheets with spices which Nicodemus had brought, more than seventy pounds weight of perfume mixture. (This is the Jewish method of burial.)

There was a large garden nearby. In it there was a new tomb—nobody had yet been buried there.

It was now getting on for six o'clock in the evening, the time when the Holy Day began. The tomb lay near at hand; so they put Jesus there.

The First Easter

It was now early on Sunday morning and it was still dark.

Mary from Magdala came along to the tomb. She looked at it—someone had taken the stone away and it was open. She ran off to Peter and the friend whom Jesus had loved dearly.

'The Master's been taken from the tomb,' she said, 'and we don't know where he's been put.'

Peter and the other friend of Jesus ran together to the tomb. The other friend got to it first; he could run faster than Peter. He peered into the tomb—the linen cloths were lying there all right—but he stayed outside. Peter came up after him and went straight inside. He gazed at the sheets lying there and at the head cloth, rolled up by itself, away from the sheets. The other friend now came in and saw it all. Mary's story was true. They both went home. They never dreamed Jesus had risen from the dead; the words of the Bible meant nothing to them.

*　　*　　*

Mary was standing outside the tomb crying. Still crying, she peered into the tomb. She saw two white-robed angels sitting on the slab where the body of Jesus had been lying, one at each end.

'What are you crying for?' they asked.

'My Master's been taken away,' she said, 'and I don't know where he's been put.'

She happened to turn round—and there was Jesus standing in the garden. She did not recognize him.

'What are you crying for?' he asked. 'Are you looking for somebody?'

She thought he must be the gardener.

'Sir,' she said, 'if you've carried him somewhere else, tell me where you've put him. I'll look after him.'

'Mary!' said Jesus.

She swung round.

'Master!' she said.

'Let go of me,' said Jesus, 'I have not yet gone up to my Father. Go to my brothers and tell them—"I go up to my Father and your Father; to my God and your God".'

Mary went off to his friends.

'I've seen the Master!' she said, and she told them what he had said to her.

*   *   *

The day passed, and it was now late in the evening.

The friends of Jesus were together in the house. They were frightened of the Jewish leaders, so they had locked the doors.

Then—there was Jesus standing among them.

'Peace be with you!' he said.

With these words, he let them see his hands and his side.

They saw it was Jesus, and were overjoyed.

'Peace be with you!' he said again. 'The Father sent me out: I now send you out.'

He there and then gave them God's power.

'Receive the Holy Spirit,' he said.

*   *   *

That evening, one of the friends of Jesus was absent—Thomas 'the twin'.

'We've seen the Master!' the others told him when he came back.

'I don't believe it!' he said. 'I must see the nail-marks in his hands and touch them first—and I must put my hand in his side.'

The following Sunday, the friends of Jesus were again in the house with locked doors. This time Thomas was there too.

Then—Jesus was with them again.

'Peace be with you!' he said.

He turned to Thomas.

'Where are your fingers?' he said. 'Here are my hands. Touch my side with your hand. You must show that you trust, not that you don't.'

'My Lord and my God!' said Thomas.

'Do you trust me,' asked Jesus, 'just because you have seen me with your own eyes? They are happy people who trust me without ever having seen me with their own eyes.'

*　　*　　*

After this Jesus showed himself again to his friends. This is what happened on the beach of Galilee Lake.

Seven of his friends were together there—Peter, Thomas 'the twin', Nathanael from Cana, Zebedee's sons (James and John) and two other of his friends.

'I'm taking the boat out fishing,' said Peter.

'We'll come along with you,' said the others.

They all got into the boat there and then. They were out all night but not a fish did they catch.

And now the day was breaking.

Jesus stood on the beach. Nobody recognized him.

'Lads!' he called out, 'have you had any luck?'

'Not a fish!' they called back.

'Try the starboard side,' he called. 'There's fish there.'

Out went the net. The mass of fish they got was so great they could not haul the net in.

'It's Jesus!' said the friend whom Jesus loved dearly to Peter.

Peter had been fishing naked. When he heard the name 'Jesus' he flung his cloak round him and jumped into the water. The others brought the boat in, dragging the net. They were only about a hundred yards off shore.

They got out of the boat—and there was a charcoal fire burning on the beach, and fish cooking on it; there was bread, too.

'Get some of the fish you've just caught,' said Jesus.

Peter went on board and dragged the net to the shore. The net had not been torn in spite of the mass of fish.

THE UNITED NATIONS. Most of the nations of the world now meet together to try to solve their problems. They do more than talk; through their organizations they bring help to people who need it. This picture shows the Assembly meeting in their headquarters in New York.

'Let's have breakfast,' said Jesus.

Nobody dared ask him who he was.

Jesus picked up the bread and the fish and gave them to his friends.

After breakfast Jesus turned to Peter as they walked along, and called him by his own name Simon.

'Simon,' he said, 'do you love me more than anything else?'

'Yes, sir,' said Peter, 'you know I love you.'

'Look after my friends,' said Jesus.

Jesus spoke to Peter a second time.

'Simon,' he said, 'do you love me?'

'Yes, sir,' said Peter, 'you know I love you.'

'Look after my friends,' said Jesus.

Then a third time Jesus spoke to Peter.

'Simon, he said, 'do you love me?'

For Jesus to ask him this question three times upset Peter.

'Sir,' he said, 'you know all about me. You, of all people, know I love you.'

'Look after my friends,' said Jesus.

'Believe me,' he went on, 'when you were a young man, you tied your own belt on and you went just where you wanted to. When you're an old man, you'll hold your hands out for someone else to tie your belt on and carry you where you don't want to go.'

Then he added—

'Follow me.'

Peter turned round and caught sight of the friend whom Jesus loved dearly. He was coming along behind. (This was the friend who was sitting on the right of Jesus at supper and leaned back and asked 'Who is it, sir, who's handing you over?').

'What about him, sir?' he asked.

'If I want him to wait till I come,' said Jesus, 'what's that got to do with you? I've given you your orders—Follow me.'

(The rumour spread among the friends of Jesus that this friend should not die. Jesus did not say this. What he said was 'If I want him to wait till I come.' This is the friend of Jesus who is our authority for this account of what happened and wrote it down. We know he is a reliable witness.)[1]

---

[1] The last sentence was added by the Christians in Ephesus who published this gospel.

Some Important Words·

Good News

This is the meaning of the word 'Gospel', a word not often used outside the New Testament. It describes all that Jesus made clear about God and men and women and the world we live in, not only in what he said, but also in what he was and did. All God had promised in the past has now been given to us ('fulfilled', said Jesus) in his coming. It is what the word 'Christianity' means—it is Good News about God and it is centred in all that Jesus was and did and said.

God's Chosen Leader and Son of Man

This translates the word 'Messiah' ('Christ' is the Greek translation of this Jewish word), the Deliverer the Jews believed God would send them. Both words mean simply 'anointed' (as kings were anointed at their coronations). Here, in Dr. Manson's words, is what they thought he would be like: he 'was an ideal figure, the embodiment of the· hopes of the godly, decent, patriotic Jew of the time. He would be a man, a descendant of the royal dynasty of David and Solomon. But he would be no ordinary man. He would be unique in wisdom and knowledge, in uprightness of character, in courage and patriotism, and in loyalty and devotion to God. He would be backed by God's power and guided by God's wisdom, and so he would overthrow all the enemies of Israel and establish an Israelite kingdom in which justice, truth, and peace would be secure, where the one true God, the God of Israel, would be worshipped and obeyed, where God's people, Israel, would enjoy permanent prosperity and happiness.'[1] Jesus did not like this word; it had so many meanings that it did not help people to understand what he came to do. He preferred the title 'Son of Man'. 'Son of Man' really means 'Man' (it is a Jewish way of saying this). If you look up the vision of Daniel (Daniel 7. 13–18), you will find that there it describes 'The People of God'. So, when Jesus uses it, he is thinking of more than himself; he is thinking of himself and his friends. So I have translated it 'I and my friends'. At the end of his life, when his friends did not prove loyal to him, and Jesus was alone, I have translated it 'I'. (Once, in the early part of the story, it means just 'Man', and here I have translated it 'men and women'—*The Beginning*, p. 18.)

---

[1] *The Beginning of the Gospel*, p. 15·

Sir, Lord

Both words, 'Sir' and 'Lord', translate one Greek word, 'Kurios'. This means, first of all, simply 'owner'; it is the word used about the owner of the donkey in the story about Jesus riding into the city (*The Beginning*, p. 31). It also means 'Sir', when you are addressing people you respect. It is also used as a title, 'Lord', for the Emperor and for the pagan title for God. When friends or strangers addressed Jesus in his lifetime as 'Kurios', they were using the word as we use the word 'Sir'. The experience of the first Easter made his friends believe that Jesus was 'more than a man'; he was for them 'God's Son', one who showed them, in his life and death and resurrection, what God was like, and who helped them to live in God's Way. To them he was no longer just 'Sir'; he was 'Lord'. When anyone was baptized and became a Christian, he confessed his faith in the words, 'Jesus is "Lord".' This is the meaning of the word for both Paul and John—and for all Christians.

Friends of Jesus

I have used this phrase to translate 'disciples' and 'apostles'. The early Christians probably called themselves just 'friends' (see Acts 27. 3); and John tells us that it was the name Jesus gave them (p. 338). 'Christians' was the nickname given to them by others (see *From Galilee to Rome*, p. 166); they also called themselves 'The People of the Way'. Today we use the name 'Christians' for all who follow Jesus. So I have used 'friends of Jesus' for all who followed him, though in later volumes I have also used the word 'Christians', which is the word we now use. (Jesus gave the name 'apostle' to those he 'sent out'; the wider name 'disciple' probably meant, when Jesus used the word, something like our word 'apprentice'.) When the friends of Jesus thought of themselves as a group, they used the word 'church', and I have used this word in this volume. But 'friends of Jesus' helps us to remember that what makes people 'Christian' is their loyalty to Jesus; and what makes them a 'church' is their carrying on the work Jesus began in Galilee.

Jewish Leaders

The Jews thought of religion and politics together, and their leaders were both their religious and political leaders. They were divided into different parties—the 'Pharisees' and the 'Sadducees' were the most famous. I have used 'Jewish leaders' for them all; you can find out from your Bibles which they actually were.

Resistance Movement

This translates the word 'Zealots', the party that believed in armed rebellion against Rome.

Where to find the Passages in your Bible

ABBREVIATIONS

The following abbreviations have been used:

Col.	Colossians	M	Matthew
Cor.	Corinthians	Mk	Mark
Eph.	Ephesians	Phil.	Philemon
Gal.	Galatians	Rom.	Romans
L	Luke	Thess.	Thessalonians

THE BEGINNING

THE MESSAGE

FROM GALILEE TO ROME

PAUL THE EXPLORER

PAUL'S OWN STORY

The passage from Paul's statement which I used as a 'framework' for all the other passages, **Galatians** 1. 11-2. 21 (see p. 185) are printed in heavier type for you to pick out easily.

JESUS, LEADER AND LORD

PAUL OF TARSUS